Dr. Nancy L. Roser
Professor, Language and Literacy Studies
The University of Texas
College of Education
Austin, Texas

Dr. Jean Wallace Gillet
Reading Specialist
Charlottesville Public Schools
Charlottesville, VA

SRA McGraw-Hill
Columbus, Ohio

A Division of The McGraw·Hill Companies

Program Reviewers

Wendy Fries
Teacher GATE Coordinator
Kings River Union School District
Kingsburg, CA

Cynthia W. Gardner
Exceptional Children's Teacher
Balls Creek Elementary School
Newton, NC

Diane Jones
Teacher
East Clayton Elementary School
Clayton, NC

Sheryl Kurtin
Curriculum Teacher
Tuttle Elementary School
Sarasota, FL

Ann Ogburn
Curriculum Coordinator
Johnston County Schools
Smithfield, NC

Michael Reck
Teacher
Big Walnut Schools
Sunbury, OH

Dr. Sherry V. Reynolds
Classroom Teacher/Elementary
 Curriculum Specialist
Will Rogers Elementary School
Stillwater, OK

Review Lesson Illustrations: Steve McInturff

Photo Credits: p.3, ©Van Gogh Museum, Amsterdam, Netherlands/Superstock; **5,** ©Richard Shock/Tony Stone Images; **7,** ©The National Geographic Society/The Everett Collection; **9,** ©David Woodfall/Tony Stone Images; **11,** ©Corbis-Bettmann; **13,** ©Myrleen Ferguson/PhotoEdit; **15,** ©Dante Gabriel Rossetti/Tony Stone Images; **17,** ©Tony Freeman/PhotoEdit; **19,** ©Hulton Getty Picture Collection/Tony Stone Images; **21,** ©Bob Daemmrich/Stock Boston; **25,** ©Everett Collection, Inc.; **29,** ©UPI/Corbis-Bettmann; **31,** ©Superstock; **33,** ©1990 Michael Keller/The Stock Market; **35,** ©Michael P. Gadomski/Earth Scenes; **37,** ©Superstock; **39,** ©Ken Biggs/Tony Stone Images; **41,** ©1994 J.B. Diederich/The Stock Market; **43,** ©David Young-Wolff/PhotoEdit; **45,** ©M. Reardon/Photo Researchers; **47,** ©Myrleen Cate/Tony Stone Images; **51,** From THE TRUE STORY OF THE THREE LITTLE PIGS by Jon Scieszka, illustrated by Lane Smith. Copyright (c) 1989 by Jon Scieszka, text. Copyright (c) 1989 by Lane Smith, illustrations. Used by permission of Viking Penguin, a division of Penguin Books USA Inc.; Cover photo/Aaron Haupt; **55,** ©John Neubauer/PhotoEdit; **57, 59,** ©Superstock; **61,** ©1997 Ariel Skelley/The Stock Market; **63,** ©1993 Paul Barton/The Stock Market; **65,** ©David Young-Wolff/PhotoEdit; **67,** ©UPI/Corbis-Bettmann; **69,** ©1997 Jose L. Pelaez/The Stock Market; **71,** ©UPI/Corbis-Bettmann; **73,** ©1991 Michael Kevin Daly/The Stock Market; **77,** ©1995 Jim Erickson/The Stock Market; **81,** ©Spencer Grant/PhotoEdit; **83,** ©Bob Daemmrich/Bob Daemmrich Photo, Inc.; **85,** ©Michael Newman/PhotoEdit; **87,** ©A. Kaye/Superstock; **89,** ©1997 Peter Beck/The Stock Market; **91,** ©Aaron Haupt; **93,** ©Peter D. Byron/PhotoEdit; **95,** ©1988 Faith Ringgold, Inc./The High Museum, Atlanta; **97,** © Jonathan Nourok/PhotoEdit; **99,** ©Mary Kate Denny/PhotoEdit; **103,** ©Aaron Haupt; **107,** ©Karl Weatherly/Tony Stone Images; **109,** © Peter Cade/Tony Stone Images; **111,** ©Deborah Davis/PhotoEdit; **113,** ©Mark E. Gibson/The Stock Market; **115,** ©Carol Havens/Tony Stone Images; **117,** ©Gay Bumgarner/Tony Stone Images; **119,** ©Michael Newman/PhotoEdit; **121,** ©1997 T&D McCarthy/The Stock Market; **123,** ©Doug Armand/Tony Stone Images; **125,** ©Jeff Greenberg/PhotoEdit; **129,** ©1995 Paul Barton/The Stock Market; **133,** ©Corbis; **135,** ©Felicia Martinez/PhotoEdit; **136,** ©Mark Steinmetz; **137,** ©UPI/Corbis-Bettmann; **139,** ©Stephen Frisch/Stock Boston; **141,** ©John Lund/Tony Stone Images; **143,** ©1997 Michelle Bridwell/PhotoEdit; **145,** ©I.M. House/Tony Stone Images; **147,** ©Earth Imaging/Tony Stone Images; **149,** ©Rich Iwasaki/Tony Stone Images; **151,** ©B. Seitz/Photo Researchers; **152,** ©Mark Steinmetz; **155,** ©Ian Shaw/Tony Stone Images.
All other photos © 1998 PhotoDisc, Inc.

SRA/McGraw-Hill
A Division of The McGraw·Hill Companies

Copyright © 1999 by SRA/McGraw-Hill.

All rights reserved. Except as permitted under the United States Copyright Act, no part of this publication may be reproduced or distributed in any form or by any means, or stored in a database or retrieval system, without the prior written permission of the publisher, unless otherwise indicated.

Send all inquiries to:
SRA/McGraw-Hill
250 Old Wilson Bridge Road
Suite 310
Worthington, Ohio 43085

Printed in the United States of America.

ISBN 0-02-674574-7

2 3 4 5 6 7 8 9 POH 04 03 02 01 00 99

How to Study a Word

1 **Look** at the word.
What does it mean?
How is it spelled?

print

2 **Say** the word.
What sounds do you hear?
Are there any silent letters?

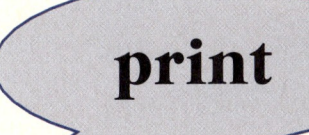

3 **Think** about the word.
How is each sound spelled?
Do you see any word parts?

pr i nt

4 **Write** the word.
Did you copy all the letters carefully?
Did you think about the sounds
and letters?

print

5 **Check** the spelling.
Did you spell the word correctly?
Do you need to write it again?

print

Contents

UNIT 1

Lesson 1	The /a/ and /o/ Sounds	2
Lesson 2	The /e/, /i/, and /u/ Sounds	6
Lesson 3	The /ā/ and /ō/ Sounds	10
Lesson 4	The /ē/ and /ī/ Sounds	14
Lesson 5	The /o͞o/ Sound	18
Lesson 6	**Review**	**22**

UNIT 2

Lesson 7	The /oi/ Sound	28
Lesson 8	The /ou/ Sound	32
Lesson 9	The /ô/ Sound	36
Lesson 10	Final Double Consonants	40
Lesson 11	The Final /əl/ Sound	44
Lesson 12	**Review**	**48**

UNIT 3

Lesson 13	Words with *-ed* or *-ing*	54
Lesson 14	Words with *spl*, *spr*, and *str*	58
Lesson 15	Words with Double Consonants	62
Lesson 16	Contractions	66
Lesson 17	Easily Misspelled Words	70
Lesson 18	**Review**	**74**

UNIT 4

Lesson 19	The /s/ Sound	80
Lesson 20	The /j/ Sound	84
Lesson 21	Plurals	88
Lesson 22	Homophones	92
Lesson 23	Days of the Week and Time Words	96
Lesson 24	**Review**	**100**

UNIT 5

Lesson 25	Words with *ld* and *ft*	106
Lesson 26	The /âr/ Sound	110
Lesson 27	The /kw/ and /skw/ Sounds	114
Lesson 28	More Contractions	118
Lesson 29	Names of Holidays	122
Lesson 30	**Review**	**126**

UNIT 6

Lesson 31	The /ûr/ and /or/ Sounds	132
Lesson 32	Words with Silent *k* and *w*	136
Lesson 33	Words with *lf, mb,* and *tch*	140
Lesson 34	Compound Words	144
Lesson 35	Names of Months	148
Lesson 36	**Review**	**152**

Student Handbook

Commonly Misspelled Words......158
Steps in the Writing Process.......159
Continuous Stroke
    Handwriting Models................160
Ball and Stick
    Handwriting Models................161

Dependable Spelling
    Patterns....................................162
Spelling Strategies 163
How to Use a Dictionary...............164
Speller Dictionary 166

Sorting Spelling Patterns

11-1-09

1 The /a/ and /o/ Sounds

Spelling Focus—The /a/ sound can be spelled *a*. The /o/ sound can be spelled *o*.

SORT Write the Core Words with the /a/ and /o/ sounds spelled the following ways. One word will be used in both sets.

Core Words

1. path
2. shot ✓
3. lamp
4. clock
5. tramp
6. sock
7. crash
8. plant
9. rot
10. math ✓
11. crop
12. trash ✓
13. stamp ✓
14. flock ✓
15. hatbox

My Words

anxious
sumunded
glad

Core Word Sentences

Walk on the wide **path**.
Take a careful **shot** with the bow.
My **lamp** has a bright light.
That **clock** has a loud tick.
Let's **tramp** through the forest.
Her **sock** has a hole.
The plane did not **crash**.
I want to **plant** flower seeds.
The potato began to **rot**.
My favorite subject is **math**.
Cotton is the **crop** we grow.
I will take out the **trash**.
Does the card have a **stamp**?
I have a large **flock** of sheep.
The **hatbox** is bright pink.

(a)
1. path
2. lamp
3. tramp
4. crash
5. plant
6. math
7. trash
8. stamp
9. hatbox

(o)
1. shot
2. clock
3. sock
4. rot
5. crop
6. flock
7. _____

Aley did not do

WRITE Write a sentence for each Core Word on a separate sheet of paper.

2 The /a/ and /o/ Sounds

Spelling Words in Context

11-6-09

 REAL-WORLD CONNECTION Write the Core Words that best complete the story. Use each word only once.

❖ Vincent van Gogh ❖

As a boy, Vincent van Gogh studied languages, **math**, and other subjects. In his twenties, he gave away everything he owned and lived like a _____. That is when Vincent started painting.

Van Gogh often walked along his favorite _____, stopping to paint scenes that caught his eye. He loved to paint flowers and other _____ life. He also painted people and animals. He might paint a **flock** of birds flying over a field. One of his paintings is of a man planting a wheat _____.

When he was painting, van Gogh did not keep track of time, or watch the _____. He would often work by the light of a _____.

Van Gogh made more than 800 paintings. Only one sold before he died. Many were thrown in the **trash**. Today his paintings are among the most expensive in the world. ❖

 CONTEXT CLUES Write the Core Word that will complete each sentence.

1. I need a **stamp** to mail this letter.
2. Will the doctor give me a **shot** today?
3. James wore one red and one blue _____.
4. We threw out the fruit that was starting to _____.
5. Keep a hat in a **hatbox**.
6. The ball might _____ through the window.

Unit 1 • Lesson 1   3

Building Spelling Vocabulary

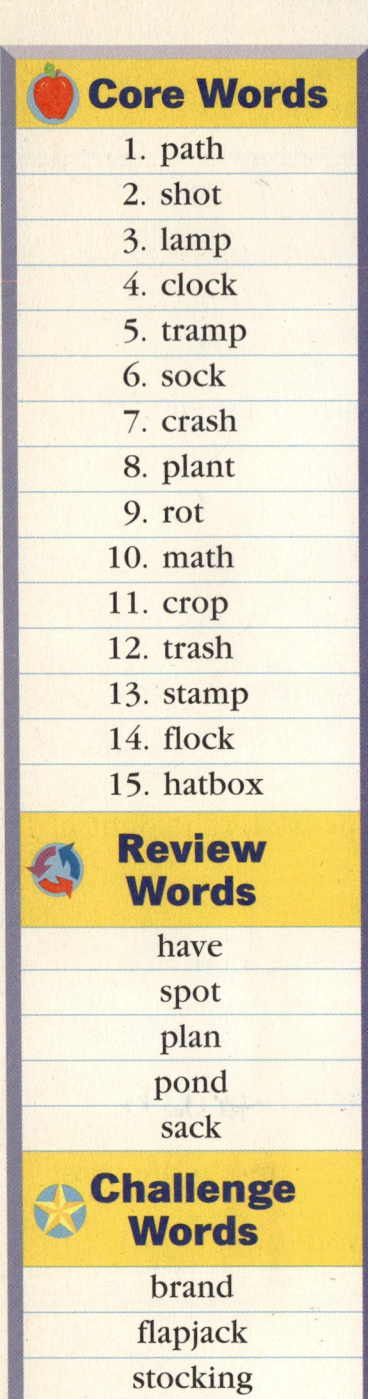

Core Words
1. path
2. shot
3. lamp
4. clock
5. tramp
6. sock
7. crash
8. plant
9. rot
10. math
11. crop
12. trash
13. stamp
14. flock
15. hatbox

Review Words
have
spot
plan
pond
sack

Challenge Words
brand
flapjack
stocking
candy
lobby

PLURALS Adding *-s* or *-es* to many nouns makes them plural. Make these Core Words plural.

1. sock _____   7. path _____
2. clock _____ 8. plant _____
3. lamp _____   9. shot _____
4. stamp _____ 10. crop _____
5. tramp _____ 11. hatbox _____
6. crash _____ 12. flock _____

Which Core Words are the same in their singular and plural forms?

13. _____   14. _____

WORD PARTS Add the underlined word parts together to make the Review Words.

1. <u>s</u>pin + h<u>ot</u> = _____
2. <u>p</u>ot + b<u>ond</u> = _____
3. <u>play</u> + <u>can</u> = _____
4. <u>s</u>ing + t<u>ack</u> = _____
5. <u>hat</u> + do<u>ve</u> = _____

CHANGING LETTERS Write the Challenge Words formed by adding, dropping, or changing one or more letters in each word.

1. blackjack _____
2. handy _____
3. rocking _____
4. branded _____
5. hobby _____

4 The /a/ and /o/ Sounds

Proofreading and Writing

Proofreading Marks

○ misspelling ≡ make a capital letter
∧ insert / make a small letter
⌿ delete ⊙ add a period

Practice Proofreading

Here is a draft of one student's journal entry about Saturday activities. Find three misspelled Core Words. Circle them and write them correctly.

> Saturday is better than any other day of the week. I have a few jobs to do, like taking out the tresh. But mostly I have fun. My friend Joey and I pretend we are on a peth in the jungle where a flouck of monster birds is chasing us.

1. _____
2. _____
3. _____

Write on Your Own: Journal Entry

Plan to write a journal entry about what you like to do on Saturdays. Think about whether you like to help your parents around the house or create art. Choose and write at least four Core Words and other words that you will use in your journal entry. Write your journal entry on a separate sheet of paper, following the steps on page 159.

1. _____   4. _____
2. _____   5. _____
3. _____   6. _____

Now proofread your word list and journal entry and correct any errors.

Unit 1 • Lesson 1   5

Sorting Spelling Patterns

2 The /e/, /i/, and /u/ Sounds

Spelling Focus—The /e/ sound can be spelled *e* and *ea*. The /i/ sound can be spelled *i*. The /u/ sound can be spelled *u*.

🍎 **SORT** Write the Core Words with the /e/, /i/, and /u/ sounds spelled the following ways.

Core Words

1. deck
2. blush
3. risk
4. fence
5. head
6. grip
7. crust
8. pick
9. spent
10. film
11. dead
12. dusk
13. tent
14. bread
15. thump

My Words

Core Word Sentences

The **deck** of the ship was wet.
A **blush** spread across his face.
Jumping off the rock was a **risk**.
A **fence** circles the house.
She is the **head** of the company.
He held on with a strong **grip**.
The pie had a crisp **crust**.
I used a **pick** and a shovel.
We **spent** all our money.
Put **film** in the camera.
The dry leaf was **dead**.
The best part of the day is **dusk**.
We all slept in the **tent**.
I like to eat **bread** and butter.
The book fell with a **thump**.

e
1. _____
2. _____
3. _____
4. _____

ea
1. _____
2. _____
3. _____

i
1. _____
2. _____
3. _____
4. _____

u
1. _____
2. _____
3. _____
4. _____

🍎 **WRITE** Write a sentence for each Core Word on a separate sheet of paper.

Spelling Words in Context

 REAL-WORLD CONNECTION Write the Core Words that best complete the story. Use each word only once.

❖ Digging Up the Past ❖

Mary Leakey never wanted a house with a _____ and a picket _____. She lived much of her life in a _____. She took water, _____, and food with her into the field. Mary was an archaeologist.

On July 17, 1959, Mary and her husband Louis were setting up camp. They were waiting for a photographer who wanted to _____ them. It was a while until _____, and Mary decided to take a walk.

Not too far from camp, Mary spotted something in the ground. When she tapped it with her fingers, it made a small _____. She carefully brushed away the _____ of dirt to find two teeth. Mary was so excited, she began to _____. She ran to tell Louis. Later she went back and dug out more. She had to _____ out more than 400 pieces of bone. When she put them together, she had the skull of a human ancestor that had been _____ for almost two million years.

Mary Leakey's work was sometimes a _____. But she _____ her life doing what she loved most—digging in the sun. ❖

 ANTONYMS Write the Core Word that is an antonym, or opposite, of each word.

1. tail _____
2. drop _____

Unit 1 • Lesson 2   7

Building Spelling Vocabulary

Core Words

1. deck
2. blush
3. risk
4. fence
5. head
6. grip
7. crust
8. pick
9. spent
10. film
11. dead
12. dusk
13. tent
14. bread
15. thump

Review Words

desk
shut
brick
dump
give

Challenge Words

thread
stitch
scrub
sweater
finish

CHANGING LETTERS Write the Core Words formed by adding, dropping, or changing one or more letters in each word.

1. gripped _____
2. tick _____
3. crusty _____
4. spend _____
5. fences _____
6. neck _____
7. flush _____
8. rent _____
9. tusk _____
10. had _____
11. films _____
12. death _____
13. risky _____
14. breaded _____
15. thumper _____

WORD BUILDING Write the Review Words. Then build and write new words by adding letters to and subtracting letters from the Review Words.

1. t + brick – b = _____ _____
2. l + give – g = _____ _____
3. p + dump – d = _____ _____
4. b + shut – sh = _____ _____
5. desk – sk + ck = _____ _____

LETTER CLUES Write the Challenge Words that fit these clues.

1. They begin with three consonants. _____
   _____
2. It ends in **er**. _____
3. It ends with three consonants. _____
4. It ends with two consonants. _____

The /e/, /i/, and /u/ Sounds

Proofreading and Writing

Proofreading Marks

⊙	misspelling	≡	make a capital letter
∧	insert	/	make a small letter
ℓ	delete	⊙	add a period

Practice Proofreding

Here is a draft of one student's descriptive paragraph about baking bread. Find three misspelled Core Words. Circle them and write them correctly.

    The bakers peck up their tall white
hats and put them on their heads. Now
they are ready to work. Each baker throws
a ball of dough on the table to make
bred. The dough lands with a thomp.

1. _____
2. _____
3. _____

Write on Your Own: Descriptive Paragraph

Plan to write a descriptive paragraph about something you do with your hands. The student above wrote about making bread. Mary Leakey used her hands to dig. Choose and write at least four Core Words and other words that you will use in your description. Write your description on a separate sheet of paper, following the steps on page 159.

1. _____   4. _____
2. _____   5. _____
3. _____   6. _____

Now proofread your word list and paragraph and correct any errors.

Unit 1 • Lesson 2   9

Sorting Spelling Patterns

3 The /ā/ and /ō/ Sounds

Spelling Focus—The /ā/ sound can be spelled *a_e*, *ai*, and *ay*. The /ō/ sound can be spelled *o_e* and *oa*.

SORT Write the Core Words with the /ā/ and /ō/ sounds spelled the following ways.

Core Words

1. cone
2. blaze
3. spoke
4. fail
5. goal
6. froze
7. play
8. away
9. flame
10. vote
11. spade
12. stain
13. chose
14. coal
15. mail

My Words

Core Word Sentences

This **cone** is from a redwood tree.
The campfire's **blaze** is warm.
We **spoke** on the phone.
If you **fail**, try again.
She kicked the winning **goal**.
My hands **froze** in the cold.
They like to **play** games.
My friend lives far **away**.
The **flame** was very hot.
I wanted to **vote** for her.
He used a **spade** to dig.
The shirt had a **stain** on it.
He **chose** her for the team.
We burn **coal** for heat.
Did you **mail** the letter?

a_e
1. _____
2. _____
3. _____

ai
1. _____
2. _____
3. _____

ay
1. _____
2. _____

o_e
1. _____
2. _____
3. _____
4. _____
5. _____

oa
1. _____
2. _____

WRITE Write a sentence for each Core Word on a separate sheet of paper.

Spelling Words in Context

 REAL-WORLD CONNECTION Write the Core Words that best complete the story. Use each word only once.

❖ Mother Jones ❖

In 1867, Mary Jones's husband and children died of yellow fever. In 1871, the Great Fire swept a huge _____ through Chicago. Mary lost everything in the _____.

Mary stayed in a building owned by the Knights of Labor. This group helped workers. In those days, children were forced to work long, hard hours in factories. They sweated through the summers and _____ through the winters. They never had time to _____.

Mary started making speeches. She would often _____ letters to the president. She led children on a march to show others how they were treated.

The police took her _____ to jail many times. Still, she _____ to fight. The people started calling her "Mother." Her _____ was to get children out of the factories and into schools. It took a long time, but she did not _____.

Mother also went to _____ mines and railroad yards. She asked the workers to _____ for unions that would help them. Mother Jones _____ out for workers everywhere. ❖

 CONTEXT CLUES Write the Core Word that will complete each sentence.

1. A _____ is a tool for digging.
2. An ice-cream _____ is a real treat on a hot day.
3. Sometimes bleach will remove a _____.

Unit 1 • Lesson 3   11

Building Spelling Vocabulary

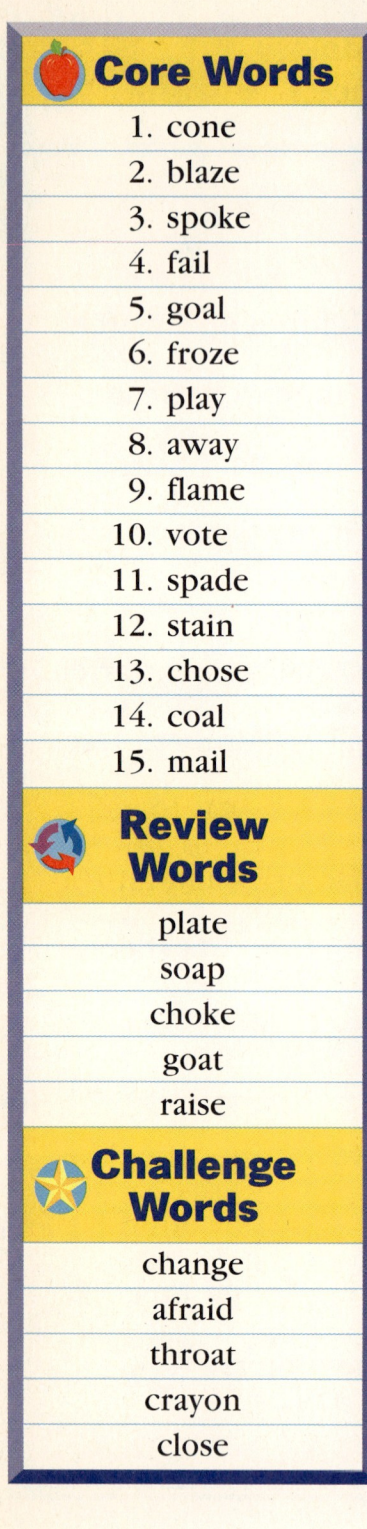

Core Words
1. cone
2. blaze
3. spoke
4. fail
5. goal
6. froze
7. play
8. away
9. flame
10. vote
11. spade
12. stain
13. chose
14. coal
15. mail

Review Words
plate
soap
choke
goat
raise

Challenge Words
change
afraid
throat
crayon
close

🍎 **WORD FORMS** Most past tense verbs end with *-ed*. Some words, like the following, have unusual patterns. Write the Core Word that is the past tense of each verb.

1. freeze _____   3. choose _____
2. speak _____

🍎 **PLURALS** Adding *-s* to many nouns makes them plural. Make these Core Words plural.

4. flame _____   8. spade _____
5. goal _____   9. vote _____
6. blaze _____   10. cone _____
7. coal _____   11. stain _____

🍎 **WORD ENDINGS** Adding *-s* to a verb makes it agree with some subjects (*she sings*). Add *-s* to these Core Words.

12. fail _____   13. play _____

🧭 **PHONETIC PATTERNS** Write the Review Word that matches each respelling.

1. /plāt/ _____   4. /chōk/ _____
2. /sōp/ _____   5. /rāz/ _____
3. /gōt/ _____

⭐ **LETTER CLUES** Write the Challenge Words that fit these clues.

1. It begins with the same letters as *choose*. _____
2. It begins with the same letters as *clock*. _____
3. It starts with three consonants. _____
4. It has the word *aid* in it. _____
5. It begins with the same letters as *crow*. _____

12 The /ā/ and /ō/ Sounds

Proofreading and Writing

Proofreading Marks

- ⊙ misspelling
- ∧ insert
- ℯ delete
- ≡ make a capital letter
- / make a small letter
- ⊙ add a period

Practice Proofreading

Here is a draft of one student's list of questions to a person who has moved to a new community. Find four misspelled Core Words. Circle them and write them correctly.

1. Are there many places to playe?
2. Do you mind being awaye from your old home?
3. How often do you get male from your old friends?
4. Are you glad that your family chos to move there?

1. _____
2. _____
3. _____
4. _____

Write on Your Own: List of Ideas

Plan to write a list of ideas of how you can help your community. Choose and write at least four Core Words and other words that you will use in your list. Write your list on a separate sheet of paper, following the steps on page 159.

1. _____   4. _____
2. _____   5. _____
3. _____   6. _____

Now proofread your word list and list of ideas and correct any errors.

Unit 1 • Lesson 3   13

Sorting Spelling Patterns

4 The /ē/ and /ī/ Sounds

Spelling Focus—The /ē/ sound can be spelled *ea* and *ee*. The /ī/ sound can be spelled *i_e* and *igh*.

🍎 **SORT** Write the Core Words with the /ē/ and /ī/ sounds spelled the following ways.

Core Words

1. high
2. deal
3. clean
4. please
5. fright
6. smile
7. street
8. line
9. pipe
10. wise
11. keep
12. glide
13. beast
14. sigh
15. neat

My Words

Core Word Sentences

The kite flew very **high**.
They agreed to the **deal**.
Did you **clean** your room?
Say "**please**" and "thank you."
The scary mask gave us a **fright**.
She has a pretty **smile**.
My house is on the next **street**.
Use a ruler to draw a **line**.
The **pipe** had a leak.
It is not **wise** to play with fire.
I **keep** my toys in a closet.
It was easy to **glide** on the ice.
A lion is a wild **beast**.
Her **sigh** sounded so sad.
His writing is **neat**.

ea
1. _____
2. _____
3. _____
4. _____
5. _____

ee
1. _____
2. _____

i_e
1. _____
2. _____
3. _____
4. _____
5. _____

igh
1. _____
2. _____
3. _____

 WRITE Write a sentence for each Core Word on a separate sheet of paper.

14 The /ē/ and /ī/ Sounds

Spelling Words in Context

 REAL-WORLD CONNECTION Write the Core Words that best complete the story. Use each word only once.

❖ Christina Rossetti ❖

As a child, Christina Rossetti loved scary stories that filled her with _____. A story about a horrible _____ was always welcome.

When she grew up, Christina loved to write stories and poems. At first, she did not make much money as a writer. To help earn money, Christina worked as a governess. Her job was to watch the children and to _____ the house _____ and _____. Finally, she gave up this job and went back to writing.

Christina spent a great _____ of time alone. From a window _____ on the second floor, she watched the people on the _____ below. Sometimes she was sad and would look out the window and _____. Other times she would look out and _____. Often she would write down her feelings in a poem. She worked carefully to get each _____ just right. People started buying more and more of her books. ❖

 DEFINITIONS Write the Core Word that fits each definition.

1. a tube made of metal, plastic, or other material _____
2. to move smoothly _____
3. to be smart _____
4. a polite word _____

Unit 1 • Lesson 4

Building Spelling Vocabulary

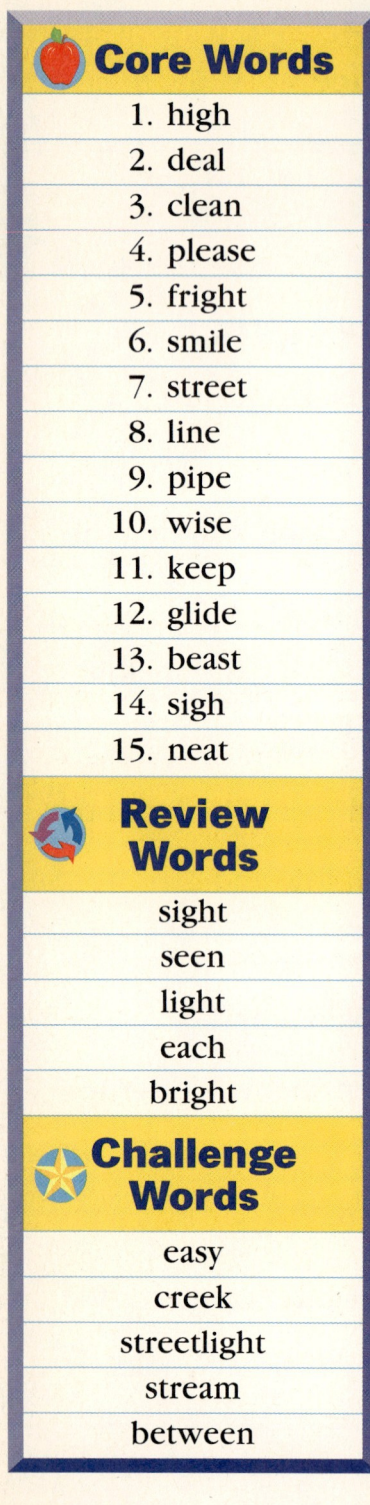

Core Words
1. high
2. deal
3. clean
4. please
5. fright
6. smile
7. street
8. line
9. pipe
10. wise
11. keep
12. glide
13. beast
14. sigh
15. neat

Review Words
sight
seen
light
each
bright

Challenge Words
easy
creek
streetlight
stream
between

RHYMING WORDS Write the Core Words that rhyme with the last word in each sentence.

1. The cake you made was *sweet*. _____
2. I like all vegetables except *peas*. _____
3. On the farm we saw some *sheep*. _____
4. My baby brother has blue *eyes*. _____
5. That is the nicest card I've ever *seen*. _____
6. A chair is a good *seat*. _____
7. She always walks one *mile*. _____
8. The new boy in school is very *shy*. _____
9. My family ate a huge *feast*. _____
10. I couldn't get to sleep last *night*. _____

WORD PARTS Put these puzzle parts together to make the Review Words and one new word.

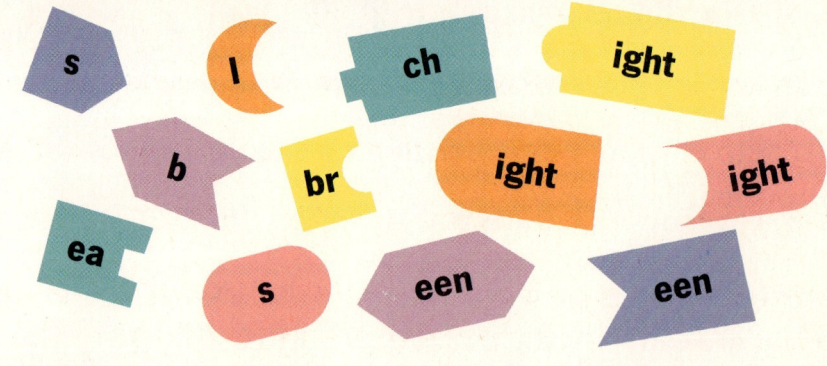

1. _____   4. _____
2. _____   5. _____
3. _____   6. _____

LETTER SCRAMBLE Unscramble these letters to write the Challenge Words.

1. seay _____   4. steamr _____
2. beenwet _____   5. kreec _____
3. strightleet _____

16 The /ē/ and /ī/ Sounds

Proofreading and Writing

Proofreading Marks

- ◯ misspelling
- ∧ insert
- ℓ delete
- ≡ make a capital letter
- / make a small letter
- ⊙ add a period

Practice Proofreading

Here is a draft of one student's newspaper article about a girl who kept a beast. Find four misspelled Core Words. Circle them and write them correctly.

> While skating one day, Kim found a beest in the street. At first Kim's parents did not want her to kepe the beast. They were afraid that it might give the neighbors a frite. The beast gave them a sweet smil, so they changed their minds.

1. _____
2. _____
3. _____
4. _____

Write on Your Own: Newspaper Article

Plan to write a newspaper article about your favorite scary story or writer. Think about information you should include in your article, including who, what, where, when, and why. Choose and write at least four Core Words and other words that you will use in your article. Write your article on a separate sheet of paper, following the steps on page 159.

1. _____   4. _____
2. _____   5. _____
3. _____   6. _____

Now proofread your word list and article and correct any errors.

Unit 1 • Lesson 4

Sorting Spelling Patterns

5 The /oo/ Sound

Spelling Focus—The /oo/ sound can be spelled *oo*, *u_e*, and *ew*.

SORT Write the Core Words with the /oo/ sound spelled the following ways.

Core Words
1. dune
2. flew
3. noon
4. dew
5. booth
6. chew
7. stew
8. shoot
9. choose
10. new
11. root
12. grew
13. flute
14. loose
15. scoop

My Words

Core Word Sentences

Climb the sand **dune**.
The bird **flew** away.
We eat lunch at **noon**.
The grass was wet with **dew**.
We built a **booth** for the fair.
Slowly **chew** your food.
Dad cooked a tasty **stew**.
Use a camera to **shoot** pictures.
You must **choose** me or her!
My glasses are brand **new**.
I **root** for the underdog!
She **grew** two inches.
I play piano and **flute**.
The belt was too **loose**.
Let's **scoop** up some sand.

oo
1. _____
2. _____
3. _____
4. _____
5. _____
6. _____
7. _____

u_e
1. _____
2. _____

ew
1. _____
2. _____
3. _____
4. _____
5. _____
6. _____

WRITE Write a sentence for each Core Word on a separate sheet of paper.

Spelling Words in Context

 REAL-WORLD CONNECTION Write the Core Words that best complete the story. Use each word only once.

❖ Annie Oakley ❖

Annie Mozee was good with a rifle. One day, Annie saw a shooting gallery. She walked up to the _____ and fired six shots. Six targets fell. "I can shoot just about anything I _____," Annie said.

A contest was set up between Annie and a trick shooter named Frank Butler. It was just after _____. Each would have to shoot at 25 clay plates tossed into the air. The clay plates _____ through the air. Frank hit 24. Annie hit 25.

After that, Annie got a new job and a _____ name. She joined Buffalo Bill's Wild West Show. She called herself Annie Oakley. Her fame _____. People liked to say things like "Annie can _____ the _____ off a plant fifty yards away. She can shoot a drop of _____ off a blade of grass. She can shoot a _____ tooth out of your mouth. She can shoot a single grain of sand off a sand _____." Of course, some of these things weren't exactly true. But Annie Oakley was surely the best shot in the world. ❖

 CONTEXT CLUES Write the Core Word that will complete each sentence.

1. Harold plays _____ in the band.
2. Beth had one _____ of banana ice cream.
3. Beef jerky is hard to _____.
4. Put meat and vegetables in the _____.

Unit 1 • Lesson 5

Building Spelling Vocabulary

Core Words
1. dune
2. flew
3. noon
4. dew
5. booth
6. chew
7. stew
8. shoot
9. choose
10. new
11. root
12. grew
13. flute
14. loose
15. scoop

Review Words
tune
soon
moon
pool
broom

Challenge Words
due
duty
caboose
true
shampoo

HOMOPHONES Write the Core Words that are homophones for these words. A *homophone* is a word that sounds the same as another word, such as *so* and *sew*.

1. knew _____   4. flu _____
2. route _____   5. chews _____
3. do _____

CHANGING LETTERS Write the Core Words formed by adding, dropping, or changing one or more letters in each word.

6. book _____   11. scooper _____
7. shooting _____   12. grow _____
8. stews _____   13. tune _____
9. loosen _____   14. fluted _____
10. chewed _____   15. soon _____

WORD BUILDING Use the letters *oo* or *u* with the following letters to write the Review Words.

1. s, n _____
2. m, n _____
3. p, l _____
4. b, r, m _____
5. t, n, e _____

LETTER CLUES Write the Challenge Words that fit these clues.

1. They end in *ue*. _____ _____
2. They have two *o*'s. _____ _____
3. It ends in *y*. _____

20 The /oo/ Sound

Proofreading and Writing

Proofreading Marks

◯	misspelling	≡	make a capital letter
∧	insert	/	make a small letter
⌒e	delete	⊙	add a period

Practice Prooofreding

Here is a draft of one student's invitation for lunch. Find four misspelled Core Words. Circle them and write them correctly.

> We will have lunch at nune on my deck. We can look over the doone to the beach. We will listen to a newe tape of flewt music while we eat. Please call me as soon as you can.

1. _____
2. _____
3. _____
4. _____

Write on Your Own: Invitation

Plan to write an invitation to a friend for a neighborhood carnival. Think about what time and where the carnival will be. You might tell what kinds of contests, booths, and events you will have. Choose and write at least four Core Words and other words that you will use in your invitation. Write your invitation on a separate sheet of paper, following the steps on page 159.

1. _____ 4. _____
2. _____ 5. _____
3. _____ 6. _____

Now proofread your word list and invitation and correct any errors.

Unit 1 • Lesson 5 21

6 Review for Lessons 1–5

Lesson 1

Lesson 1
- trash
- tramp
- clock
- shot
- math
- rot
- crop
- crash
- lamp
- flock

WORD SORT Write two Core Words each that spell the /a/ and the /o/ sounds.

/a/
1. _____
2. _____

/o/
3. _____
4. _____

CLASSIFYING Write a Core Word that fits each group.

5. science, social studies, English, _____
6. herd, pack, group, _____

WORD PARTS Add the underlined word parts together to make the Core Words.

7. tr̲y + d̲amp = _____
8. cr̲ack + w̲ish = _____
9. r̲ip + n̲ot = _____
10. cl̲ip + d̲ock = _____

Lesson 2

Lesson 2
- spent
- blush
- dead
- risk
- film
- deck
- tent
- crust
- bread
- grip

WORD SORT Write two Core Words each that spell the /e/, the /i/, and the /u/ sounds.

/e/
1. _____
2. _____

/i/
3. _____
4. _____

/u/
5. _____
6. _____

DEFINITIONS Write a Core Word that fits each meaning.

7. to turn red _____
8. to have used all your money _____

PLURALS Adding -s to many nouns makes them plural. Make these Core Words plural.

9. tent _____
10. film _____
11. risk _____
12. grip _____

22 Lesson 6 Review

Review

Lesson 3

Lesson 3
- vote
- cone
- fail
- stain
- spade
- blaze
- coal
- away
- spoke
- flame

🍎 **WORD SORT** Write two Core Words each that spell the /ā/ and the /ō/ sounds.

/ā/   /ō/

1. _____   3. _____

2. _____   4. _____

🍎 **CONTEXT CLUES** Write a Core Word to complete each sentence. The missing word will rhyme with the underlined word.

5. A green shovel is a <u>jade</u> _____.

6. He told a <u>joke</u> when he _____.

🍎 **CHANGING LETTERS** Write the Core Words formed by adding, dropping, or changing one or more letters in each word.

7. ways _____   8. flaming _____

Lesson 4

Lesson 4
- high
- sigh
- neat
- wise
- glide
- pipe
- fright
- beast
- clean
- deal

🍎 **WORD SORT** Write two Core Words each that spell the /ē/ and the /ī/ sounds.

/ē/   /ī/

1. _____   3. _____

2. _____   4. _____

🍎 **ANTONYMS** Write a Core Word that is an antonym, or opposite, of each word.

5. dirty _____   7. foolish _____

6. low _____   8. messy _____

🍎 **RHYMING WORDS** Write the Core Word that rhymes with each word.

9. seal _____   10. feast _____

Lesson 6 Review 23

Review

Lesson 5

Lesson 5
- booth
- root
- scoop
- dune
- grew
- shoot
- flew
- chew
- flute
- dew

🍎 **WORD SORT** Write two Core Words that spell the /o͞o/ sound for each pattern.

ew	oo	u_e
1. _____	3. _____	5. _____
2. _____	4. _____	6. _____

🍎 **CONTEXT CLUES** Write a Core Word to complete each sentence.

7. The grass is wet with _____.

8. I would like a _____ of ice cream.

🍎 **WORD BUILDING** Write the Core Words. Then build and write new words by adding letters to and subtracting letters from the Core Words.

9. t + booth – b = _____, _____

10. gr + chew – ch = _____, _____

Spelling Strategy

THINK Look at the Core Word lists on pages 22–24. Choose one word from each list that is hardest for you to spell. Write the word and a strategy to help you remember how to spell each word. For example: You put *ash* in the *trash*.

Words	Spelling Strategies
1. _____	_____
2. _____	_____
3. _____	_____
4. _____	_____
5. _____	_____

Review
Practice Proofreading

Read the paragraph below. Find eight misspelled Core Words. Circle them and write them correctly.

Proofreading Marks	
◯	misspelling
∧	insert
℮	delete
≡	make a capital letter
/	make a small letter
⊙	add a period

   brenda loves to play at her grandmother's house. When Grandmother sees brenda, she smiles. Together, they spend the morning making bred and stu. They eat Lunch at nune on the sunny dek. then Grandmother gets down an old hatbocks. This is where She likes to keap interesting stamps. At duske, Brenda walks down the pathe to go home.

1. _____
2. _____
3. _____
4. _____
5. _____
6. _____
7. _____
8. _____

Now find two words that should begin with a capital letter and two words that should begin with small letters. Use the correct proofreading marks to show which letters should be capitals and which should be small.

Write on Your Own: Interview Questions

Write interview questions you would like to ask an actor you admire. Use at least six spelling words. First write the spelling words that you want to use.

1. _____
2. _____
3. _____
4. _____
5. _____
6. _____

Now proofread your word list and questions and correct any errors.

Lesson 6 Review

Review

SPELLING FUN Use Core Words from Lessons 1–5 to complete this puzzle.

Lesson 1
sock
stamp
plant

Lesson 2
fence
head
thump
pick

Lesson 3
mail
play

Lesson 4
street
smile
please
line

Lesson 5
new
loose

ACROSS
2. It's fun to _____.
3. Worn on your foot
5. Not tight
7. The magic word
8. Rhymes with *bump*
9. Found on a letter
12. Rhymes with *pine*

DOWN
1. It sits on your neck.
2. _____ flowers for a bouquet
3. Can be on your face
4. A railing or wall used to mark a boundary
6. Look both ways before crossing it.
7. Water the _____.
10. Send letters
11. Rhymes with *dew*

Review

STANDARDIZED-FORMAT TEST PRACTICE

Choose the correct spelling of the Core Words from Lessons 1–5.

ANSWERS

SAMPLE.	A. frite	B. fright	C. fryte	Ⓐ ● Ⓒ
1.	A. shoot	B. shute	C. shote	Ⓐ Ⓑ Ⓒ
2.	A. choze	B. choas	C. chose	Ⓐ Ⓑ Ⓒ
3.	A. dune	B. dewn	C. doon	Ⓐ Ⓑ Ⓒ
4.	A. piyp	B. piep	C. pipe	Ⓐ Ⓑ Ⓒ

Choose the misspelled Core Words from Lessons 1–5.

SAMPLE.	A. sok	B. play	C. dusk	● Ⓑ Ⓒ
1.	A. fail	B. ded	C. stain	Ⓐ Ⓑ Ⓒ
2.	A. shot	B. choose	C. coale	Ⓐ Ⓑ Ⓒ
3.	A. trashe	B. crop	C. flute	Ⓐ Ⓑ Ⓒ
4.	A. floo	B. glide	C. lamp	Ⓐ Ⓑ Ⓒ

Choose the correct spelling of the Core Words from Lessons 1–5 to complete each sentence.

SAMPLE. The _____ test was easy.			
A. maht	B. math	C. meth	Ⓐ ● Ⓒ

1. The lake _____ in the icy cold.

   A. frose   B. froz   C. froze   Ⓐ Ⓑ Ⓒ

2. The soccer player scored a _____.

   A. goal   B. gole   C. gowl   Ⓐ Ⓑ Ⓒ

3. The tree _____ to be very large.

   A. gru   B. grew   C. grewe   Ⓐ Ⓑ Ⓒ

4. I like the _____ of the bread.

   A. crost   B. cruste   C. crust   Ⓐ Ⓑ Ⓒ

Sorting Spelling Patterns

7 The /oi/ Sound

Spelling Focus—The /oi/ sound can be spelled *oy* or *oi*.

SORT Write the Core Words with the /oi/ sound spelled the following ways.

Core Words

1. oil
2. boil
3. boy
4. coil
5. royal
6. join
7. point
8. spoil
9. broil
10. noise
11. voice
12. soil
13. enjoy
14. coin
15. loyal

My Words

Core Word Sentences

Water and **oil** don't mix.

The hot water began to **boil.**

The **boy** sat down.

The snake lay in a **coil.**

The king has a **royal** robe.

May I **join** your club?

The pencil has a sharp **point.**

Don't **spoil** my mood.

Let's **broil** the chicken.

Drums make **noise.**

Did you **voice** a complaint?

The **soil** was good for planting.

I **enjoy** scary movies.

The **coin** I have is a dime.

The knight was honest and **loyal.**

oy

1. _____
2. _____
3. _____
4. _____

oi

1. _____
2. _____
3. _____
4. _____
5. _____
6. _____
7. _____
8. _____
9. _____
10. _____
11. _____

WRITE Write a sentence for each Core Word on a separate sheet of paper.

Spelling Words in Context

 REAL-WORLD CONNECTION Write the Core Words that best complete the story. Use each word only once.

❖ George Washington Carver ❖

George Washington Carver was born in the early 1860s. As a _____, he lived in Arkansas and Missouri. When he grew up, he traveled around doing odd jobs. He never had an extra _____ to spend.

Later, Carver studied music and art. He had a good _____ and used to _____ singing. He also loved to paint portraits of flowers, vines, and ivy twisted in a _____. Later he studied agriculture. After that, he went to _____ the staff at Tuskegee Institute in Alabama.

Soil in the South was ruined from planting too much cotton. Carver knew that planting peanuts would make the _____ rich again. He needed to find ways for people to use the peanuts. He tried to _____, _____, mix, and mash them. Carver made things like cooking _____, wood stains, milk, and soap from peanuts. In all, he found more than 300 uses for them. His main _____ was to help black farmers.

Carver had many job offers, but he stayed _____ to the South and to Tuskegee Institute. He received many honors. One came from a _____ society in London. He did not let all this _____ him, though. Carver was a very quiet man who never made much _____, but his work changed the South. ❖

Unit 2 • Lesson 7

Building Spelling Vocabulary

Core Words

1. oil
2. boil
3. boy
4. coil
5. royal
6. join
7. point
8. spoil
9. broil
10. noise
11. voice
12. soil
13. enjoy
14. coin
15. loyal

Review Words

any
many
very
every
who

Challenge Words

choice
noisy
oyster
destroy
poison

WORD ENDINGS Add *-ed* or *-ing* to these Core Words to show that an action has happened or is happening now.

1. join _____ _____
2. enjoy _____ _____
3. broil _____ _____
4. point _____ _____
5. spoil _____ _____

CHANGING LETTERS Write the Core Words formed by adding, dropping, or changing one or more letters in each word.

6. boiler _____   10. noises _____
7. boyish _____   11. coins _____
8. spoil _____   12. oily _____
9. voiced _____   13. disloyal _____

LETTER CLUES Write the Review Words that fit these clues.

1. These two words contain the letters *any*.
   _____ _____

2. These two words contain the letters *very*.
   _____ _____

3. This word contains the letters *wh*. _____

WORD BUILDING Build and write the Challenge Words by adding and subtracting letters as shown.

1. ch + oise − se + ce = _____
2. oyn + st − n + er = _____
3. desk + tr − k + oy = _____
4. poi + s + mon − m = _____
5. noi + st − t + y = _____

30 The /oi/ Sound

Proofreading and Writing

Proofreading Marks

◯ misspelling ≡ make a capital letter
∧ insert / make a small letter
⸌ delete ⊙ add a period

Practice Proofreading

Here is a draft of one student's story about a boy finding oil. Find four misspelled Core Words. Circle them and write them correctly.

> Yesterday a young boy found oyl while digging in the king's roiyal soil. Being a true and loyel young man, he told the king. The king was so pleased that he asked the boy to joyn him at the palace for a huge party.

1. _____
2. _____
3. _____
4. _____

Write on Your Own: Story

Plan to write a story about someone you know who found something or made a discovery. Think about your family, friends, or famous people. Choose and write at least four Core Words and other words to use in your story. Write your story on a separate sheet of paper, following the steps on page 159.

1. _____ 4. _____
2. _____ 5. _____
3. _____ 6. _____

Now proofread your word list and story and correct any errors.

Unit 2 • Lesson 7

Sorting Spelling Patterns

8 The /ou/ Sound

Spelling Focus—The /ou/ sound can be spelled *ou* or *ow*.

SORT Write the Core Words with the /ou/ sound spelled the following ways.

Core Words

1. gown
2. brown
3. bound
4. proud
5. crowd
6. shout
7. count
8. mouse
9. mouth
10. south
11. frown
12. cloud
13. crown
14. growl
15. scout

My Words

Core Word Sentences

The queen wore a long **gown**.
The mud was a dark **brown**.
She **bound** the box with tape.
Dad is **proud** of my success.
The **crowd** was quiet.
Do not scream or **shout**.
Is he a duke or a **count**?
The **mouse** ate the cheese.
His **mouth** was full of food.
Birds fly **south** for the winter.
Her smile turned to a **frown**.
A **cloud** blocked the sunshine.
The king wore a gold **crown**.
My dog likes to **growl** and bark.
A **scout** is an explorer.

ou
1. _____
2. _____
3. _____
4. _____
5. _____
6. _____
7. _____
8. _____
9. _____

ow
1. _____
2. _____
3. _____
4. _____
5. _____
6. _____

WRITE Write a sentence for each Core Word on a separate sheet of paper.

Spelling Words in Context

 REAL-WORLD CONNECTION Write the Core Words that best complete the story. Use each word only once.

❖ How to Be a Clown ❖

Being a clown should make a person _____. Clowns have been making people laugh for more than 3,000 years.

How a clown looks is very important. You might paint your _____ to always have a smile or a _____. You might wear a tuxedo or a fancy _____. Your clothes will have lots of different colors, like orange, red, yellow, and _____. You might also wear a _____ and look like royalty, or you might wear a coonskin cap and look like a frontier _____.

You also have to plan your act. Will you be a clown who makes a funny noise, like a _____ or a squeal? You might do magic tricks or funny skits. For example, you might say abracadabra, _____ 1, 2, 3 and pull a turnip out of a hat, or you might run from a windup _____ and _____ "Help! Help!"

Whatever you choose to look like and however you plan your act, you're sure to be a real _____ pleaser. ❖

 CONTEXT CLUES Write the Core Word that will complete each sentence.

1. Winter is usually warmer in the _____.
2. The train is _____ for Oklahoma.
3. That _____ looks like a giant marshmallow.

Unit 2 • Lesson 8   33

Building Spelling Vocabulary

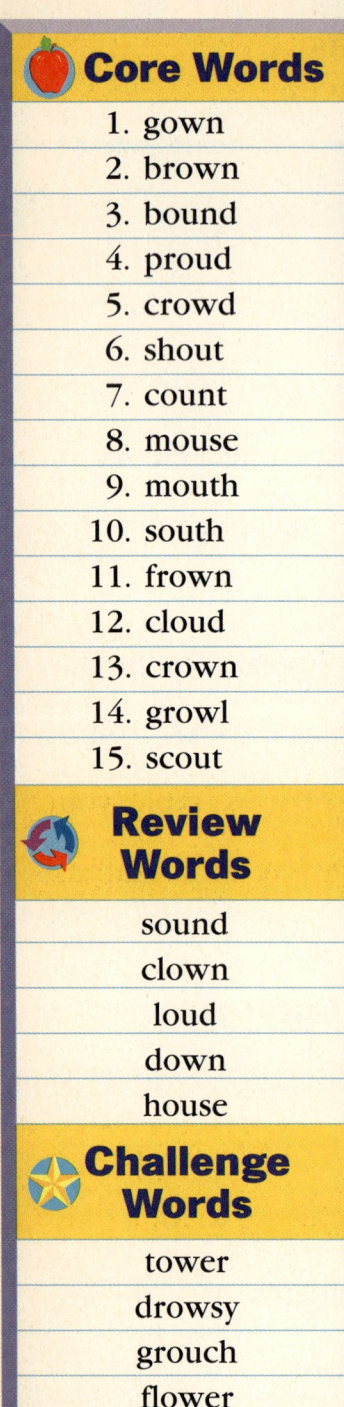

Core Words
1. gown
2. brown
3. bound
4. proud
5. crowd
6. shout
7. count
8. mouse
9. mouth
10. south
11. frown
12. cloud
13. crown
14. growl
15. scout

Review Words
sound
clown
loud
down
house

Challenge Words
tower
drowsy
grouch
flower
aloud

LETTER CLUES Write the Core Words that fit these clues.

These two words have the same five letters.

1. _____ 2. _____

This word is in *counting*.

3. _____

These four words rhyme with *drown*.

4. _____ 6. _____
5. _____ 7. _____

These four words have *out* in them.

8. _____ 10. _____
9. _____ 11. _____

These two words end in *oud*.

12. _____ 13. _____

This word rhymes with *house*.

14. _____

WORD BUILDING Write the Review Words. Then build and write new words by adding and subtracting letters as shown.

1. cr + down – d = _____ _____
2. dr + clown – cl = _____ _____
3. pr + loud – l = _____ _____
4. gr + sound – s = _____ _____
5. bl + house – h = _____ _____

WORD BUILDING Write the Challenge Words that have these smaller words in them.

1. ouch _____   4. flow _____
2. rows _____   5. loud _____
3. tow _____

The /ou/ Sound

Proofreading and Writing

Proofreading Marks

◯	misspelling	≡	make a capital letter
∧	insert	/	make a small letter
℮	delete	⊙	add a period

Practice Proofreding

Here is a draft of one student's newspaper story about a play. Find four misspelled Core Words. Circle them and write them correctly.

> The croud enjoyed the play last night even though a mowse and a clowd almost ruined the show. The children have a right to feel prod. They did a great job. Everyone should see this play because it was fun.

1. _____
2. _____
3. _____
4. _____

Write on Your Own: Newspaper Story

Plan to write a newspaper story about a birthday party or circus act that had a clown. Think about what people would like to know about the clown's act. Choose and write at least four Core Words and other words that you will use in your newspaper story. Write your newspaper story on a separate sheet of paper, following the steps on page 159.

1. _____   4. _____
2. _____   5. _____
3. _____   6. _____

Now proofread your word list and newspaper story and correct any errors.

Unit 2 • Lesson 8

Sorting Spelling Patterns

9 The /ô/ Sound

Spelling Focus—The /ô/ sound can be spelled *o*, *aw*, or *au*.

SORT Write the Core Words with the /ô/ sound spelled the following ways.

Core Words

1. moss
2. saw
3. moth
4. fawn
5. pause
6. haul
7. draw
8. crawl
9. claw
10. haunted
11. hawk
12. because
13. law
14. dawn
15. frost

My Words

Core Word Sentences

The rock was covered with **moss**.
We **saw** the game.
The **moth** flew to the light.
A **fawn** is a young deer.
She read without a **pause**.
I need a truck to **haul** wood.
I **draw** with crayons.
Babies like to **crawl**.
The lobster has one **claw**.
That's a **haunted** house.
The **hawk** flew low.
We ran **because** of the rain.
No one should break the **law**.
We woke up at **dawn**.
The **frost** melted.

o
1. _____
2. _____
3. _____

aw
1. _____
2. _____
3. _____
4. _____
5. _____
6. _____
7. _____
8. _____

au
1. _____
2. _____
3. _____
4. _____

WRITE Write a sentence for each Core Word on a separate sheet of paper.

Spelling Words in Context

 REAL-WORLD CONNECTION Write the Core Words that best complete the story. Use each word only once.

❖ A Grand Adventure ❖

One of the most beautiful places in the southwest is the Grand Canyon. A good time to visit the canyon is early morning, at _____, when there is a colorful sunrise. You may see _____ on the ground if it is cool enough. Many visitors like to _____ pictures of the canyon. If you yell into the canyon, you will hear an echo, _____ it is deep and hollow. This may make the canyon sound spooky, or _____.

When walking through the forest paths above the canyon, you may see a baby deer, or _____. If you _____ for a moment, you may get a good look before it runs away. You may also see various birds, like the _____, fly by. These birds may fly so low that you can almost touch a _____. There are also signs that tell people to beware of snakes that _____ along the ground.

There is a _____ stating that no one can cut, or _____ down, any trees and _____ them out of the forest. This helps keep the Grand Canyon a natural work of art. ❖

 CONTEXT CLUES Write the Core Word that will complete each sentence.

1. The pond was covered with green _____.
2. The _____ flew near the light.

Unit 2 • Lesson 9

Building Spelling Vocabulary

Core Words
1. moss
2. saw
3. moth
4. fawn
5. pause
6. haul
7. draw
8. crawl
9. claw
10. haunted
11. hawk
12. because
13. law
14. dawn
15. frost

Review Words
dog
log
fog
frog
hog

Challenge Words
drawn
caught
naughty
awful
taught

LETTER CLUES Complete these puzzles to make Core Words by filling in the missing letters.

1. _ a w
2. _ a w
3. l a w
4. r a w
5. _ a w k
6. _ a w n
7. _ a w n
8. _ a w l

9. _ a u l
10. _ a u n _ _
11. _ a u s e
12. _ _ a u s e

WORD BUILDING Use a spelling pattern in this lesson to write the Review Word that solves each word problem.

1. d + song − sn = _____
2. long − n = _____
3. log − l + h = _____
4. frock − ck + g = _____
5. frog − r = _____

LETTER CLUES Which Challenge Words are spelled with *aw* and which with *au*?

aw   1. _____
      2. _____
au   3. _____
      4. _____
      5. _____

The /ô/ Sound

Proofreading and Writing

Proofreading Marks

◯ misspelling   ≡ make a capital letter
∧ insert   / make a small letter
⤴ delete   ⊙ add a period

Practice Proofreading

Here is a draft of one student's letter about life in a forest. Find four misspelled Core Words. Circle them and write them correctly.

> When I woke up at don, the ground was covered with frawst. I was cold and hungry. I sau a deer and was about to shoot it. A hawk flew over to me and stopped me. Then I knew I was in a magic forest, becos the hawk talked to me.

1. _____
2. _____
3. _____
4. _____

Write on Your Own: Letter

Plan to write a letter to a friend about a forest, mountain, or canyon you have visited or would like to visit. Think about what you saw or might see and how you felt or might feel. Choose and write at least four Core Words and other words that you will use in your letter. Write your letter on a separate sheet of paper, following the steps on page 159.

1. _____   4. _____
2. _____   5. _____
3. _____   6. _____

Now proofread your word list and letter and correct any errors.

Unit 2 • Lesson 9   39

Sorting Spelling Patterns

10 Final Double Consonants

Spelling Focus—Ending sounds can be spelled with the double consonants *ll, ss, dd, ff, tt,* or *zz.*

SORT Write the Core Words with the following double consonant spellings.

Core Words
1. add
2. mess
3. fall
4. miss
5. gruff
6. small
7. buzz
8. spill
9. less
10. odd
11. hill
12. mitt
13. smell
14. cliff
15. gull

My Words

Core Word Sentences

Did you **add** the numbers?
Clean up the **mess**.
Try not to slip and **fall**.
Do not **miss** the target.
The dog was mean and **gruff**.
That ladybug sure is **small**.
Listen to the bees **buzz**.
He did not **spill** milk.
It took **less** time to get back home.
Three is an **odd** number.
Jill went up the **hill**.
Catch with your **mitt**.
That rose has a nice **smell**.
The **cliff** is steep.
The **gull** flew low.

ll
1. _____
2. _____
3. _____
4. _____
5. _____
6. _____

ss
1. _____
2. _____
3. _____

dd
1. _____
2. _____

ff
1. _____
2. _____

tt
1. _____

zz
1. _____

WRITE Write a sentence for each Core Word on a separate sheet of paper.

40 Final Double Consonants

Spelling Words in Context

🍎 **REAL-WORLD CONNECTION** Write the Core Words that best complete the story. Use each word only once.

❖ Oil Spill! ❖

On March 23, 1989, the Exxon Valdez oil ship left Valdez, Alaska. After a few hours, the captain changed course in order to _____ some icebergs that had broken off a great mountain, or _____, of ice.

The ship got around the ice, but it ran into Bligh Reef. Oil began to _____ out into the ocean. In _____ than an hour, tons of oil polluted the water. What a horrible _____! The _____ was awful.

Cleanup was no _____ task. Crews started to _____ oil-eating chemicals to the water. The _____ of machines could be heard everywhere.

Workers also tried to save oil-coated animals. They wore a special _____ on each hand to handle them. Every animal was in danger. A bird, such as a _____, cannot fly with oil on its wings. It will always _____ back to the ground.

Scientists study the area. They want to find safer ways of moving oil and better ways to clean up oil spills. ❖

🍎 **SYNONYMS** Write the Core Word that is a synonym for each word.

1. strange   _____
2. rough   _____
3. bluff   _____

Unit 2 • Lesson 10

Building Spelling Vocabulary

Core Words
1. add
2. mess
3. fall
4. miss
5. gruff
6. small
7. buzz
8. spill
9. less
10. odd
11. hill
12. mitt
13. smell
14. cliff
15. gull

Review Words
egg
full
glass
kiss
pull

Challenge Words
doll
across
unless
spell
press

LETTER CLUES Complete these puzzles by filling in the missing letters to make Core Words.

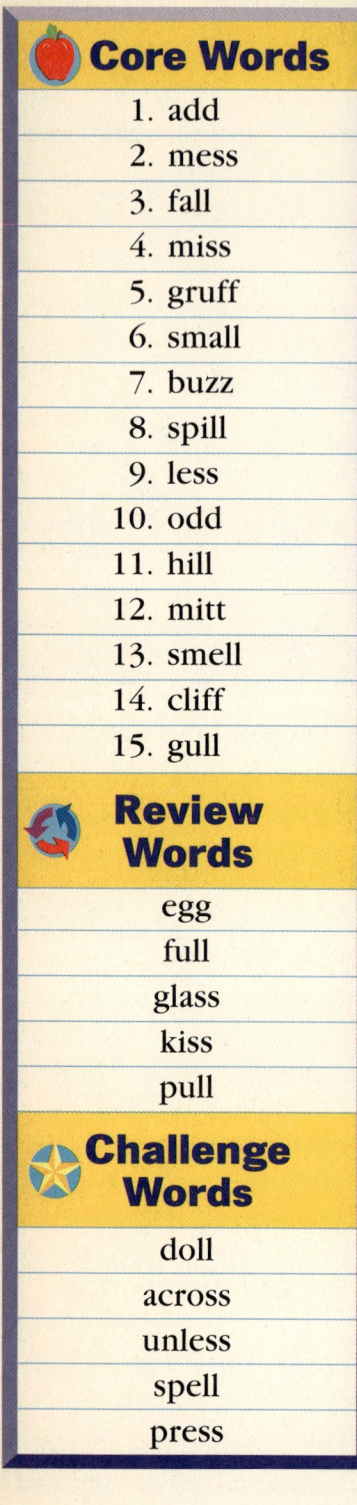

RHYMING WORDS Write the Core Word that rhymes with each word.

7. nod _____
8. ball _____
9. dull _____
10. kiss _____
11. hit _____
12. fuzz _____
13. bluff _____
14. mill _____
15. mess _____

LETTER CLUES Write the Review Words that fit these clues.

1. It ends with *gg*.
   egg

2. They end with *ll*.
   full   pull

3. They end with *ss*.
   kiss   glass

CHANGING LETTERS Write the Challenge Words formed by adding, dropping, or changing one or more letters in each word.

1. dollar _____
2. pressure _____
3. lesson _____
4. spelling _____
5. crossed _____

42 Final Double Consonants

Proofreading and Writing

Proofreading Marks

◯	misspelling	≡	make a capital letter
∧	insert	/	make a small letter
⊝	delete	⊙	add a period

Practice Prooofreding

Here is a draft of one student's paragraph about summer and winter activities. Find four misspelled Core Words. Circle them and write them correctly.

> In winter, I sled down the hil and play in the snow. But I like winter liss than summer. In summer, I swim in a smoll pond near our house. I also go on hikes with my family. We have fun climbing a rocky clif near the beach.

1. _____
2. _____
3. _____
4. _____

Write on Your Own: Paragraph

Plan to write a paragraph comparing spring and fall cleanup activities, such as washing windows or raking leaves. Think about and describe how these activities can be made fun. Choose and write at least four Core Words and other words that you will use in your paragraph. Write your paragraph on a separate sheet of paper, following the steps on page 159.

1. _____   4. _____
2. _____   5. _____
3. _____   6. _____

Now proofread your word list and paragraph and correct any errors.

Unit 2 • Lesson 10   43

Sorting Spelling Patterns

11 The Final /əl/ Sound

Spelling Focus—The final /əl/ sound can be spelled *le*.

SORT Write the Core Words with the final /əl/ sound spelled the following ways.

Core Words

1. apple
2. tumble
3. bottle
4. little
5. handle
6. puddle
7. puzzle
8. wiggle
9. candle
10. pebble
11. tangle
12. jungle
13. marble
14. bubble
15. turtle

My Words

Core Word Sentences

I ate an **apple**.

Did you **tumble** and fall?

He filled the **bottle** with water.

The **little** plant grew.

I can **handle** the work.

The rain made a **puddle**.

He has all the **puzzle** pieces.

Watch the worm **wiggle**.

She lit the **candle**.

I have a rock and a **pebble**.

Don't **tangle** the wires.

It is hot in the **jungle**.

This is a **marble** statue.

The **bubble** floated in the air.

The **turtle** had a green shell.

two different consonants before le

1. _____
2. _____
3. _____
4. _____
5. _____
6. _____
7. _____

the same two consonants before le

1. _____
2. _____
3. _____
4. _____
5. _____
6. _____
7. _____
8. _____

WRITE Write a sentence for each Core Word on a separate sheet of paper.

Spelling Words in Context

 REAL-WORLD CONNECTION Write the Core Words that best complete the story. Use each word only once.

❖ Saving the Turtles ❖

A turtle reserve in Mexico sits between the _____ of _____ vines and the ocean. The reserve is a place where people take care of sea turtles. When workers see _____ tracks on the beach, they know a mother turtle has laid her eggs. The eggs are larger than a rock, or _____, but smaller than a fruit such as an _____. The workers make sure the eggs are covered with sand.

After a few weeks, the _____ turtles start to _____. They crack the eggshells. Then they _____ out. The swirling designs on their shells look almost like _____.

Baby turtles hatch at night. They look for light shining off the water to find their way to the ocean. A large _____ of water can be like a _____ to them. They may think it's the ocean at first. Workers hold flashlights to show them the way.

As each one dives under, an air _____ comes to the top of the water. All the workers are happy.

 CONTEXT CLUES Write the Core Word that will complete each sentence.

1. A baby drinks juice from a _____.

2. That _____ smells good.

3. The _____ on this suitcase is broken.

Unit 2 • Lesson 11

Building Spelling Vocabulary

Core Words

1. apple
2. tumble
3. bottle
4. little
5. handle
6. puddle
7. puzzle
8. wiggle
9. candle
10. pebble
11. tangle
12. jungle
13. marble
14. bubble
15. turtle

Review Words

uncle
batting
cutting
mopped
tapped

Challenge Words

single
stumble
needle
jingle
trickle

WORD BUILDING Write a Core Word to go with each word. Then write the compound word that the two words make.

1. _____ + sauce = _____
2. _____ + neck = _____
3. _____ + gum = _____
4. _____ + light = _____
5. _____ + bar = _____

CHANGING LETTERS Write the Core Words formed by adding, dropping, or changing one or more letters in each word.

6. tumbling _____
7. littlest _____
8. puddles _____
9. puzzling _____
10. wiggler _____
11. tangled _____
12. jungles _____

SYLLABLES Write these Review Words and draw a line between the syllables. If a word has one syllable, write *one*.

1. uncle _____
2. batting _____
3. cutting _____
4. mopped _____
5. tapped _____

LETTER CLUES Write the Challenge Words that fit these clues.

1. They end with *gle*. _____
   _____
2. It has two vowels in the middle. _____
3. It contains the word *trick*. _____
4. It rhymes with *crumble*. _____

46 The Final /əl/ Sound

Proofreading and Writing

Proofreading Marks

○ misspelling ≡ make a capital letter
∧ insert / make a small letter
⤴ delete ⊙ add a period

Practice Proofreding

Here is a draft of one student's list of items found while exploring. Find four misspelled Core Words. Circle them and write them correctly.

1. a pebbel as round and shiny as a marbl
2. a bird's nest in an old aple tree
3. a large old turtle with a striped shell
4. a glass bottel filled with little ants

1. _____
2. _____
3. _____
4. _____

Write on Your Own: List

Plan to write a list of things you might see while exploring a new place or walking on the beach. Choose and write at least four Core Words and other words that you will use in your list. Write your list on a separate sheet of paper, following the steps on page 159.

1. _____   4. _____
2. _____   5. _____
3. _____   6. _____

Now proofread both lists and correct any errors.

Unit 2 • Lesson 11 47

12 Review for Lessons 7–11

Lesson 7

Lesson 7
- broil
- voice
- boy
- join
- noise
- boil
- point
- soil
- oil
- royal

🍎 **WORD SORT** Write two Core Words that spell the /oi/ sound for each pattern.

oi
1. _____
2. _____

oy
3. _____
4. _____

🍎 **SYNONYMS** Rewrite these sentences. Replace the underlined word with a Core Word.

5. Flowers grow in <u>dirt</u>. _____
6. Jack wants to <u>bake</u> the vegetables. _____

🍎 **PREFIXES** The prefix *re-* means "again." Write a single word that means the same as each phrase.

7. to oil again _____   8. to join again _____

Lesson 8

Lesson 8
- frown
- crown
- scout
- shout
- cloud
- south
- crowd
- gown
- bound
- brown

🍎 **WORD SORT** Write two Core Words that spell the /ou/ sound for each pattern.

ou
1. _____
2. _____

ow
3. _____
4. _____

🍎 **ANTONYMS** Write a Core Word that is an antonym, or opposite, of each word.

5. whisper _____   7. smile _____
6. free _____   8. north _____

🍎 **WORD PARTS** Add the underlined word parts together to make the Core Words.

9. <u>cl</u>ap + l<u>oud</u> = _____   10. <u>sc</u>are + p<u>out</u> = _____

48 Lesson 12 Review

Review

Lesson 9

Lesson 9
- frost
- moth
- law
- claw
- haunted
- pause
- crawl
- draw
- haul
- moss

🍎 **WORD SORT** Write two Core Words that spell the /ô/ sound for each pattern.

au	aw	o
1. _____	3. _____	5. _____
2. _____	4. _____	6. _____

🍎 **RIDDLES** Write the Core Word that fits each clue.

7. Babies do this before they walk. _____

8. It is an insect that looks like a butterfly. _____

🍎 **PHONETIC PATTERNS** Write the Core Word that matches each respelling.

9. /drô/ _____   10. /hôn′tid/ _____

Lesson 10

Lesson 10
- buzz
- gull
- gruff
- mitt
- mess
- cliff
- spill
- small
- miss
- fall

🍎 **WORD SORT** Write two Core Words that spell double consonant endings for each pattern.

ff	ll	ss
1. _____	3. _____	5. _____
2. _____	4. _____	6. _____

🍎 **CONTEXT CLUES** Write a Core Word to complete each sentence. The missing word will rhyme with the underlined word.

7. After you clean, there is <u>less</u> _____.

8. If you tear your baseball glove, it is a <u>split</u> _____.

🍎 **SUFFIXES** The suffix *-ing* can be used to tell about the present. Make these Core Words show action that is happening now by adding *-ing*.

9. spill _____   10. buzz _____

Lesson 12 Review 49

Review

Lesson 11

Lesson 11
- tangle
- wiggle
- marble
- little
- pebble
- apple
- candle
- handle
- puddle
- bottle

🍎 **WORD SORT** Write two Core Words that spell the final /əl/ sound for each pattern.

same two consonants before the /əl/ sound

1. _____   2. _____

different two consonants before the /əl/ sound

3. _____   4. _____

🍎 **CLASSIFYING** Write the Core Word that fits each group.

5. jar, can, cup, _____

6. squirm, wag, shake, _____

🍎 **PLURALS** Adding -s to many nouns makes them plural. Make these Core Words plural.

7. apple _____   8. marble _____

Spelling Strategy

THINK Look at the Core Word lists on pages 48–50. Choose one word from each list that is the hardest for you to spell. Write the word and a strategy to help you remember how to spell each word. For example: To spell *royal,* remember that *Roy* and *Al* are *kings.*

Words	Spelling Strategies
1. _____	_____
2. _____	_____
3. _____	_____
4. _____	_____
5. _____	_____

Review
Practice Proofreading

Read the letter. Find nine misspelled Core Words. Circle them and write them correctly.

July 15, 1997

Dear Barry,

   I always enjoi your gifts This puzzel is fun.
All the pieces add up to a a beautiful picture of a jungal at daun. There are many animals in the picture There is is a turtel, a hauk, a fon, a prowd lion, and a snake in a coyl.
Thank you very much.

Love,

Cindy

Proofreading Marks	
◯	misspelling
∧	insert
⁄e⁄	delete
≡	make a capital letter
⁄	make a small letter
⊙	add a period

1. _____
2. _____
3. _____
4. _____
5. _____
6. _____
7. _____
8. _____
9. _____

Now find two places where a period should be added and two places where a word should be deleted. Use the correct proofreading marks to show where periods should be added and where words should be deleted.

Write on Your Own: Letter

Write a letter to a friend about a folktale that you like or would like to write a new ending for. Use at least six spelling words. First list the spelling words that you want to use.

1. _____
2. _____
3. _____
4. _____
5. _____
6. _____

Now proofread your word list and letter and correct any errors.

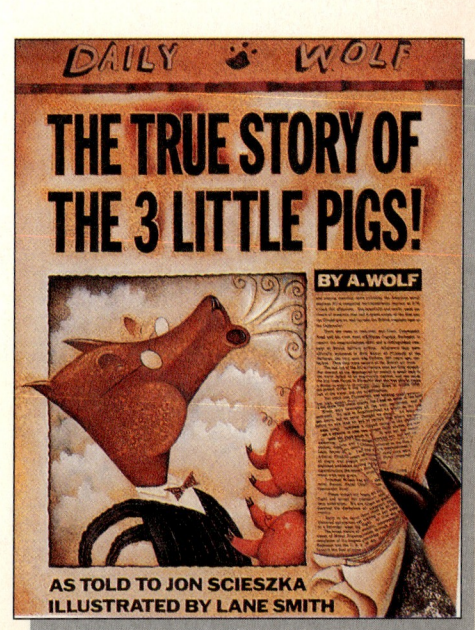

Lesson 12 Review 51

Review

 **SPELLING FUN** Use these Core Words from Lessons 7–11 to complete this puzzle.

Lesson 7
spoil
coin
loyal

Lesson 8
mouse
mouth
growl

Lesson 9
saw
haul
because

Lesson 10
add
odd
smell

Lesson 11
tumble
pebble
bubble

ACROSS
3. Where teeth are
4. A stomach does this
6. Why? _____ I said so.
8. A small stone
9. A penny
10. Carry on a truck
12. What your nose does
13. Different and strange

DOWN
1. To take a fall
2. A small rodent
5. Rhymes with *royal*
6. Blow a _____
7. Starts like *spot*, ends like *toil*
11. A math term
12. To cut down

52 Lesson 12 Review

Review

STANDARDIZED-FORMAT TEST PRACTICE

Choose the correct spelling of the Core Words from Lessons 7–11.

ANSWERS

SAMPLE	A. hawke	B. hawk	C. houk	Ⓐ ● Ⓒ
1.	A. voyce	B. voic	C. voice	Ⓐ Ⓑ Ⓒ
2.	A. candel	B. candle	C. candl	Ⓐ Ⓑ Ⓒ
3.	A. small	B. smal	C. smoll	Ⓐ Ⓑ Ⓒ
4.	A. clif	B. cliff	C. clife	Ⓐ Ⓑ Ⓒ

Choose the misspelled Core Words from Lessons 7–11.

SAMPLE	A. brown	B. ad	C. puddle	Ⓐ ● Ⓒ
1.	A. gul	B. crowd	C. crown	Ⓐ Ⓑ Ⓒ
2.	A. claw	B. tangle	C. gruf	Ⓐ Ⓑ Ⓒ
3.	A. litle	B. less	C. moss	Ⓐ Ⓑ Ⓒ
4.	A. roile	B. law	C. gown	Ⓐ Ⓑ Ⓒ

Choose the correct spelling of the Core Words from Lessons 7–11 to complete each sentence.

SAMPLE	My mom gave me a shiny new _____.			
	A. coyne	B. coin	C. koin	Ⓐ ● Ⓒ

1. My baby sister can _____ to ten.

   A. count   B. cownt   C. cont   Ⓐ Ⓑ Ⓒ

2. I climbed the big _____.

   A. hil   B. hill   C. hile   Ⓐ Ⓑ Ⓒ

3. A new _____ moved next door to me.

   A. boi   B. boye   C. boy   Ⓐ Ⓑ Ⓒ

4. The tractor makes a lot of _____.

   A. nois   B. noise   C. noize   Ⓐ Ⓑ Ⓒ

Sorting Spelling Patterns

13 Words with -ed or -ing

Spelling Focus—The endings *-ed* and *-ing* can be added to base words.

SORT Write the Core Words that end with the following letters.

Core Words

1. make
2. hike
3. bite
4. prized
5. skated
6. shaking
7. making
8. diving
9. shake
10. hiking
11. skate
12. prize
13. skating
14. dive
15. biting

My Words

Core Word Sentences

Try to **make** it better.
I like to **hike** in the woods.
Take a big **bite** of bread.
The book is a **prized** possession.
They **skated** on the ice.
Trees were **shaking** in the wind.
I am **making** a paper airplane.
He likes **diving** into the pool.
Do not **shake** the ladder!
We were **hiking** along the trail.
He tied his **skate**.
She won the science **prize**.
It is too warm to go **skating**.
Do not **dive** into the water.
Kicking and **biting** are not nice.

e
1. _____
2. _____
3. _____
4. _____
5. _____
6. _____
7. _____

-ing
1. _____
2. _____
3. _____
4. _____
5. _____
6. _____

-ed
1. _____
2. _____

WRITE Write a sentence for each Core Word on a separate sheet of paper.

Spelling Words in Context

 REAL-WORLD CONNECTION Write the Core Words that best complete the story. Use each word only once.

❖ Summer and Winter Sports ❖

Many people enjoy outdoor sports. Some people engage in a sport just because they enjoy it. Others do it for the money or to win a _____.

Water sports are very popular in summer. People love swimming, waterskiing, and _____. Have you ever watched pro swimmers get ready to _____ into a race? Often they will _____ their arms first. This _____ helps to loosen and stretch the muscles. _____ is another favorite warm-weather sport. People _____ in city parks and through wilderness areas. Some hikers carry a backpack with food, water, and a small tent. They also take a first-aid kit in case they get a cut, a sprain, or an insect _____.

In winter, many people like to ski, sled, and _____ snowballs. _____ a snowman is also fun. A lot of people like to ice-_____ outdoors in the winter. Many cities have indoor ice-_____ rinks that are open all year. If you've never _____ on ice, you might want to try it. ❖

 DEFINITIONS Write the Core Word that fits each definition.

1. having great value   _____
2. cutting with the teeth   _____

Unit 3 • Lesson 13   55

Building Spelling Vocabulary

Core Words
1. make
2. hike
3. bite
4. prized
5. skated
6. shaking
7. making
8. diving
9. shake
10. hiking
11. skate
12. prize
13. skating
14. dive
15. biting

Review Words
hide
shine
hiding
shining
smiling

Challenge Words
move
paste
score
dance
prove

RHYMING WORDS Write the Core Word that rhymes with each word.

1. shake _____
2. kite _____
3. writing _____
4. five _____
5. make _____
6. size _____
7. sized _____
8. bike _____
9. late _____
10. shaking _____
11. driving _____
12. making _____
13. rated _____
14. dating _____
15. biking _____

SYLLABLES Write the Review Words that have one syllable, then those that have two syllables.

one syllable

1. _____   2. _____

two syllables

3. _____   5. _____
4. _____

PLURALS Adding -s to many nouns makes them plural. Make these Challenge Words plural.

1. score _____
2. dance _____

WORD ENDINGS Adding -s to a verb makes it agree with some subjects (*she sings*). Add -s to these Challenge Words.

3. move _____
4. prove _____
5. paste _____

56 Words with -ed or -ing

Proofreading and Writing

Proofreading Marks

◯	misspelling	≡	make a capital letter
∧	insert	/	make a small letter
⌒	delete	⊙	add a period

Practice Prooofreding

Here is a draft of one student's poem about spring. Find four misspelled Core Words. Circle them and write them correctly.

```
Spring
The wind is makeing soft sounds.
The maple tree is shakeing its branches.
The robin is diveing for twigs to make a nest.
Will you hik with me in the warm sunshine?
```

1. _____
2. _____
3. _____
4. _____

Write on Your Own: Poem

Plan to write a poem about your favorite season. Think of a title for your poem. Choose and write at least four Core Words and other words that you will use in your poem. Write your poem on a separate piece of paper, following the steps on page 159.

1. _____   4. _____
2. _____   5. _____
3. _____   6. _____

Now proofread your word list and poem and correct any errors.

Unit 3 • Lesson 13   57

Sorting Spelling Patterns

14 Words with *spl*, *spr*, and *str*

Spelling Focus—The /spl/ sound can be spelled *spl*. The /spr/ sound can be spelled *spr*. The /str/ sound can be spelled *str*.

SORT Write the Core Words with the /spl/, /spr/, and /str/ sounds spelled the following ways.

Core Words

1. split
2. sprinkle
3. splash
4. strain
5. strap
6. spread
7. sprout
8. string
9. splint
10. spray
11. strike
12. spring
13. strong
14. splatter
15. streak

My Words

Core Word Sentences

They **split** the pie into two pieces.
Do not **sprinkle** sugar on the cake.
The whale made a huge **splash**.
Her back **strain** hurts a lot.
I bought a new watch **strap**.
He **spread** jam on the bread.
Flowers will **sprout** in the spring.
She used **string** to tie a knot.
His broken leg was in a **splint**.
She likes to **spray** perfume.
You should not **strike** the match.
Robins return in the **spring**.
Steel is very **strong**.
Do not **splatter** the paint.
I had a **streak** of good luck.

spl
1. _____
2. _____
3. _____
4. _____

spr
1. _____
2. _____
3. _____
4. _____
5. _____

str
1. _____
2. _____
3. _____
4. _____
5. _____
6. _____

WRITE Write a sentence for each Core Word on a separate sheet of paper.

Spelling Words in Context

🍎 **REAL-WORLD CONNECTION** Write the Core Words that best complete the story. Use each word only once.

❖ No Brush Needed ❖

Did you ever _____ paint with a butter knife, a finger, or a rag? It's fun! Here are some other ideas for painting without a brush.

Put thin paint in a capped bottle and poke holes in the lid. The paint will _____ out. If the holes are too big, the paint will come out in a big _____.

Drag a thin _____ through paint. Then _____ it across the paper. This can be messy. Wear an old shirt and work outside.

Dip a _____ in paint. Lay it on a sheet of paper to make a design. Gently press another sheet of paper on top. You don't need to _____.

You can also make prints by dipping a key or a _____ in paint. Press it on your paper to make a design.

Dip a toothbrush in paint and then rub it across a screen. The paint will _____ onto the paper underneath.

Fill a squirt gun with thin tempera paint. When you pull the trigger, you paint a _____ of color across the paper. Watch out! It might _____ on you, too. ❖

🍎 **DEFINITIONS** Write the Core Word that fits each definition.

1. new growth of a plant _____
2. something used to hold a broken bone in place _____
3. having power _____
4. divide _____

Unit 3 • Lesson 14   59

Building Spelling Vocabulary

Core Words
1. split
2. sprinkle
3. splash
4. strain
5. strap
6. spread
7. sprout
8. string
9. splint
10. spray
11. strike
12. spring
13. strong
14. splatter
15. streak

Review Words
spin
sting
stay
stack
speed

Challenge Words
splendid
strange
straddle
splinter
straight

WORD BUILDING Write the Core Words hidden in the letters of two words next to each other in these sentences.

1. This is the biggest ring in the store. _____
2. Which month gets the most rain? _____
3. "Let's trap the thief," said the police. _____
4. Was the wasp ready to sting you? _____

WORD PARTS Add the underlined word parts together to make the Core Words.

5. <u>sp</u>in + <u>little</u> = _____
6. <u>spa</u>re + <u>flint</u> = _____
7. <u>split</u> + <u>fl</u>ash = _____
8. <u>sp</u>ill + <u>clatter</u> = _____
9. <u>spread</u> + <u>tr</u>ay = _____
10. <u>sprout</u> + <u>br</u>ing = _____
11. <u>str</u>ay + <u>b</u>ike = _____
12. <u>str</u>ing + <u>leak</u> = _____

RHYMING WORDS Write the Review Word that rhymes with each word.

1. twin _____   4. back _____
2. need _____   5. day _____
3. ring _____

CHANGING LETTERS Write the Challenge Words formed by dropping one or more letters in each word.

1. straddled _____   4. straighten _____
2. splendidly _____   5. splintering _____
3. stranger _____

60 Words with *spl*, *spr*, and *str*

Proofreading and Writing

Proofreading Marks

◯ misspelling   ≡ make a capital letter
∧ insert   / make a small letter
⌒ delete   ⊙ add a period

Practice Proofreading

Here is a draft of one student's directions for planting seeds. Find four misspelled Core Words. Circle them and write them correctly.

Shake the seeds from a bean pod. Next spred the tiny seeds in the soil in a sunny spot. The sun will help the bean plants to sprot and grow stong. Then cover the seeds with soil and spinkle them with water.

1. _____
2. _____
3. _____
4. _____

Write on Your Own: Directions

Plan to write directions telling how to do something. Think about how to make a snack, catch a ball, or ride a bike. Choose and write at least four Core Words and other words that you will use in your directions. Write your directions on a separate sheet of paper, following the steps on page 159.

1. _____   4. _____
2. _____   5. _____
3. _____   6. _____

Now proofread your word list and directions and correct any errors.

Unit 3 • Lesson 14

Sorting Spelling Patterns

15 Words with Double Consonants

Spelling Focus—The /ər/ sound can be spelled *er* in words with the double consonants *tt, bb, cc, dd, ll, ff, mm, nn,* or *pp.*

SORT Write the Core Words with the /ər/ sound and double consonants spelled the following ways.

Core Words

1. ladder
2. soccer
3. offer
4. taller
5. rubber
6. dinner
7. hammer
8. supper
9. summer
10. slippers
11. better
12. butter
13. letter
14. potter
15. scatter

My Words

Core Word Sentences

Climb the **ladder.**
She has a **soccer** ball.
He made an **offer** to help.
The giraffe is **taller** than I am.
A **rubber** ball bounces.
Did you eat **dinner?**
Use the **hammer.**
We cooked **supper.**
I went to **summer** camp.
I wore socks and **slippers.**
She feels **better** now.
I put **butter** on my cracker.
The **letter** "e" comes after "d."
The **potter** uses clay.
We have to **scatter** the seeds.

tt

1. _____
2. _____
3. _____
4. _____
5. _____

bb, cc, dd, ll, or ff

1. _____
2. _____
3. _____
4. _____
5. _____

mm, nn, or pp

1. _____
2. _____
3. _____
4. _____
5. _____

WRITE Write a sentence for each Core Word on a separate sheet of paper.

Spelling Words in Context

 REAL-WORLD CONNECTION Write the Core Words that best complete the story. Use each word only once.

❖ Summertime Fixings ❖

_____ is a good time to help with odd jobs around the house. Here are some things you might _____ to do:

1. Work in the garden. _____ seeds and water them with a _____ hose.

2. Help someone who is working on the house outside. Get a _____ and _____ when they need it. Make sure the ladder can be pulled out and made _____.

3. Help roast corn on the grill. Don't forget the _____ to spread on it. Invite a friend over for _____ or _____.

4. Clean out the garage to make it look _____.

5. Write a card or _____ to a relative. After you've done a good job, you can relax in your pajamas and _____. ❖

 CONTEXT CLUES Write the Core Word that will complete each sentence.

1. Someone who works with clay is called a _____.

2. Someone who guards the goal in a _____ game is called a goalie.

Unit 3 • Lesson 15   63

Building Spelling Vocabulary

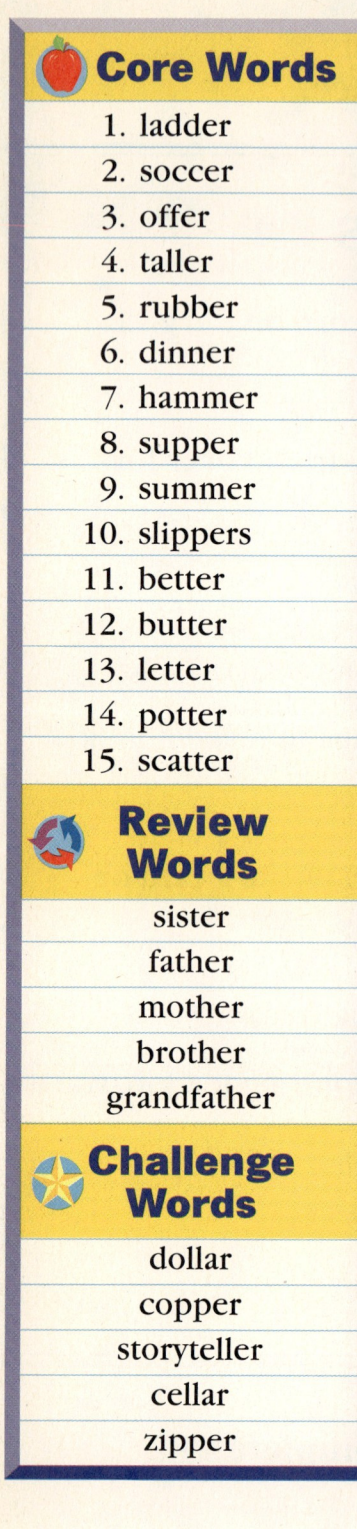

Core Words
1. ladder
2. soccer
3. offer
4. taller
5. rubber
6. dinner
7. hammer
8. supper
9. summer
10. slippers
11. better
12. butter
13. letter
14. potter
15. scatter

Review Words
sister
father
mother
brother
grandfather

Challenge Words
dollar
copper
storyteller
cellar
zipper

SYLLABLES Write the Core Words and draw a line between the syllables.

1. dinner _____   9. butter _____
2. rubber _____   10. letter _____
3. hammer _____   11. taller _____
4. slippers _____   12. potter _____
5. soccer _____   13. better _____
6. supper _____   14. offer _____
7. scatter _____   15. summer _____
8. ladder _____

PLURALS Adding -s to many nouns makes them plural. Make these Review Words plural.

1. father _____
2. grandfather _____
3. mother _____
4. sister _____
5. brother _____

WORD BUILDING Write the Challenge Words that have these smaller words in them.

1. doll _____
2. zip _____
3. cop _____
4. tell _____
5. cell _____

Words with Double Consonants

Proofreading and Writing

Proofreading Marks

⭕ misspelling	≡ make a capital letter
∧ insert	/ make a small letter
⌒e delete	⊙ add a period

Practice Prooofreding

Here is a draft of one student's poster for a summer job. Find four misspelled Core Words. Circle them and write them correctly.

I WANT TO HELP
Do you want beter help at cheaper prices?
I am a hard worker who can ofer you a great deal. I know how to use a hamer.
I can work all sumer.

1. _____
2. _____
3. _____
4. _____

Write on Your Own: Poster

Plan to make a poster about jobs you can do in the summer to earn money. Think about and tell why people should hire you, and tell where and when they can reach you. Choose and write at least four Core Words and other words that you will include in your poster. Write the copy for your poster on a separate sheet of paper, following the steps on page 159.

1. _____   4. _____
2. _____   5. _____
3. _____   6. _____

Now proofread your word list and poster and correct any errors.

Unit 3 • Lesson 15   65

16 Contractions

Sorting Spelling Patterns

Spelling Focus—Contractions are made from two words with some letters left out. An apostrophe replaces the missing letters.

SORT Write the Core Words that are contractions made from the following words.

Core Words
1. I'd
2. we'll
3. she'd
4. I'm
5. that's
6. I'll
7. he'll
8. it's
9. he'd
10. you'll
11. they'll
12. we'd
13. she'll
14. you'd
15. what's

My Words

Core Word Sentences

I'd like to go to the zoo.
I think **we'll** go tomorrow.
Mom said **she'd** also like to go.
I'm happy that she is coming.
She said **that's** a great idea.
I'll tell her how to get there.
Sam said **he'll** go by himself.
It's been delightful.
Sam said **he'd** have a hot dog.
You'll see all the animals.
He said, "**They'll** be asleep."
We said **we'd** wait for you.
I know **she'll** have a great time.
It would be better if **you'd** come.
Let's do **what's** right.

will/shall
1. _____
2. _____
3. _____
4. _____
5. _____
6. _____

had/would
1. _____
2. _____
3. _____
4. _____
5. _____

is/has/am
1. _____
2. _____
3. _____
4. _____

WRITE Write a sentence for each Core Word on a separate sheet of paper.

Spelling Words in Context

🍎 **REAL-WORLD CONNECTION** Write the Core Word that is the contraction of each pair of words in parentheses. Use each word only once.

❖ Jackie Robinson ❖

Before 1946, black baseball players were banned from the major leagues. In 1946, Branch Rickey and Jackie Robinson changed that.

Branch Rickey was the manager of the Brooklyn Dodgers. (He had) _____ seen Jackie play and knew he was good. Branch Rickey asked to meet with him.

"(I would) _____ like you to play on my team," he said. "A lot of people won't like it. (They will) _____ call you names and throw things at you. (You will) _____ have to take it and not fight back. (It is) _____ not going to be easy. (You had) _____ better be sure before you answer."

Jackie looked at Branch Rickey. "(I will) _____ do it," he said. Branch Rickey told Jackie he'd help any way he could.

When the other players found out, they were mad. "(We will) _____ quit if you hire him," they said. "(We would) _____ rather not play at all." Branch Rickey stood his ground. "(I am) _____ not going to fight about this," he said. "Jackie is playing, and (that is) _____ that. (He will) _____ be good for us. Just wait and see."

Branch Rickey was right. Jackie helped the Dodgers win many games.

🍎 **CONTRACTIONS** Write the Core Word that is a contraction of each pair of words.

1. what is _____ 2. she would _____ 3. she will _____

Unit 3 • Lesson 16   67

Building Spelling Vocabulary

Core Words
1. I'd
2. we'll
3. she'd
4. I'm
5. that's
6. I'll
7. he'll
8. it's
9. he'd
10. you'll
11. they'll
12. we'd
13. she'll
14. you'd
15. what's

Review Words
she
you
they
that
what

Challenge Words
could
should
I've
would
it'll

WORD PARTS Circle the letters that are left out to make a contraction from each pair of words. Then write the Core Word.

1. he would _____
2. she would _____
3. we would _____
4. he will _____
5. she will _____
6. we will _____
7. they will _____
8. you would _____
9. you will _____
10. I am _____
11. what is _____
12. I would _____
13. that is _____
14. I will _____
15. it is _____

LETTER CLUES Write the Review Words that fit these clues.

1. It starts with *s*. _____
2. It ends with *y*. _____
3. It starts with *y*. _____
4. They end with *at*. _____
   _____

PHONETIC PATTERNS Write the Challenge Word that matches each respelling.

1. /kŏŏd/ _____
2. /shŏŏd/ _____
3. /wŏŏd/ _____

WORD PARTS Write the words that make up the two Challenge Words that are contractions. Then write the contractions.

4. _____ _____
5. _____ _____

Contractions

Proofreading and Writing

Proofreading Marks

◯ misspelling
∧ insert
℮ delete
= make a capital letter
/ make a small letter
⊙ add a period

Practice Proofreading

Here is a draft of one student's thank-you note for a party invitation. Find four misspelled Core Words. Circle them and write them correctly.

> Dear Jeff,
> Thank you for inviting me to your party. Ide be very happy to come. Ill be so glad to see you again. Its always fun to get together. Thats for sure!
> Your friend,
> Jess

1. _____
2. _____
3. _____
4. _____

Write on Your Own: Thank-You Note

Plan to write a thank-you note to someone you know who has helped others. Think about how your teacher, parent, or a famous person helps others. Choose and write at least four Core Words and other words that you will include in your note. Write your note on a separate sheet of paper, following the steps on page 159.

1. _____   4. _____
2. _____   5. _____
3. _____   6. _____

Now proofread your word list and thank-you note and correct any errors.

Unit 3 • Lesson 16

Sorting Spelling Patterns

17 Easily Misspelled Words

Spelling Focus—Some words don't follow regular spelling rules. These words are not spelled the way they sound.

SORT Write the Core Words that have the following number of syllables.

Core Words

1. work
2. once
3. friend
4. been
5. done
6. guess
7. shoe
8. their
9. school
10. other
11. nothing
12. only
13. always
14. again
15. color

My Words

Core Word Sentences

I **work** in an office.
I was late only **once**.
My boss is my **friend**.
She has **been** there two years.
She has **done** her job well.
He made a lucky **guess**.
I stopped to tie my **shoe**.
Where is **their** car parked?
We met during a **school** play.
She had some **other** jobs.
I had **nothing** to eat today.
I want **only** one apple.
We **always** have fun.
We will go out **again**.
My favorite **color** is green.

one syllable

1. _____
2. _____
3. _____
4. _____
5. _____
6. _____
7. _____
8. _____
9. _____

two syllables

1. _____
2. _____
3. _____
4. _____
5. _____
6. _____

WRITE Write a sentence for each Core Word on a separate sheet of paper.

Spelling Words in Context

 REAL-WORLD CONNECTION Write the Core Words that best complete the story. Use each word only once.

❖ Mary McLeod Bethune ❖

Mary McLeod Bethune started the first _____ for black children in Daytona, Florida. She started with _____ five students. All the children and _____ families shared the _____ at the school. They planted gardens, cleaned, and cooked. They did whatever needed to be _____. After one year, the school had 100 students. Mary needed a bigger building. She called every _____ and helper she knew. They built a new school on land where a trash dump had _____.

Mary _____ said that people were like flowers in a garden, all different colors growing together. _____ a little girl said that black people couldn't be in the garden because there were no black flowers. When Mary was in Holland, she saw black tulips. Later, she saw roses of the same _____. You can probably _____ what she did. She brought some of the flowers home with her and planted them at the school. ❖

 CONTEXT CLUES Write the Core Word that will complete each sentence.

1. Can you help me find my tennis _____?
2. The _____ team won.
3. There was _____ stopping us from winning.
4. Once _____, she won the race.

Unit 3 • Lesson 17

Building Spelling Vocabulary

Core Words

1. work
2. once
3. friend
4. been
5. done
6. guess
7. shoe
8. their
9. school
10. other
11. nothing
12. only
13. always
14. again
15. color

Review Words

are
said
your
were
thing

Challenge Words

movie
people
trouble
almost
double

LETTER CLUES Fill in the missing letters and write the Core Words.

1. _ or _ _____
2. _ _ _ oo _ _____
3. _ ee _ _____
4. _ _ ai _ _____
5. _ _ ei _ _____
6. _ th _ _ _____
7. _ _ ie _ _ _____
8. al _ _ _ _ _____
9. d _ n _ _____
10. on _ _ _____
11. _ _ th _ _ _ _____
12. o _ _ _ _____

CHANGING LETTERS Write the Core Words formed by dropping letters in each word.

13. shoebox _____
14. guessing _____
15. colorful _____

WORD BUILDING Write the Review Words formed by adding and subtracting letters as shown.

1. part – pt + e = _____
2. this – s + ring – ir = _____
3. you're – 'e = _____
4. says – ys + hid – h = _____
5. weren't – n – 't = _____

CHANGING LETTERS Write the Challenge Words formed by adding, dropping, or changing one or more letters in each word.

1. movies _____
2. troubled _____
3. most _____
4. peopled _____
5. doubling _____

72 Easily Misspelled Words

Proofreading and Writing

Proofreading Marks

- ⭕ misspelling
- ∧ insert
- ℯ delete
- ≡ make a capital letter
- / make a small letter
- ⊙ add a period

Practice Prooofreding

Here is a draft of one student's paragraph about shaping clay. Find four misspelled Core Words. Circle them and write them correctly.

> I like to werk with clay. There is allways a new thing that I want to make. I have onle made things out of clay for a short while. It is fun to feel the clay and make shapes with it. My freind says I smile while I work!

1. _____
2. _____
3. _____
4. _____

Write on Your Own: Paragraph

Plan to write a paragraph about something you have built, such as a sand castle, model airplane, or snowman. Think about what type of materials you used as you did it. Choose and write at least four Core Words and other words that you will include in your paragraph. Write your paragraph on a separate sheet of paper, following the steps on page 159.

1. _____   4. _____
2. _____   5. _____
3. _____   6. _____

Now proofread your word list and paragraph and correct any errors.

Unit 3 • Lesson 17   73

18 Review for Lessons 13–17

Lesson 13

Lesson 13
- bite
- diving
- shake
- skate
- skated
- hike
- prize
- prized
- dive
- skating

WORD SORT Write two Core Words each that end with *-e*, *-ed*, or *-ing*.

-e	-ed	-ing
1. _____	3. _____	5. _____
2. _____	4. _____	6. _____

CONTEXT CLUES Write a Core Word to complete each sentence. Each word will end with *-e*, *-ed*, or *-ing*.

7. The first _____ of a peach tastes the best.

8. Her feet hurt after her three-mile _____.

WORD PARTS Write the Core Words that are formed by combining the underlined parts of each word.

9. d<u>i</u>et + l<u>ive</u> = _____   10. <u>sk</u>in + r<u>ated</u> = _____

Lesson 14

Lesson 14
- strain
- strap
- splatter
- spread
- sprinkle
- streak
- spray
- split
- sprout
- splash

WORD SORT Write two Core Words each that spell the /spl/, /spr/, or /str/ sounds.

spl	spr	str
1. _____	3. _____	5. _____
2. _____	4. _____	6. _____

CONTEXT CLUES Write a Core Word to complete each sentence. The missing word will rhyme with the underlined word.

7. Throwing coins in a lake makes a <u>cash</u> _____.

8. Thinking hard can be a <u>brain</u> _____.

SUFFIXES Add the suffix *-er* to these Core Words. Write the word that means *someone who*, or *something that*, *sprays or spreads*.

9. _____   10. _____

74 Lesson 18 Review

Review

Lesson 15

Lesson 15
- ladder
- butter
- supper
- letter
- soccer
- slippers
- better
- potter
- hammer
- taller

🍎 **WORD SORT** Write two Core Words that spell the /ər/ sound with each pattern.

        pp   **tt**

1. _____   3. _____

2. _____   4. _____

🍎 **CLASSIFYING** Write a Core Word that fits each group of words.

5. saw, nails, _____   6. rugby, football, _____

🍎 **CHANGING LETTERS** Write the Core Words formed by changing one or two letters in each word.

7. smaller _____

8. madder _____

Lesson 16

Lesson 16
- what's
- you'll
- she'd
- she'll
- he'd
- I'd
- it's
- I'm
- I'll
- that's

🍎 **WORD SORT** Write two Core Words that spell contractions with each word or words.

   will/shall   *is*   *had/would*

1. _____   3. _____   5. _____

2. _____   4. _____   6. _____

🍎 **CONTEXT CLUES** Use Core Word contractions in place of the underlined words.

7. <u>I would</u> like to go to the museum with you. _____

8. <u>You will</u> be the first to arrive. _____

🍎 **WORD PARTS** Write the contraction for each pair of words.

9. he would _____   10. I am _____

Lesson 18 Review   **75**

Review

Lesson 17

Lesson 17
- once
- again
- nothing
- their
- shoe
- only
- always
- guess
- other
- color

🍎 **WORD SORT** Write two Core Words each that fit the following descriptions.

        one syllable   two syllables

1. _____   3. _____

2. _____   4. _____

🍎 **DEFINITIONS** Write the Core Word that fits each definition.

5. The opposite of *never* _____

6. The opposite of *something* _____

🍎 **PHONETIC PATTERNS** Write the Core Word that matches each respelling.

7. /wuns/ _____   9. /ōnˊ lē/ _____

8. /thâr/ _____   10. /ə genˊ/ _____

Spelling Strategy

THINK Look at the Core Word lists on pages 74–76. Choose one word from each list that is the hardest for you to spell. Write the word and a strategy to help you remember how to spell each word. For example: A *sprout* grows *out* of the ground.

      Words   Spelling Strategies

1. _____   _____

2. _____   _____

3. _____   _____

4. _____   _____

5. _____   _____

Review
Practice Proofreading

Read this paragraph. Find ten misspelled Core Words. Circle them and write them correctly.

Its sring The boy is makeing a garden. first, he'll scater seeds. They'll sprowt after a sprinkal of rain. There will be flowers and vegetables. the colors of the flowers will be beautiful The boy and his family will have fresh vegetables for diner. They'll be good plain or with buter.

Proofreading Marks	
◯	misspelling
∧	insert
ℯ	delete
≡	make a capital letter
/	make a small letter
⊙	add a period

1. _____
2. _____
3. _____
4. _____
5. _____
6. _____
7. _____
8. _____
9. _____
10. _____

Now find two words that should begin with a capital letter and two places where a period should be added. Use the correct proofreading marks to show which letters should be capitals and where periods should be added.

 **on Your Own:** Story

Write a story about something you enjoy doing in nature using at least six spelling words. First write the spelling words that you want to use.

1. _____   4. _____
2. _____   5. _____
3. _____   6. _____

Now proofread your word list and story and correct any errors.

Lesson 18 Review 77

Review

SPELLING FUN Use the Core Words from Lessons 13–17 to complete this puzzle.

Lesson 13
- make
- prized

Lesson 14
- string
- strike
- strong

Lesson 15
- offer
- summer
- slippers

Lesson 16
- what's

Lesson 17
- work
- friend
- been
- done
- shoe
- color
- school

ACROSS
1. Contraction with *what* and *is*
3. Not weak
4. Red is one
7. Suggest
9. Create
10. Soft shoes
13. Finished
14. I've _____ thinking about going.

DOWN
2. A place to learn
3. Hit or slap
5. _____ vacation
6. Whistle while you _____.
8. A person to keep
10. It holds a balloon.
11. Valued
12. It fits on your foot.

Review
STANDARDIZED-FORMAT TEST PRACTICE

Choose the correct spelling of the Core Words from Lessons 13–17.

ANSWERS

SAMPLE	A. splahsh	B. splah	C. splash	Ⓐ Ⓑ **Ⓒ**
1.	A. spladder	B. splatter	C. splater	Ⓐ Ⓑ Ⓒ
2.	A. shaking	B. shakeing	C. shakin	Ⓐ Ⓑ Ⓒ
3.	A. streek	B. streke	C. streak	Ⓐ Ⓑ Ⓒ
4.	A. you'd	B. you'de	C. you'ded	Ⓐ Ⓑ Ⓒ

Choose the misspelled Core Words from Lessons 13–17.

SAMPLE	A. bite	B. I'le	C. other	Ⓐ **Ⓑ** Ⓒ
1.	A. rubber	B. skateing	C. splint	Ⓐ Ⓑ Ⓒ
2.	A. split	B. uther	C. we'd	Ⓐ Ⓑ Ⓒ
3.	A. we'll	B. hiking	C. strape	Ⓐ Ⓑ Ⓒ
4.	A. biteing	B. diving	C. potter	Ⓐ Ⓑ Ⓒ

Choose the correct spelling of the Core Words from Lessons 13–17 to complete each sentence.

SAMPLE	My favorite _____ is red.			**Ⓐ** Ⓑ Ⓒ
	A. color	B. colore	C. cullor	

1. I can't find my other ice _____.

   A. scate   B. skate   C. skait   Ⓐ Ⓑ Ⓒ

2. Sally said _____ buy me lunch.

   A. she'de   B. shed   C. she'd   Ⓐ Ⓑ Ⓒ

3. Can you _____ my age?

   A. gess   B. guess   C. ghess   Ⓐ Ⓑ Ⓒ

4. I sent a _____ to my sister.

   A. letter   B. leter   C. ledder   Ⓐ Ⓑ Ⓒ

Lesson 18 Review

Sorting Spelling Patterns

19 The /s/ Sound

Spelling Focus—The /s/ sound can be spelled *s* or *c*.

SORT Write the Core Words with the /s/ sound spelled the following ways. Some words will appear on more than one list.

Core Words

1. safe
2. face
3. since
4. sauce
5. mice
6. trace
7. rice
8. city
9. race
10. place
11. nice
12. police
13. pencil
14. sink
15. circus

My Words

Core Word Sentences

Home is a **safe** place.
Please **face** forward.
He's been sick **since** Monday.
The **sauce** tastes great.
The cat chased the **mice**.
We saw a **trace** of snow.
I like **rice** with my meal.
The **city** is full of people.
Did you **race** to the finish?
Florida is a sunny **place**.
Did you have a **nice** nap?
The **police** stopped the thief.
The tip of my **pencil** broke.
The **sink** is full of dishes.
I saw elephants at the **circus**.

c
1. _____
2. _____
3. _____
4. _____
5. _____
6. _____
7. _____
8. _____
9. _____
10. _____
11. _____
12. _____
13. _____

s
1. _____
2. _____
3. _____
4. _____
5. _____

s and c
1. _____
2. _____
3. _____

WRITE Write a sentence for each Core Word on a separate sheet of paper.

Spelling Words in Context

REAL-WORLD CONNECTION Write the Core Words that best complete the story. Use each word only once.

❖ Keeping Our Neighborhood Safe ❖

The job of the _____ department is to keep our community, or _____, and state _____ from crime. It is _____ to know that they are there to help us.

You may have seen a police car _____ down the street after another car. Police must also look for a _____ of evidence, or clue, at the scene of a crime.

When they catch a lawbreaker, they make the person stand in a line next to other people and _____ forward. Then they ask anyone who saw the crime take _____ to pick out the guilty person. A police artist may also use a _____ to sketch the criminal from a description.

Ever _____ there were laws, there were people to make sure the laws were obeyed. Even when the sun must _____ out of sight, the police are working for us. That is why the job of a police officer is important. ❖

DEFINITIONS Write the Core Word that fits each definition.

1. a food that looks like small white or brown grains _____
2. small animals that like cheese _____
3. something you put over spaghetti _____
4. a place where there are clowns and elephants _____

Unit 4 • Lesson 19

Building Spelling Vocabulary

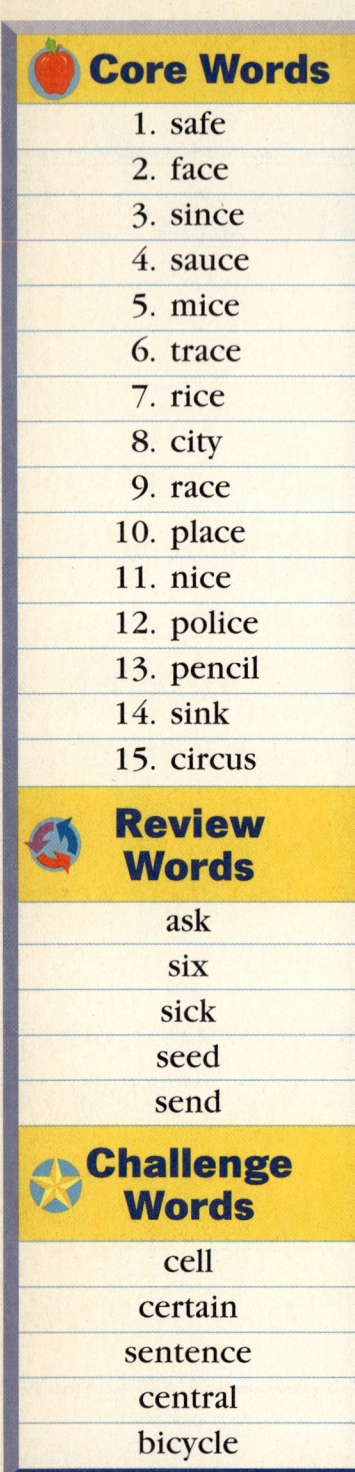

Core Words
1. safe
2. face
3. since
4. sauce
5. mice
6. trace
7. rice
8. city
9. race
10. place
11. nice
12. police
13. pencil
14. sink
15. circus

Review Words
ask
six
sick
seed
send

Challenge Words
cell
certain
sentence
central
bicycle

CHANGING LETTERS Write the Core Words formed by adding, dropping, or changing one or more letters in each word.

1. prince _____
2. saucy _____
3. mouse _____
4. nicer _____
5. slice _____
6. faces _____
7. racy _____
8. placed _____
9. tracer _____
10. policeman _____
11. safety _____
12. sinks _____
13. penciled _____
14. cities _____
15. circuit _____

WORD PARTS Write the Review Words formed by adding together the underlined parts of each word.

1. <u>as</u>p + tic<u>k</u> = _____
2. <u>seem</u> + le<u>d</u> = _____
3. <u>s</u>ad + <u>fix</u> = _____
4. <u>s</u>uch + b<u>end</u> = _____
5. <u>s</u>ome + <u>p</u>ick = _____

LETTER CLUES Write the Challenge Words that fit these clues.

1. They start with **ce**.

   _____

   _____

2. It has two **c**'s with two different sounds.

   _____

3. It ends with **ce**.

   _____

82 The /s/ Sound

Proofreading and Writing

Proofreading Marks

◯	misspelling	≡	make a capital letter
∧	insert	/	make a small letter
⌒	delete	⊙	add a period

Practice Prooofreding

Here is a draft of one student's thank-you letter about finding a lost cat. Find four misspelled Core Words. Circle them and write them correctly.

> It has been two weeks cinse you helped me find my cat. Thank you for finding Tootles and for being so nis to me. When Tootles was gone without a trase, I was very sad. You brought a smile to my fase when you found him.

1. _____
2. _____
3. _____
4. _____

Write on Your Own: Thank-You Letter

Plan to write a thank-you letter to someone in your neighborhood who provides a service for you. Think about why you appreciate this person's help. Choose and write at least four Core Words and other words that you will include in your letter. Write your letter on a separate sheet of paper, following the steps on page 159.

1. _____   4. _____
2. _____   5. _____
3. _____   6. _____

Now proofread your word list and letter and correct any errors.

Unit 4 • Lesson 19

20 The /j/ Sound

Sorting Spelling Patterns

Spelling Focus—The /j/ sound can be spelled *g*.

SORT Write the Core Words with the /j/ sound spelled *g* at the beginning, middle, or end of the word.

Core Words

1. hinge
2. germ
3. stage
4. gentle
5. plunge
6. cage
7. magic
8. giant
9. huge
10. large
11. range
12. gym
13. fringe
14. age
15. page

My Words

Core Word Sentences

The door **hinge** squeaks.
A **germ** can cause disease.
He sang on the **stage**.
My pet rabbit is **gentle**.
She took a **plunge** in the lake.
I keep my parakeet in a **cage**.
Can you do **magic** tricks?
The **giant** was ten feet tall.
I ate a **huge** meal.
My father has **large** feet.
The mountain **range** is ancient.
Jerry works out in a **gym**.
His scarf had **fringe**.
Her **age** is 8 years old.
Turn the **page**.

beginning
1. _____
2. _____
3. _____
4. _____

middle
1. _____

end
1. _____
2. _____
3. _____
4. _____
5. _____
6. _____
7. _____
8. _____
9. _____
10. _____

WRITE Write a sentence for each Core Word on a separate sheet of paper.

Spelling Words in Context

 REAL-WORLD CONNECTION Write the Core Words that best complete the story. Use each word only once.

❖ A Trip to the Zoo ❖

No matter what _____ you are, a trip to the zoo can seem like _____. Monkeys are always a favorite. Their _____ may look like a _____, full of swings, beams, and balls. Other favorites are the birds of prey. They often perform on a _____. A hawk might fly from the trainer's arm up and over the crowd. Or, it might dive, or _____, toward the crowd. Then it will glide back to its trainer.

Many animals live in open _____ areas where they can walk around freely. You might see a _____ giraffe nibbling at a high branch. You might see a _____ African elephant or a _____ rhino prancing around slowly. You might even see a _____ hippo cooling off in a pond.

If you need to cool off, you can stop at one of the colorful carts with _____ around the top and buy a lemonade. You can also visit the gift store. They will have toys, T-shirts, and books with page after _____ of animal pictures.

What's your favorite part of a trip to the zoo? ❖

 CONTEXT CLUES Write the Core Word that will complete each sentence.

1. A _____ is too small to see without a microscope.
2. Somebody should oil that squeaking _____.

Unit 4 • Lesson 20   85

Building Spelling Vocabulary

Core Words
1. hinge
2. germ
3. stage
4. gentle
5. plunge
6. cage
7. magic
8. giant
9. huge
10. large
11. range
12. gym
13. fringe
14. age
15. page

Review Words
jam
jog
jeep
jump
just

Challenge Words
gypsy
general
sponge
gently
pigeon

PLURALS Adding -s to many nouns makes them plural. Make these Core Words plural.

1. giant _____
2. germ _____
3. age _____
4. page _____
5. hinge _____
6. cage _____
7. stage _____
8. gym _____
9. range _____
10. fringe _____

SUFFIXES The suffix -er, when added to an adjective, means "more." Add -er to a Core Word to match each phrase.

11. more than large _____
12. more than huge _____
13. more than gentle _____

RHYMING WORDS Write the Review Word that rhymes with each word.

1. ham _____
2. rust _____
3. bump _____
4. log _____
5. deep _____

LETTER SCRAMBLE Write the Challenge Words hidden in these letters.

1. pigeonrnyx _____
2. fpuvgypsy _____
3. knlspongeto _____
4. swuvgently _____
5. lfmgeneralosd _____

The /j/ Sound

Proofreading and Writing

Proofreading Marks

◯ misspelling ≡ make a capital letter
∧ insert / make a small letter
⦚ delete ⊙ add a period

Practice Prooofreding

Here is a draft of one student's story about an animal he saw at the zoo. Find four misspelled Core Words. Circle them and write them correctly.

A Horse Named Jump

Once there was a jentle horse named Jump. Jump had a majic saddle with golden frinje on its edges. Whoever sat on Jump's saddle could travel anywhere in the world. One day, Jump was roaming on the ranje when he saw a giant.

1. _____
2. _____
3. _____
4. _____

Write on Your Own: Story

Plan to write a story about your favorite zoo animal. Think about why the animal is your favorite. What does it do? Choose and write at least four Core Words and other words that you will include in your story. Write your story on a separate sheet of paper, following the steps on page 159.

1. _____   4. _____
2. _____   5. _____
3. _____   6. _____

Now proofread your word list and story and correct any errors.

Unit 4 • Lesson 20

Sorting Spelling Patterns

21 Plurals

Spelling Focus—The singular form of a word, or a word meaning *only one,* can end in *-y.* The plural form of a word, or a word meaning *more than one,* can end in *-ies.*

SORT Write the singular Core Words that end in *-y* and the plural ones that end in *-ies.*

Core Words

1. berry
2. hobbies
3. puppies
4. bunnies
5. pennies
6. guppies
7. hobby
8. berries
9. penny
10. guppy
11. puppy
12. pony
13. bunny
14. ponies
15. babies

My Words

Core Word Sentences

The **berry** was blue.
I have many **hobbies**.
My dog had six **puppies**.
The **bunnies** ate the carrots.
Bill saves his **pennies** in a jar.
The fish store sells **guppies**.
What is your favorite **hobby?**
The **berries** tasted sweet.
The gum costs one **penny.**
My **guppy** swims.
Jon bought a **puppy.**
The **pony** has a long mane.
Keith keeps his **bunny** in a pen.
I like to ride **ponies.**
Little **babies** can cry a lot.

singular or -y

1. _____
2. _____
3. _____
4. _____
5. _____
6. _____
7. _____

plural or -ies

1. _____
2. _____
3. _____
4. _____
5. _____
6. _____
7. _____
8. _____

WRITE Write a sentence for each Core Word on a separate sheet of paper.

88 Plurals

Spelling Words in Context

 REAL-WORLD CONNECTION Write the Core Words that best complete the story. Use each word only once.

❖ Hobbies Are Fun ❖

People have many different kinds of _____, or things they do for fun. Some people even make money with their _____. For example, a person might collect stamps or coins, such as _____. A 1939 _____ could be very valuable. Someone else might grow something, like _____. That person could make and sell _____ pies and jellies.

Many people like to raise and sell animals. Some people may keep _____ in a fishbowl. It's fun to watch a _____ swim around in the water. A mother guppy has lots of _____. Other people may raise and care for _____ with long ears. They love to feel the soft fur of a _____. Maybe you know someone who raises _____. Playing with a _____ can be so much fun. Another person may raise horses or _____. This person might sell a _____ to make money.

Hobbies can be great fun. Sometimes you can even make money, too. ❖

Unit 4 • Lesson 21

Building Spelling Vocabulary

Core Words

1. berry
2. hobbies
3. puppies
4. bunnies
5. pennies
6. guppies
7. hobby
8. berries
9. penny
10. guppy
11. puppy
12. pony
13. bunny
14. ponies
15. babies

Review Words

drum
boy
spy
baby
family

Challenge Words

donkey
library
strawberry
country
butterfly

SYLLABLES Write the Core Words and draw a line between the two syllables in each word.

1. puppy _____
2. berry _____
3. hobbies _____
4. pennies _____
5. bunny _____
6. pony _____
7. guppy _____
8. ponies _____
9. guppies _____
10. puppies _____
11. babies _____
12. bunnies _____
13. hobby _____
14. berries _____
15. penny _____

WORD BUILDING Build and write the Review Words by adding and subtracting letters as shown.

1. d + strum – st = _____
2. s + pry – r = _____
3. fast – st + mily = _____
4. bake – ke + by = _____
5. boat – at + y = _____

LETTER CLUES Write the Challenge Words that fit these clues.

1. They end in **ry**.
   _____ _____ _____

2. It has the word *fly* in it.
   _____

3. It has the word *key* in it.
   _____

Plurals

Proofreading and Writing

Proofreading Marks

◯ misspelling ≡ make a capital letter
∧ insert / make a small letter
⌿ delete ⊙ add a period

Practice Proofreading

Here is a draft of one student's list of questions about raising animals. Find four misspelled Core Words. Circle them and write them correctly.

1. Why is raising bunnys a good hobbi?
2. Do rabbits like to eat berrys and other fruit?
3. Is it easier to raise puppies or ponies?
4. What happens if a puppy swallows a pennie?

1. _____
2. _____
3. _____
4. _____

Write on Your Own: List of Questions

Plan to write a list of questions you would ask people who have collections. Think about how they got started, or where they find their collectibles. Choose and write at least four Core Words and other words to use in your list. Write your list on a separate sheet of paper, following the steps on page 159.

1. _____   4. _____
2. _____   5. _____
3. _____   6. _____

Now proofread your word list and list of questions and correct any errors.

Unit 4 • Lesson 21

Sorting Spelling Patterns

22 Homophones

Spelling Focus—Homophones are words that sound the same but are spelled differently and have different meanings.

SORT Write the pairs of Core Words that are homophones. Then write the homophone for the word *mane*.

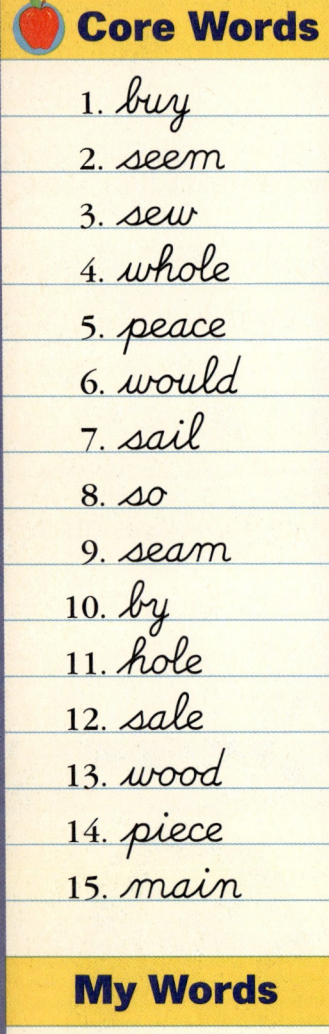

Core Words

1. buy
2. seem
3. sew
4. whole
5. peace
6. would
7. sail
8. so
9. seam
10. by
11. hole
12. sale
13. wood
14. piece
15. main

My Words

Core Word Sentences

Maureen wants to **buy** a jacket.
They **seem** angry.
Can you **sew** up the hole?
She ate the **whole** pie.
Let's make **peace**.
She **would** like to go.
The **sail** of the boat was raised.
It is **so** cold outside!
The **seam** of my pants ripped.
We camped **by** a lake.
There is a **hole** in the bag.
The store had a **sale**.
The desk is made of **wood**.
Let's **piece** the puzzle together.
Follow the **main** street.

1. by
   buy
2. _____
3. _____
4. _____
5. _____
6. _____
7. _____
8. _____

WRITE Write a sentence for each Core Word on a separate sheet of paper.

Spelling Words in Context

 REAL-WORLD CONNECTION Write the Core Words that best complete the story. Use each word only once.

❖ Quilts ❖

It takes a long time to make a quilt. First, you choose a design. Then you choose your colors and fabrics. Then you cut out each _____ of the design and start sewing the pieces together. You can _____ the pieces _____ hand or use a sewing machine. Either way, you try to make a straight _____.

When all the pieces are together, the _____ thing goes on a quilting frame. Most frames are made of _____. The frame holds the layers of a quilt while you sew them together. The _____ thing is to keep the layers even.

Some quilts look like paintings or drawings. One quilt may show a fleet of boats that _____ the seas. The Peace Quilt was made to remind people who see it to work for _____.

Many quilters put their quilts on _____. People like to _____ quilts as gifts or to keep for themselves. If you made a quilt, what design _____ you use? ❖

 CONTEXT CLUES Write the Core Word that will complete each sentence.

1. I _____ to have lost my homework paper.
2. My mother is _____ smart.
3. Which do you like better, the doughnut or the _____?

Unit 4 • Lesson 22

Building Spelling Vocabulary

Core Words

1. buy
2. seem
3. sew
4. whole
5. peace
6. would
7. sail
8. so
9. seam
10. by
11. hole
12. sale
13. wood
14. piece
15. main

Review Words

sea
son
four
road
right

Challenge Words

cent
scent
through
sent
threw

WORD BUILDING Fill in the missing letters and write the Core Word. Then write the Core Word that is a homophone for each word.

1. _ o _____ _____
2. _ ea _ _____ _____
3. _ ou _ _ _____ _____
4. _ _ o _ e _____ _____
5. _ uy _____ _____
6. _ ie _ e _____ _____
7. _ a _ e _____ _____

This Core Word has a homophone that does not appear on the word list. Write the Core Word and its homophone.

8. _ ai _ _____ _____

CHANGING LETTERS Write the Review Words formed by changing one letter in each word.

1. tea _____
2. sight _____
3. ton _____
4. foul _____
5. roam _____

RHYMING WORDS Write the Challenge Words that fit these clues.

1. They rhyme with *bent*.

   _____ _____ _____

2. They rhyme with *grew*.

   _____ _____

94 Homophones

Proofreading and Writing

Proofreading Marks

- ◯ misspelling
- ∧ insert
- ℯ delete
- ≡ make a capital letter
- / make a small letter
- ⊙ add a period

Practice Prooofreding

Here is a draft of one student's descriptive paragraph about taking a bus trip. Find four misspelled Core Words. Circle them and write them correctly.

Every spring I go to a baseball game with my friends. We get on the bus buy our apartment building. The hole bus is usually packed with people sew we never get a seat. The ride does not seam to take very long.

1. _____
2. _____
3. _____
4. _____

Write on Your Own: Descriptive Paragraph

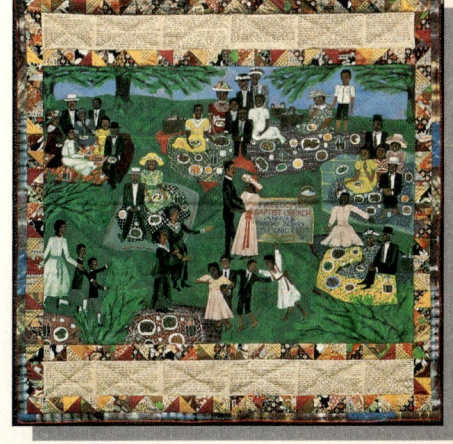

Plan to write a descriptive paragraph about how you might make a quilt that tells a story. Think about what shapes of cloth or scraps of clothing you could use in your quilt. Choose and write at least four Core Words and other words that you will include in your story. Write your story on a separate sheet of paper, following the steps on page 159.

1. _____   4. _____
2. _____   5. _____
3. _____   6. _____

Now proofread your word list and paragraph and correct any errors.

Unit 4 • Lesson 22

Sorting Spelling Patterns

23 Days of the Week and Time Words

Spelling Focus—Some words name the days of the week. These words are spelled with capital letters. Some words name different times of day.

SORT Write the Core Words that fit the following categories.

Core Words

1. afternoon
2. Monday
3. sunrise
4. week
5. Thursday
6. yesterday
7. Saturday
8. Wednesday
9. today
10. Friday
11. Tuesday
12. sunset
13. morning
14. Sunday
15. evening

My Words

Core Word Sentences

Let's eat this **afternoon.**

I don't like **Monday.**

The **sunrise** is colorful.

Thanksgiving is next **week.**

We are leaving on **Thursday.**

He saw a movie **yesterday.**

The game is this **Saturday.**

My birthday is **Wednesday.**

Is the play **today?**

Last **Friday** she left.

The day after **Monday** is **Tuesday.**

Did you see the **sunset?**

I am not a **morning** person.

They went hiking last **Sunday.**

"Good **evening**," said the man.

days of week

1. _____
2. _____
3. _____
4. _____
5. _____
6. _____
7. _____

times of day

1. _____
2. _____
3. _____
4. _____
5. _____

other time words

1. _____
2. _____
3. _____

WRITE Write a sentence for each Core Word on a separate sheet of paper.

Spelling Words in Context

 REAL-WORLD CONNECTION Write the Core Words that best complete the story. Use each word only once.

❖ Name That Day! ❖

We use words like day, _____, month, and year to tell about time. We call right now _____. A day ago is _____. The early part of a day is the _____. We call the time after lunch _____. We call the time between afternoon and night _____.

Did you ever wonder where our words about time came from? Words like _____ and _____ are easy to figure out. They tell about the rising and setting of the sun. But what about the names of the days of the week? Where did they come from?

Thousands of years ago, most people believed in many gods and goddesses. They named the days after their gods. Most English names came from Norse gods. Look at the list. Can you fill in the blanks to show the names we use today? ❖

1. Sun's day   _____   Many cultures had sun gods.
2. Moon's day   _____   Many cultures had moon gods.
3. Tiw's day   _____   Tiw was the Norse god of war.
4. Woden's day   _____   Woden was the ruler of all the Norse gods.
5. Thor's day   _____   Thor was the Norse god of thunder.
6. Frigga's day   _____   Frigga was the Norse goddess of love.
7. Saturn's day   _____   Saturn was the Roman god of time.

Unit 4 • Lesson 23

Building Spelling Vocabulary

Core Words

1. afternoon
2. Monday
3. sunrise
4. week
5. Thursday
6. yesterday
7. Saturday
8. Wednesday
9. today
10. Friday
11. Tuesday
12. sunset
13. morning
14. Sunday
15. evening

Review Words

now
time
days
night
seven

Challenge Words

begin
midnight
future
daybreak
tomorrow

🍎 **WORD BUILDING** Write Core Words to fill in the spaces on the calendar pages.

1. S _ _ _ _ _
2. no school _ _ _ _ _
3. _ on _ _ _
4. watch the s _ _ _ _ _ _
5. T _ _ _ _ ay
6. bring lunch this w _ _ _
7. _ e _ _ _ _ day
8. piano lesson 7 P.M. this _ _ _ _ ing
9. _ _ _ _ sd _ _
10. soccer practice at 3 P.M. in the _ _ _ ern _ _ _
11. _ _ _ day
12. watch the s _ _ _ _ _
13. S _ _ _ rd _ _
14. go hiking 8 A.M. this _ _ _ _ ing

🔄 **LETTER SCRAMBLE** Unscramble the letters to write the Review Words.

1. yads _____
2. neevs _____

🔄 **ANAGRAMS** Write the three Review Words that use these same letters to spell a different word.

1. won _____
2. mite _____
3. thing _____

⭐ **SYLLABLES** Write the Challenge Words and draw a line between the syllables.

1. midnight _____
2. daybreak _____
3. future _____
4. tomorrow _____
5. begin _____

Days of the Week and Time Words

Proofreading and Writing

Proofreading Marks

◯	misspelling	≡	make a capital letter
∧	insert	/	make a small letter
ℯ	delete	⊙	add a period

Practice Proofreading

Here is a draft of one student's schedule for several days. Find four misspelled Core Words. Circle them and write them correctly.

> Wensday: school, go to library in afturnoon
> Thersday: school, gym today
> Friday: school
>   Janet's party in evning
> Saturday: rest in morning

1. _____
2. _____
3. _____
4. _____

Write on Your Own: Schedule

Plan to write out your schedule for the week. Think about everything you do during the week. Choose and write at least four Core Words and other words that you will include in your schedule. Write your schedule on a separate sheet of paper, following the steps on page 159.

1. _____ 4. _____
2. _____ 5. _____
3. _____ 6. _____

Now proofread your word list and schedule and correct any errors.

24 Review for Lessons 19–23

Lesson 19

Lesson 19
- nice
- trace
- pencil
- mice
- place
- sink
- face
- city
- safe
- race

🍎 **WORD SORT** Write two Core Words that spell the /s/ sound for each pattern.

       s   c

1. _____ 3. _____

2. _____ 4. _____

🍎 **DEFINITIONS** Write the Core Word that fits each definition.

5. friendly and kind _____

6. small rodents _____

Lesson 20

Lesson 20
- fringe
- plunge
- huge
- gentle
- range
- age
- page
- cage
- giant
- stage

🍎 **WORD SORT** Write two Core Words with the /j/ sound spelled g at the beginning or the end of the word.

    beginning   end

1. _____ 3. _____

2. _____ 4. _____

🍎 **ANALOGIES** Write a Core Word to complete each analogy.

5. *Cow* is to *herd* as *mountain* is to _____.

6. *Jump* is to *rise* as *dive* is to _____.

🍎 **CHANGING LETTERS** Write the Core Words formed by adding, dropping, or changing one or more letters in each word.

7. ageless _____ 9. cagey _____

8. staged _____ 10. fringed _____

Review

Lesson 21

Lesson 21
- bunnies
- pony
- babies
- puppy
- hobbies
- pennies
- hobby
- guppy
- puppies
- berry

🍎 **WORD SORT** Write two Core Words for each group.

singular words   plural words

1. _____   3. _____

2. _____   4. _____

🍎 **CONTEXT CLUES** Write a Core Word to complete each sentence.

5. Two one-cent coins are a couple of _____.

6. Four rabbits are a bunch of _____.

🍎 **PLURALS** Write the Core Words by changing these words from plural to singular, or singular to plural.

7. guppies _____   8. baby _____

Lesson 22

Lesson 22
- peace
- seam
- wood
- sale
- piece
- hole
- sail
- seem
- whole
- buy

🍎 **PHONETIC PATTERNS** Write two Core Words that fit each group.

1. homophones with the /ē/ sound

_____   _____

2. homophones with the /ā/ sound

_____   _____

🍎 **CONTEXT CLUES** Write a Core Word to complete each sentence. Each word will be a homophone of the underlined word.

3. I went <u>by</u> the store to _____ some food.

4. <u>Would</u> someone please carry the _____?

🍎 **PHONETIC PATTERNS** Write the Core Words that match each respelling.

5. /hōl/ _____, _____   6. /sāl/ _____, _____

Lesson 24 Review   101

Review

Lesson 23

Lesson 23
Wednesday
Thursday
morning
sunrise
Friday
Monday
afternoon
Sunday
Tuesday
Saturday

🍎 **WORD SORT** Write two Core Words that fit each category.

days of the week   times of the day

1. _____   3. _____

2. _____   4. _____

🍎 **CLASSIFYING** Write the Core Word that fits in each group of words.

5. Tuesday, _____, Thursday

6. Saturday, _____, Monday

🍎 **WORD ORIGINS** These word origins contain clues to the English words based on them. Write the Core Word that matches each word origin.

7. From the Old English *mōna*, meaning *moon*. _____

8. From the Latin *Sāturnus*, meaning *Saturn*. _____

Spelling Strategy

THINK Look at the Core Word lists on pages 100–102. Choose one word from each list that is the hardest for you to spell. Write the word and a strategy to help you remember how to spell each word. For example: You cannot *see* the *seam*.

Words   Spelling Strategies

1. _____   _____

2. _____   _____

3. _____   _____

4. _____   _____

5. _____   _____

Review
Practice Prooofreding

Read the paragraph. Find ten misspelled Core Words. Circle them and write them correctly.

Proofreading Marks	
◯	misspelling
∧	insert
ℯ	delete
≡	make a capital letter
/	make a small letter
⊙	add a period

At sunrize, Angie will leave for for the majic island. She will sail there with a jentle morening wind. She take some rise and berrys sew she can have a picnic. She will also take her her puppie, Woof, with her. He keep her saif. Wood you like to come along?

1. _____
2. _____
3. _____
4. _____
5. _____
6. _____
7. _____
8. _____
9. _____
10. _____

Now find two words that should be inserted and two words that should be deleted. Use the correct proofreading marks to show which words should be inserted and which words should be deleted.

on Your Own: Rap Song

Write a rap song about a character from a book you like. Use at least six spelling words. First write the spelling words that you want to use.

1. _____
2. _____
3. _____
4. _____
5. _____
6. _____

Now proofread your word list and song and correct any errors.

Review

🍎 **SPELLING FUN** Use Core Words from Lessons 19–23 to complete this puzzle.

Lesson 19
place
police
pencil
circus

Lesson 20
germ
giant
large
gym

Lesson 21
penny
bunny

Lesson 22
sew
whole
peace
by

Lesson 23
yesterday
sunset
evening

ACROSS
3. Animals and clowns perform here.
4. When the sun goes down
5. Not small
8. _____ and quiet
9. All of it
11. Made of wood and graphite
12. A _____ rabbit
13. Can make you sick
14. Where basketball is played

DOWN
1. Day before today
2. Oversized
6. Opposite of morning
7. Use a needle and thread
8. People who enforce the law
10. Take _____; occur
11. Is made of copper
12. Made _____ hand

Review

STANDARDIZED-FORMAT TEST PRACTICE

Choose the correct spelling of the Core Words from Lessons 19–23.

ANSWERS

| SAMPLE | A. bunny | B. bunnie | C. buny | Ⓐ Ⓑ Ⓒ |

1. A. hinje   B. hinj   C. hinge   Ⓐ Ⓑ Ⓒ
2. A. sause   B. sauce   C. sawce   Ⓐ Ⓑ Ⓒ
3. A. hobies   B. hobbys   C. hobbies   Ⓐ Ⓑ Ⓒ
4. A. aftrnoon   B. afternoon   C. afternune   Ⓐ Ⓑ Ⓒ

Choose the misspelled Core Words from Lessons 19–23.

| SAMPLE | A. huge | B. pennies | C. gim | Ⓐ Ⓑ Ⓒ |

1. A. today   B. guppies   C. paje   Ⓐ Ⓑ Ⓒ
2. A. main   B. seam   C. ponys   Ⓐ Ⓑ Ⓒ
3. A. Toosday   B. sink   C. would   Ⓐ Ⓑ Ⓒ
4. A. berry   B. sinse   C. Friday   Ⓐ Ⓑ Ⓒ

Choose the correct spelling of the Core Words from Lessons 19–23 to complete each sentence.

SAMPLE	I ate the _____ sandwich.
	A. whole B. hole C. wole Ⓐ Ⓑ Ⓒ

1. Seven days are in one _____.
   A. week   B. weak   C. weik   Ⓐ Ⓑ Ⓒ
2. We bought a _____ pumpkin for Halloween.
   A. yuge   B. huje   C. huge   Ⓐ Ⓑ Ⓒ
3. My dog had three _____.
   A. puppies   B. puppys   C. pupies   Ⓐ Ⓑ Ⓒ
4. The day before Friday is _____.
   A. Thirsday   B. Thursday   C. Thurzday   Ⓐ Ⓑ Ⓒ

Lesson 24 Review

Sorting Spelling Patterns

25 Words with *ld* and *ft*

Spelling Focus—The /ft/ sound can be spelled *ft*. The /ld/ sound can be spelled *ld*.

🍎 **SORT** Write the Core Words with the /ft/ and /ld/ sounds spelled the following ways.

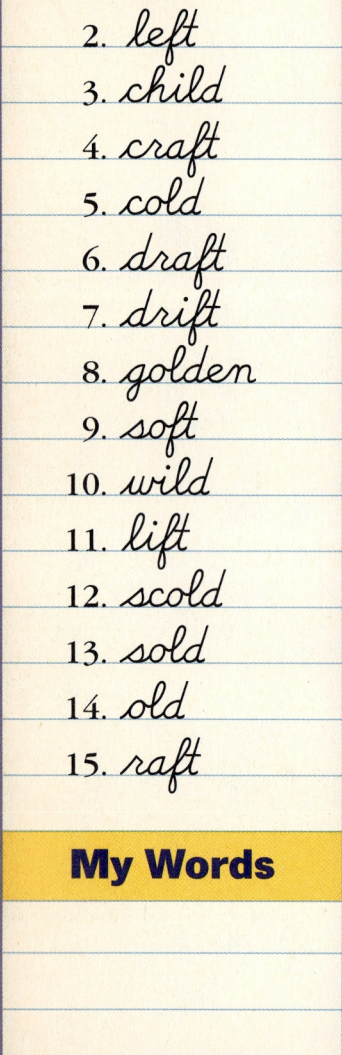

Core Words
1. held
2. left
3. child
4. craft
5. cold
6. draft
7. drift
8. golden
9. soft
10. wild
11. lift
12. scold
13. sold
14. old
15. raft

My Words

Core Word Sentences

Mom **held** my hand.
Dad turned **left** on the road.
The **child** took a nap.
Model-making is a fun **craft**.
Winter is a **cold** season.
A **draft** comes in this window.
The leaves **drift** in the breeze.
Our dog has **golden** fur.
A tissue is very **soft**.
Some **wild** animals are scary.
Can you **lift** the heavy books?
Mom had to **scold** my sister.
I **sold** drinks for five cents.
I'll replace my **old** bookbag.
I floated on my **raft**.

ft
1. _____
2. _____
3. _____
4. _____
5. _____
6. _____
7. _____

ld
1. _____
2. _____
3. _____
4. _____
5. _____
6. _____
7. _____
8. _____

🍎 **WRITE** Write a sentence for each Core Word on a separate sheet of paper.

Words with *ld* and *ft*

Spelling Words in Context

REAL-WORLD CONNECTION Write the Core Words that best complete the story. Use each word only once.

❖ Rafting the New River ❖

New River in West Virginia is a great place for a _____ trip. In some places the water is rough and _____. In other places, the water is calm. You _____ along slowly. The sunlight coming through the trees is _____ in color. You can see _____ mining shacks along the banks.

The rafts are full of air, so they're _____ to sit on. They have straps inside for your feet. These straps help you stay in the raft when you're going through rough water. If you do go overboard, you won't be _____ behind. Someone will help you back into the raft.

At lunchtime, you stop at a shady spot to eat. You _____ the _____ out of the water and pull one end up on the bank. You don't want it to float away while you're eating lunch. If you're _____, you can wrap up in a towel for a few minutes. Then it's back into the raft for the rest of your trip. ❖

 CONTEXT CLUES Write the Core Word that will complete each sentence.

1. My brother _____ me his bicycle.
2. I wish my dad wouldn't _____ the puppy.
3. There's a cool _____ in this hallway.
4. I _____ a baby chick in my hands today.
5. I am an only _____, with no brothers or sisters.

Unit 5 • Lesson 25 107

Building Spelling Vocabulary

Core Words
1. held
2. left
3. child
4. craft
5. cold
6. draft
7. drift
8. golden
9. soft
10. wild
11. lift
12. scold
13. sold
14. old
15. raft

Review Words
hand
bend
lend
test
thank

Challenge Words
bald
gift
theft
mold
swift

SUFFIXES The suffix *-er* means "more," and the suffix *-est* means "most." Add *-er* and *-est* to these Core Words.

1. cold _____ _____
2. wild _____ _____
3. old _____ _____
4. soft _____ _____

RELATED WORDS Write the Core Words that are related forms of these words.

5. sell _____
6. gold _____
7. children _____
8. lifted _____
9. hold _____
10. drifting _____
11. drafty _____
12. crafted _____
13. leftover _____
14. rafting _____
15. scolded _____

LETTER SCRAMBLE Write the Review Words hidden in these letters.

1. rkshand _____
2. lpubendth _____
3. lendyrf _____
4. jutestco _____
5. lmthank _____

CHANGING LETTERS Write the Challenge Words formed by adding, dropping, or changing one or more letters in each word.

1. ball _____
2. swiftly _____
3. thief _____
4. molding _____
5. gifted _____

108 Words with *ld* and *ft*

Proofreading and Writing

Proofreading Marks

- ◯ misspelling
- ∧ insert
- ꭱ delete
- ≡ make a capital letter
- / make a small letter
- ⊙ add a period

Practice Proofreding

Here is a draft of one student's folktale about a fisherman and his wife. Find four misspelled Core Words. Circle them and write them correctly.

> A fisherman and his wife lived in a colde house, with little to eat. Every day as the man lefed his house, his wife would scoled him. "Why can't you catch enough fish from the raff to feed us?" she would yell.

1. _____
2. _____
3. _____
4. _____

Write on Your Own: Story

Plan to write a story about a water-park ride you have been on or a water sport you enjoy. Think about what happens when you are doing it and how you feel. Choose and write at least four Core Words and other words that you will include in your story. Write your story on a separate sheet of paper, following the steps on page 159.

1. _____   4. _____
2. _____   5. _____
3. _____   6. _____

Now proofread your word list and story and correct any errors.

Unit 5 • Lesson 25   109

Sorting Spelling Patterns

26 The /âr/ Sound

Spelling Focus—The /âr/ sound can be spelled *are*, *air*, and *ear*.

SORT Write the Core Words with the /âr/ sound spelled the following ways.

Core Words

1. pear
2. fair
3. hair
4. mare
5. rare
6. bear
7. dare
8. fare
9. chair
10. stair
11. share
12. stare
13. bare
14. air
15. wear

My Words

Core Word Sentences

The **pear** was sweet and juicy.
We saw cows at the **fair**.
I need to comb my **hair**.
The gray **mare** ate the oats.
Snow in July is **rare**.
The athlete can **bear** the strain.
Take a chance if you **dare**.
The bus **fare** is two dollars.
Sit on the **chair**.
Don't trip on the **stair**.
I **share** my toys with friends.
Don't **stare** at the sun.
Trees are **bare** in winter.
Jets fly through the **air**.
Which shirt will you **wear**?

are
1. _____
2. _____
3. _____
4. _____
5. _____
6. _____
7. _____

air
1. _____
2. _____
3. _____
4. _____
5. _____

ear
1. _____
2. _____
3. _____

WRITE Write a sentence for each Core Word on a separate sheet of paper.

Spelling Words in Context

 REAL-WORLD CONNECTION Write the Core Words that best complete the story. Use each word only once.

❖ Ferry Ride ❖

A ferry ride is a _____ treat for most people. Lake Erie is a place people can go for a ferry ride. Ferries take people back and forth to islands out in the lake. The _____ is about six dollars, and most trips take about thirty minutes.

Most ferries have more than one level. You board on a lower deck. Then you can climb each _____ to the top deck. If you don't want to stand, you can usually find a _____ to sit in. Some ferries have long benches that several people _____. If you don't want to sit, you can stand out against the rail. There you can feel the wind blow through your _____. You can also _____ across the lake at the island you will visit.

Make sure you _____ a sweater, even if you think the weather will be _____. The _____ on the lake can be very cold against your _____ skin. ❖

 CONTEXT CLUES Write the Core Word that will complete each sentence.

1. We saw a gray _____ and her colt at the farm.
2. A grizzly _____ can be very dangerous.
3. Would you rather have the apple or the _____?
4. I _____ you to do it.

Unit 5 • Lesson 26

Building Spelling Vocabulary

Core Words
1. pear
2. fair
3. hair
4. mare
5. rare
6. bear
7. dare
8. fare
9. chair
10. stair
11. share
12. stare
13. bare
14. air
15. wear

Review Words
first
dirt
shirt
third
bird

Challenge Words
spare
glare
narrow
aware
declare

WORD ENDINGS Add -ing to each of these Core Words. Remember to drop the final e before adding -ing.

1. bare _____
2. dare _____
3. stare _____
4. share _____
5. fare _____
6. bear _____
7. wear _____
8. air _____

WORD PARTS Use air, are, or ear to write these Core Words.

9. h _ _ _ _____
10. ch _ _ _ _____
11. st _ _ _ _____
12. m _ _ _ _____
13. r _ _ _ _____
14. p _ _ _ _____
15. f _ _ _ _____

RHYMING WORDS Write the Review Word that rhymes with each word.

1. third _____
2. thirst _____
3. skirt _____
4. bird _____

BASE WORDS Write the Challenge Word that is the base word for each of these words.

1. spared _____
2. glaring _____
3. narrowly _____
4. declaration _____
5. awareness _____

112 The /âr/ Sound

Proofreading and Writing

Proofreading Marks

- ⭘ misspelling
- ∧ insert
- ⤴ delete
- ≡ make a capital letter
- / make a small letter
- ⊙ add a period

Practice Proofreading

Here is a draft of one student's tall tale about a turtle and rabbit race. Find three misspelled Core Words. Circle them and write them correctly.

> A turtle and rabbit decided to race. The rabbit could run through the aire like the wind. The turtle, who had to wair a heavy shell on his back, went very slowly. "Do you think this race will be faire?" the other animals asked.

1. _____
2. _____
3. _____

Write on Your Own: Tall Tale

Plan to write a tall tale about a ferry ride. Think about what could happen as the ferry cruises to an island in the middle of a lake. Choose and write at least four Core Words and other words that you will include in your tall tale. Write your tall tale on a separate sheet of paper, following the steps on page 159.

1. _____   4. _____
2. _____   5. _____
3. _____   6. _____

Now proofread your word list and tall tale and correct any errors.

Unit 5 • Lesson 26

Sorting Spelling Patterns

27 The /kw/ and /skw/ Sounds

Spelling Focus—The /kw/ sound can be spelled *qu*. The /skw/ sound can be spelled *squ*.

 SORT Write the Core Words with the /kw/ and /skw/ sounds spelled the following ways.

Core Words

1. quit
2. square
3. squirrel
4. quiet
5. quite
6. squeal
7. quail
8. squid
9. squint
10. squirt
11. quilt
12. squeak
13. queen
14. squeeze
15. quick

My Words

Core Word Sentences

The player **quit** the game.
Let's meet in the town **square**.
The **squirrel** climbed the tree.
Be **quiet** in the library.
It is **quite** warm in August.
We heard the pig **squeal**.
The **quail** flew south.
A **squid** is a strange fish.
I must **squint** my eyes in the sun.
Let's **squirt** water on these plants.
Mom made a **quilt** for our bed.
The rocking chair may **squeak**.
The **queen** sits on her throne.
Please **squeeze** the melon gently.
The runner is **quick**.

qu
1. _____
2. _____
3. _____
4. _____
5. _____
6. _____
7. _____

squ
1. _____
2. _____
3. _____
4. _____
5. _____
6. _____
7. _____
8. _____

 WRITE Write a sentence for each Core Word on a separate sheet of paper.

Spelling Words in Context

 REAL-WORLD CONNECTION Write the Core Words that best complete the story. Use each word only once.

❖ The Princess and the Pea ❖

Once upon a time, there was a girl who said she was a princess. The _____ was not _____ sure. She came up with a _____ way to find out. She invited the princess to spend the night. She put a pea on the bed the princess would sleep in and stacked mattresses on top. "There," she said. "Only a real princess will feel that pea."

That night, they ate _____ for dinner. For dessert, they had tiny _____ cakes with a _____ of chocolate sauce on top. Then the queen showed the princess to her room. The princess had to climb a ladder to get on the bed. A soft _____ was on top.

The castle was _____. There was not so much as the _____ of a mouse or the scurry of a _____. But the princess could not sleep. A lump in the bed kept her awake.

The next morning at breakfast, the princess could barely keep her eyes open. She had to _____ and blink. She had trouble holding her head up. She couldn't keep her _____ eggs on her fork. Finally, she said, "I _____. I can't go on. I'm too sleepy."

The queen let out a little _____. She ran over to hug and _____ the princess. "You really are a princess!" she cried. ❖

Unit 5 • Lesson 27

Building Spelling Vocabulary

Core Words
1. quit
2. square
3. squirrel
4. quiet
5. quite
6. squeal
7. quail
8. squid
9. squint
10. squirt
11. quilt
12. squeak
13. queen
14. squeeze
15. quick

Review Words
park
sharp
hard
art
dark

Challenge Words
quarter
quietly
squawk
question
squash

LETTER CLUES Write the Core Words that fit these clues.

1. They have the same five letters.
   _____   _____

2. When you subtract *e* from *quite*, you get this word.
   _____

3. When you change one letter in *squint* and *squeak*, you get these two words.
   _____   _____

4. When you change one letter in *quack*, you get this word.
   _____

PLURALS Adding *-s* or *-es* to many nouns makes them plural. Make these Core Words plural.

5. quilt _____   9. square _____
6. queen _____   10. squeak _____
7. quail _____   11. squeeze _____
8. squid _____   12. squirrel _____

RHYMING WORDS Write the Review Words that rhyme with these words.

1. lark _____   3. card _____
2. harp _____   4. part _____

LETTER CLUES Write the Challenge Words that begin with these letters.

squa   qua
1. _____   4. _____

2. _____   qui

que   5. _____

3. _____

116 The /kw/ and /skw/ Sounds

Proofreading and Writing

Proofreading Marks

- ⟲ misspelling
- ∧ insert
- ℯ delete
- ≡ make a capital letter
- / make a small letter
- ⊙ add a period

Practice Prooƒreding

Here is a draft of one student's report about the squid. Find four misspelled Core Words. Circle them and write them correctly.

> The squid is qite an interesting animal that lives in the kwiet of the sea. It has ten arms and a round body. When another animal comes near, the squid will skwert out dark ink. Not many animals are quik enough to catch a squid.

1. _____
2. _____
3. _____
4. _____

Write on Your Own: Report

Plan to write a report on squirrels, quails, or another animal. Think about and describe what your animal looks like, where it lives, and what it eats. Choose and write at least four Core Words and other words to use in your report. Write your report on a separate sheet of paper, following the steps on page 159.

1. _____   4. _____
2. _____   5. _____
3. _____   6. _____

Now proofread your word list and report and correct any errors.

Unit 5 • Lesson 27

Sorting Spelling Patterns

28 More Contractions

Spelling Focus—In a contraction, *'s* stands for *is* or *us*. The letters *n't* stand for *not*.

SORT Write the Core Word contractions that fit each category.

Core Words

1. here's
2. hasn't
3. wouldn't
4. can't
5. don't
6. won't
7. aren't
8. wasn't
9. didn't
10. let's
11. hadn't
12. haven't
13. couldn't
14. isn't
15. shouldn't

My Words

Core Word Sentences

Here's the dog!
She **hasn't** called us.
You **wouldn't** like this food.
I **can't** go to the movies.
Don't cross the street.
He **won't** come to the party.
You **aren't** going to the park.
She **wasn't** home today.
You **didn't** ask the teacher.
Let's have a picnic!
We **hadn't** heard the news.
They **haven't** come home yet.
We **couldn't** go to the beach.
Mom **isn't** at the office.
They **shouldn't** be late.

contraction with is
1. _____

contraction with us
1. _____

contractions with not
1. _____
2. _____
3. _____
4. _____
5. _____
6. _____
7. _____
8. _____
9. _____
10. _____
11. _____
12. _____
13. _____

WRITE Write a sentence for each Core Word on a separate sheet of paper.

Spelling Words in Context

 REAL-WORLD CONNECTION Write the Core Words that best complete the story. Use each word only once.

❖ Neighborhood Safety ❖

Everyone should live in a safe neighborhood. _____ a list of some simple safety tips that can help keep any neighborhood safe:

• Remind children that they _____ play with matches.

• In case there is a fire in your home, plan more than one escape path, so your family _____ be trapped inside.

• Have fire drills every couple of months if you _____ already been doing so.

• Make sure your pets _____ able to reach any poisonous cleaning products.

• If you _____ reach something, ask an adult to get it for you.

• Make sure you _____ ever tell anyone that your parents aren't home.

• If someone _____ already done so, put a list of emergency numbers by the phone.

• Never talk to strangers; it _____ safe. Even if a stranger asks you for help, think to yourself, "Why _____ this person ask an adult for help?"

Now _____ all practice these safety tips. ❖

 CONTEXT CLUES Write the Core Word that will complete each sentence.

1. He _____ prepared for the test.
2. She _____ go to school yesterday.
3. We _____ seen the play before tonight.
4. I _____ believe what I was seeing.

Unit 5 • Lesson 28

Building Spelling Vocabulary

Core Words

1. here's
2. hasn't
3. wouldn't
4. can't
5. don't
6. won't
7. aren't
8. wasn't
9. didn't
10. let's
11. hadn't
12. haven't
13. couldn't
14. isn't
15. shouldn't

Review Words

does
that's
what's
she'll
you'll

Challenge Words

you're
they're
there's
where's
doesn't

WORD BUILDING Fill in the missing letters and write the Core Words. Remember to add apostrophes in the correct places.

1. is _ _ _____
2. are _ _ _____
3. do _ _ _____
4. was _ _ _____
5. should _ _ _____
6. has _ _ _____
7. can _ _____
8. did _ _ _____
9. had _ _ _____
10. have _ _ _____
11. would _ _ _____
12. here _ _____
13. wo _ _ _____
14. let _ _____
15. could _ _ _____

RELATED WORDS Write the Review Words that are related forms of these words.

1. doesn't _____
2. that _____
3. she'd _____
4. what _____
5. you'd _____

LETTER CLUES Write the Challenge Words that fit these clues.

1. They end with 're.

   _____ _____

2. They end with 's.

   _____ _____

3. It is made by combining *does* and *not*.

   _____

120 More Contractions

Proofreading and Writing

Proofreading Marks

◯ misspelling   ≡ make a capital letter
∧ insert   / make a small letter
⌿ delete   ⊙ add a period

Practice Prooofreding

Here is a draft of one student's speech about winning a game. Find four misspelled Core Words. Circle them and write them correctly.

> You might think this team could'nt win a game even if it tried. Well, we wont win unless we change. Heres the way we can get better. Lets care more about the game. Come to practice ready to work hard.

1. _____
2. _____
3. _____
4. _____

Write on Your Own: Speech

Plan to write a speech on safety tips for your school. Think about some of the things at your school that students need to be careful about. Choose and write at least four Core Words and other words that you will use in your speech. Write your speech on a separate sheet of paper, following the steps on page 159.

1. _____   4. _____
2. _____   5. _____
3. _____   6. _____

Now proofread your word list and speech and correct any errors.

Unit 5 • Lesson 28

Sorting Spelling Patterns

29 Names of Holidays

Core Words

1. Mother's Day
2. Hanukkah
3. Valentine's Day
4. birthday
5. holidays
6. Thanksgiving
7. New Year's Day
8. Labor Day
9. Columbus Day
10. Christmas
11. Father's Day
12. children
13. Flag Day
14. Groundhog Day
15. Halloween

My Words

Spelling Focus—Names of holidays are proper nouns. They are spelled with capital letters. Some words that describe special days are not proper nouns. They do not have capital letters.

SORT Write the Core Words that fit the following categories.

Core Word Sentences

Mother's Day is here.
Hanukkah is a Jewish festival.
I sent a **Valentine's Day** card.
My **birthday** is in March.
Holidays are happy times.
We eat on **Thanksgiving.**
New Year's Day is in January.
Labor Day honors workers.
I love a **Columbus Day** parade.
It snowed during **Christmas.**
I saw Dad on **Father's Day.**
The **children** are home today.
Flag Day honors the U.S. flag.
Groundhog Day is in winter.
I wore a mask on **Halloween.**

holidays
1. _____
2. _____
3. _____
4. _____
5. _____
6. _____
7. _____
8. _____
9. _____
10. _____
11. _____
12. _____

special days
1. _____
2. _____

people
1. _____

WRITE Write a sentence for each Core Word on a separate sheet of paper.

Spelling Words in Context

 REAL-WORLD CONNECTION Write the Core Words that best complete the story. Use each word only once.

❖ Special Days ❖

Everyone has a _____. Everyone loves _____. These are special days for _____ and adults to enjoy. They are days for giving and celebrating.

On _____, people celebrate the end of one year and the beginning of another. _____ is the day that Punxatawney Phil comes out of his hole and predicts the weather for the next six weeks. Will we have more winter or an early spring? February also has _____.

_____ is the day you give your mother a special gift. On _____, it's Dad's turn. On _____, we honor the flag, but we don't have to buy a gift.

Fall and winter are full of holidays. In September, we honor workers on _____. In October, we celebrate _____, and we go trick-or-treating on _____.

_____ comes on the fourth Thursday of November. In December, people celebrate _____ and _____.

What's your favorite holiday? ❖

Unit 5 • Lesson 29 123

Building Spelling Vocabulary

Core Words

1. Mother's Day
2. Hanukkah
3. Valentine's Day
4. birthday
5. holidays
6. Thanksgiving
7. New Year's Day
8. Labor Day
9. Columbus Day
10. Christmas
11. Father's Day
12. children
13. Flag Day
14. Groundhog Day
15. Halloween

Review Words

best
food
meal
games
noise

Challenge Words

celebrate
Memorial Day
April Fools' Day
Independence Day
Veterans Day

 LETTER CLUES Fill in the missing consonants and write these Core Words.

1. _ o _ u _ _ u _   _ ay _____
2. _ a _ o _   _ ay _____
3. _ a _ _ o _ ee _ _____
4. _ a _ _ e _ _   _ ay _____
5. _ _ a _   _ ay _____
6. _ a _ u _ _ a _ _____
7. _ o _ _ e _ _   _ ay _____
8. _ _ _ i _ _ _ a _ _____
9. _ e _   _ ea _ _   _ ay _____
10. _ _ ou _ _ _ o _   _ ay _____
11. _ a _ e _ _ i _ e _   _ ay _____
12. _ _ a _ _ _ _ i _ i _ _ _____

CHANGING LETTERS Write the Review Words formed by changing one letter in each word.

1. west _____   4. gates _____
2. noisy _____   5. meat   _____
3. fool _____

SYLLABLES Write the Challenge Words that fit each description.

1. It has three syllables. _____
2. They have four syllables.

   _____   _____

3. They have five syllables.

   _____

124 Names of Holidays

Proofreading and Writing

Proofreading Marks

- ◯ misspelling
- ∧ insert
- ꝸ delete
- ≡ make a capital letter
- / make a small letter
- ⊙ add a period

Practice Prooofreding

Here is a draft of one student's booklet about holidays. Find three misspelled Core Words. Circle them and write them correctly.

> Valentime's Day—On February 14, people give candy, flowers, and cards as a sign of love.
> Indipendance Day—On July 4, people have picnics and watch fireworks to celebrate America's birthday.
> Thanxgiving—On the fourth Thursday in November, people give thanks for all their blessings.

1. _____
2. _____
3. _____

Write on Your Own: Booklet

Plan to make a holiday booklet. Choose three holidays to write about and think about pictures to go with each holiday. Choose and write at least four Core Words and other words that you will use in your booklet. Write your booklet on a separate sheet of paper, following the steps on page 159.

1. _____   4. _____
2. _____   5. _____
3. _____   6. _____

Now proofread your word list and booklet and correct any errors.

Unit 5 • Lesson 29

30 Review for Lessons 25–29

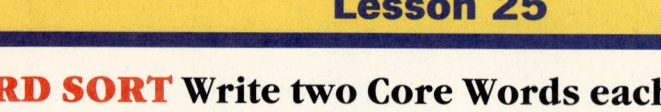

Lesson 25

Lesson 25
- drift
- raft
- draft
- cold
- sold
- wild
- lift
- soft
- craft
- old

🍎 **WORD SORT** Write two Core Words each that spell the /ft/ and the /ld/ sounds.

/ft/   /ld/

1. _____   3. _____

2. _____   4. _____

🍎 **ANTONYMS** Write a Core Word that means the opposite of each word.

5. tame _____   6. hard _____

🍎 **PLURALS** Adding -s to many nouns makes them plural. Make these Core Words plural.

7. craft _____   8. drift _____

Lesson 26

Lesson 26
- stare
- pear
- bare
- chair
- wear
- share
- dare
- fair
- fare
- mare

🍎 **WORD SORT** Write two Core Words that spell the /âr/ sound for each pattern.

air   are   ear

1. _____   3. _____   5. _____

2. _____   4. _____   6. _____

🍎 **CONTEXT CLUES** Write a Core Word to complete each sentence.

7. He had picked the pear tree _____.

8. He rode off to the _____.

🍎 **SUFFIXES** Make these words show action in the past by adding the suffix -ed. Drop the final e before adding -ed.

9. fare _____   10. stare _____

126 Lesson 30 Review

Review

Lesson 27

Lesson 27
- squirt
- squint
- quail
- squeak
- queen
- squeal
- squid
- squeeze
- quilt
- quick

🍎 **WORD SORT** Write two Core Words each that spell the /kw/ and the /skw/ sounds.

           qu   **squ**

1. _____ 3. _____

2. _____ 4. _____

🍎 **DEFINITIONS** Write a Core Word for each definition.

5. Speedy or fast _____

6. A royal woman _____

🍎 **WORD ENDINGS** Add *-ing* to these Core Words to show that an action is happening now.

7. squeal _____ 8. squeak _____

Lesson 28

Lesson 28
- wasn't
- isn't
- wouldn't
- can't
- hasn't
- aren't
- let's
- didn't
- won't
- here's

🍎 **WORD PARTS** Write two contraction Core Words that use these words.

          not   **us *or* is**

1. _____ 3. _____

2. _____ 4. _____

🍎 **LETTER CLUES** Find the words in each sentence that can be made into one of the Core Words. Write the Core Word.

5. She did not want to go to the doctor. _____

6. Jose was not afraid of the snake. _____

🍎 **WORD BUILDING** A contraction is made up of two words with some letters replaced by an apostrophe. Write a contraction for each pair of words.

7. is not _____ 8. will not _____

Lesson 30 Review   127

Review

Lesson 29

Lesson 29
Father's Day
Christmas
Columbus Day
Hanukkah
Labor Day
Valentine's Day
birthday
New Year's Day
Groundhog Day
Mother's Day

🍎 **WORD SORT** Write two holiday Core Words each that have the following number of syllables.

1. three syllables

_____ _____

2. four syllables

_____ _____

🍎 **RIDDLES** Write the Core Word that fits each clue.

3. On this holiday, a candle is lit on each of eight days.

_____

4. On this day, people honor the workers of the country.

_____

🍎 **WORD BUILDING** Add and subtract letters as shown to write the Core Words.

5. choral − oal + ist + mas = _____

6. bird − d + the − e + day = _____

Spelling Strategy

THINK Look at the Core Word lists on pages 126–128. Choose one word from each list that is the hardest for you to spell. Write the word and a strategy to help you remember how to spell each word. For example: There is no *air* in a *pear*.

Words	Spelling Strategies
1. _____	_____
2. _____	_____
3. _____	_____
4. _____	_____
5. _____	_____

128 Lesson 30 Review

Review

Practice Prooofreding

Read the paragraph. Find ten misspelled Core Words. Circle them and write them correctly.

Proofreading Marks	
◯	misspelling
∧	insert
ℯ	delete
≡	make a capital letter
/	make a small letter
⊙	add a period

It was Fred's Haloween party. "Dont forget to ware special costumes," Fred had told his friends. Kevin dressed up as bear. Carol came as a skuid with long tentacles. Suddenly the lights went out. It was so Dark you couldn't see anything. The childrn were qiet. Then someone let out a squeal. Something white came the stairs. "Lets get out of here," one chiled screamed. But it wasn't a ghost. It was only Fred's mom with a qilt over her head. Kevin laughed and Said, "That gave me quiet a scare!"

1. _____
2. _____
3. _____
4. _____
5. _____
6. _____
7. _____
8. _____
9. _____
10. _____

Now find two words that should begin with a small letter and two places where a word should be inserted. Use the correct proofreading marks to show which letters should be small and where words should be inserted.

on Your Own: Paragraph

Write a paragraph describing your favorite holiday using at least six spelling words. First write the spelling words that you want to use.

1. _____
2. _____
3. _____
4. _____
5. _____
6. _____

Now proofread your word list and paragraph and correct any errors.

Lesson 30 Review

Review

SPELLING FUN Use Core Words from Lessons 25–29 to complete this puzzle.

Lesson 25
held
left
golden
scold

Lesson 26
hair
rare
bear
stair
air

Lesson 27
quit
square
squirrel
squirt

Lesson 28
here's

Lesson 29
Thanksgiving
Flag Day

ACROSS

2. Abandoned
5. To find fault
6. A grizzly
9. Has four equal sides
10. Stop
11. A step to climb
12. Grows on your head
13. What we breathe
14. Not common
15. A day for red, white, and blue

DOWN

1. Here is
3. Looks like gold
4. Turkey day
7. It gathers nuts
8. A _____ gun full of water
12. Rhymes with *yelled*

Review
STANDARDIZED-FORMAT TEST PRACTICE

Choose the correct spelling of the Core Words from Lessons 25–29.

ANSWERS

SAMPLE	A. dare	B. dair	C. dayr
1.	A. holidays	B. holydays	C. holidayes
2.	A. shoodn't	B. shuldn't	C. shouldn't
3.	A. payr	B. peare	C. pear
4.	A. Valentien's Day	B. Valentine's Day	C. Valentines Day

Choose the misspelled Core Words from Lessons 25–29.

SAMPLE	A. wans't	B. golden	C. hair
1.	A. Mothers' Day	B. wouldn't	C. let's
2.	A. quial	B. couldn't	C. Groundhog Day
3.	A. hadn't	B. solde	C. Columbus Day
4.	A. mare	B. Father's Day	C. caint

Choose the correct spelling of the Core Words from Lessons 25–29 to complete each sentence.

SAMPLE	The _____ sat on her throne.		
	A. queen	B. kween	C. cween

1. I sat in the soft _____.
    A. char B. chare C. chair

2. They _____ finished their work.
    A. haven't B. havn't C. havent

3. The _____ shirt was torn.
    A. oald B. ole C. old

4. January 1 is _____.
    A. New Yere's Day B. New Yer's Day C. New Year's Day

Lesson 30 Review

31 The /ûr/ and /or/ Sounds

Spelling Focus—The /or/ sound can be spelled *or* or *ore*. The /ûr/ sound can be spelled *ur*.

SORT Write the Core Words with the /or/ and the /ûr/ sounds spelled the following ways.

Core Words

1. murmur
2. fort
3. burn
4. forest
5. story
6. curb
7. surprise
8. porch
9. hurry
10. nurse
11. order
12. sport
13. tore
14. storm
15. hurt

My Words

Core Word Sentences

We heard the wind **murmur**.
The soldiers are in the **fort**.
The sun can **burn** your skin.
Trees in the **forest** are tall.
Mom read me a **story**.
The car is parked at the **curb**.
The **surprise** party is a secret.
I like the view from the **porch**.
Let's **hurry** or we'll be late!
The **nurse** took my pulse.
Please **order** the book.
Football is a team **sport**.
She **tore** her coat pocket.
The **storm** damaged the house.
The hammer **hurt** my finger.

or
1. _____
2. _____
3. _____
4. _____
5. _____
6. _____
7. _____

ore
1. _____

ur
1. _____
2. _____
3. _____
4. _____
5. _____
6. _____
7. _____

WRITE Write a sentence for each Core Word on a separate sheet of paper.

Spelling Words in Context

 REAL-WORLD CONNECTION Write the Core Words that best complete the story. Use each word only once.

❖ Clara Barton ❖

Clara Barton was a _____ during the Civil War. When she heard about the wounded and dying soldiers in the field, she knew she had to help. "I must _____," she said. "My boys need me." First she had to get a pass from the government. When the _____ came, Clara went straight to the battlefields.

After a battle, Clara searched the field and _____ for men who were _____. She listened for a loud yell or a low _____.

Some soldiers looked at her with _____ when she stopped to comfort them. They did not think help would come. Clara treated every bullet wound, every _____, every broken bone. She made splints from tree branches and _____ old sheets to make bandages. Even when cannons blasted like thunder in a _____, Clara worked to save the soldiers. People called her "The Angel of the Battlefield." ❖

 CONTEXT CLUES Write the Core Word that will complete each sentence.

1. Baseball is a great _____.
2. Don't step off the _____ until you know it's safe.
3. We built a _____ with a big box and some wood.
4. My dad likes to sit on the _____ and read.
5. My favorite _____ is *Alice in Wonderland*.

Unit 6 • Lesson 31   133

Building Spelling Vocabulary

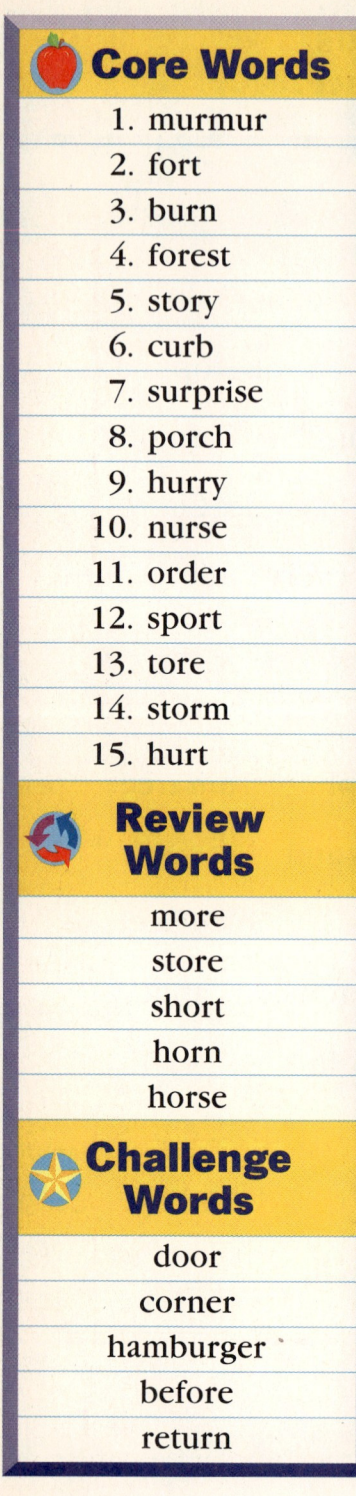

Core Words
1. murmur
2. fort
3. burn
4. forest
5. story
6. curb
7. surprise
8. porch
9. hurry
10. nurse
11. order
12. sport
13. tore
14. storm
15. hurt

Review Words
more
store
short
horn
horse

Challenge Words
door
corner
hamburger
before
return

🍎 **PLURALS** Adding -s or -es to many nouns makes them plural. Make these Core Words plural. Change the *y* to *i* before adding -es to one word.

1. forest _____
2. order _____
3. fort _____
4. sport _____
5. burn _____
6. curb _____
7. nurse _____
8. surprise _____
9. murmur _____
10. porch _____
11. story _____

🍎 **BASE WORDS** Write the Core Words based on these words.

12. hurried _____
13. stormy _____
14. torn _____
15. hurting _____

🔄 **CHANGING LETTERS** Write the Review Words formed by adding or changing one or more letters in each word.

1. bore _____
2. chore _____
3. port _____
4. corn _____
5. hoarse _____

⭐ **LETTER CLUES** Write the Challenge Word that fits each spelling pattern for the /or/ and /ûr/ sounds.

1. *oor* _____
2. *ore* _____
3. *ur* _____
    _____
4. *or* _____

134 The /ûr/ and /or/ Sounds

Proofreading and Writing

Proofreading Marks

- ◯ misspelling
- ∧ insert
- ℮ delete
- ≡ make a capital letter
- / make a small letter
- ⊙ add a period

Practice Proofreading

Here is a draft of one student's story about a storm. Find four misspelled Core Words. Circle them and write them correctly.

> Connie was sitting on her pourch when she heard a loud clap of thunder. Dark sturm clouds blew over. Suddenly she was surprised to hear a strange noise coming from the fourest behind her house. "Please hurey," the voice called.

1. _____
2. _____
3. _____
4. _____

Write on Your Own: Story

Plan to write a story about what it might be like to do your schoolwork during a storm. Think about what the sky, wind, and weather would be like outside. Choose and write at least four Core Words and other words that you will use in your story. Write your story on a separate sheet of paper, following the steps on page 159.

1. _____   4. _____
2. _____   5. _____
3. _____   6. _____

Now proofread your word list and story and correct any errors.

Unit 6 • Lesson 31

Sorting Spelling Patterns

32) Words with Silent *k* and *w*

Spelling Focus—The /n/ sound can be spelled *kn*. The *k* is silent. The /r/ sound can be spelled *wr*. The *w* is silent.

SORT Write the Core Words with the /n/ and /r/ sounds spelled the following ways.

Core Words

1. wrap
2. wren
3. knit
4. knew
5. write
6. know
7. wrong
8. kneel
9. knee
10. wrist
11. knife
12. wreck
13. knot
14. wrote
15. knock

My Words

Core Word Sentences

Let's **wrap** the gift in paper.
The **wren** has black wings.
Can she **knit** a wool sweater?
I **knew** the right answer.
We will **write** a letter.
Do you **know** the facts?
He dialed the **wrong** number.
Bend your knees to **kneel**.
I scraped my left **knee**.
Her watch is on her **wrist**.
Slice bread with a **knife**.
The old car was a **wreck**.
The ship's speed was one **knot**.
The author **wrote** a book.
Please **knock** on the door.

kn
1. _____
2. _____
3. _____
4. _____
5. _____
6. _____
7. _____
8. _____

wr
1. _____
2. _____
3. _____
4. _____
5. _____
6. _____
7. _____

WRITE Write a sentence for each Core Word on a separate sheet of paper.

Spelling Words in Context

 REAL-WORLD CONNECTION Write the Core Words that best complete the story. Use each word only once.

❖ The Great Houdini ❖

Harry Houdini, the great magician, is on stage. "My brother Dash will hold out one _____ and then the other. I will _____ a rope around them and tie a _____. Dash will _____ down inside this heavy _____ bag. Finally, he will get inside this trunk and will be locked in."

People come and _____ on the trunk. They look to see if anything is _____ with it. Houdini ties Dash into the bag and locks him in the trunk. A big screen is pushed in front of the trunk. People look at each other and say, "I _____ he can't get out." Houdini steps behind the screen and counts 1-2-3. The screen moves away. Dash is pushing it!

Dash takes the chains off the trunk. He unties the bag. There is Harry on one _____, smiling at the people. How did they do it?

Dash had used a hidden _____ to cut the bag. Then he had climbed out a trapdoor. Harry had climbed in. It was a trick, but only the brothers _____ it. ❖

 CONTEXT CLUES Write the Core Word that will complete each sentence.

1. My grandmother _____ me a letter.
2. I forgot to _____ my name on my paper.
3. We had a _____ last week, but nobody was hurt.
4. A _____ is building a nest in our backyard.

Unit 6 • Lesson 32   137

Building Spelling Vocabulary

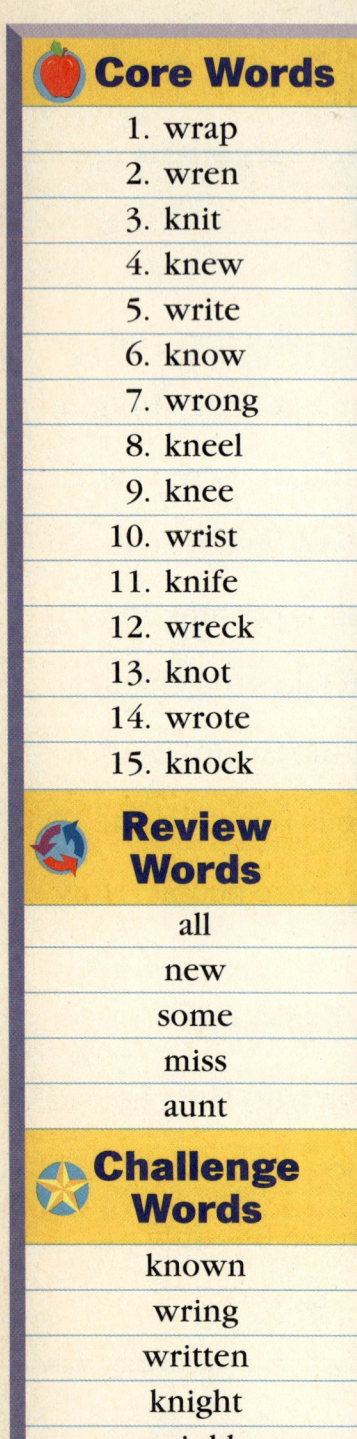

Core Words
1. wrap
2. wren
3. knit
4. knew
5. write
6. know
7. wrong
8. kneel
9. knee
10. wrist
11. knife
12. wreck
13. knot
14. wrote
15. knock

Review Words
all
new
some
miss
aunt

Challenge Words
known
wring
written
knight
wrinkle

🍎 **PHONETIC PATTERNS** Write the Core Word that matches each respelling.

1. /rōt/ _____
2. /rap/ _____
3. /nīf/ _____
4. /nēl/ _____
5. /ren/ _____
6. /rông/ _____
7. /no͞o/ _____
8. /nē/ _____
9. /nit/ _____
10. /not/ _____
11. /nok/ _____
12. /rīt/ _____
13. /nō/ _____
14. /rist/ _____
15. /rek/ _____

🔁 **WORD PARTS** Add the underlined word parts together to write the Review Words.

1. dr<u>a</u>w + she<u>ll</u> = _____
2. <u>so</u>n + co<u>me</u> = _____
3. <u>ne</u>utral + <u>w</u>et = _____
4. mi<u>x</u> + ki<u>ss</u> = _____

🔁 **HOMOPHONES** Write the homophone Review Word that sounds the same as the following word.

5. ant _____

⭐ **WORD BUILDING** Fill in the missing letters and write the Challenge Words.

1. _ _ ow _ _____
2. _ _ _ gh _ _____
3. wr _ _ _ _____
4. _ _ ink _ _ _____
5. _ _ it _ _ _ _____

138 Words with Silent *k* and *w*

Proofreading and Writing

Proofreading Marks

- ◯ misspelling
- ∧ insert
- ℯ delete
- ≡ make a capital letter
- / make a small letter
- ⊙ add a period

Practice Proofreading

Here is a draft of one student's journal entry about a storm at sea. Find four misspelled Core Words. Circle them and write them correctly.

> As I rite in my journal, I do not no if we will make it through this storm. I am worried that our ship will become a reck if it is blown against the rocks. Yesterday one of the crew members slipped on deck and broke his rist.

1. _____
2. _____
3. _____
4. _____

Write on Your Own: Journal Entry

Plan to write a journal entry about a magic act you would like to perform. Think about whether you would like to use cards, shadow puppets, or a friend in your act. Choose and write at least four Core Words and other words that you will use in your entry. Write your journal entry on a separate sheet of paper, following the steps on page 159.

1. _____   4. _____
2. _____   5. _____
3. _____   6. _____

Now proofread your word list and journal entry and correct any errors.

Unit 6 • Lesson 32

Sorting Spelling Patterns

33 Words with *lf*, *mb*, and *tch*

Spelling Focus—The /ch/ sound can be spelled *tch*. The *t* is silent. The /m/ sound can be spelled *mb*. The *b* is silent. The /f/ sound can be spelled *lf*. The *l* is silent.

SORT Write the Core Words with the /ch/, /m/, and /f/ sounds spelled the following ways.

Core Words

1. match
2. half
3. batch
4. limb
5. ditch
6. climb
7. crumb
8. calf
9. lamb
10. catch
11. latch
12. thumb
13. comb
14. pitch
15. switch

My Words

Core Word Sentences

The two shoes do not **match**.
We cut the pizza in **half**.
Dad baked a **batch** of cookies.
I broke a **limb** while skating.
The ball fell in the **ditch**.
Can you **climb** the steep hill?
Wipe up the **crumb**.
The **calf** followed the cow.
Get wool from a **lamb**.
Use a mitt to **catch** the ball.
The brass **latch** is on the door.
I can't bend my sore **thumb**.
Please **comb** your hair.
She can **pitch** a no-hit game.
We can **switch** off the program.

tch
1. _____
2. _____
3. _____
4. _____
5. _____
6. _____
7. _____

mb
1. _____
2. _____
3. _____
4. _____
5. _____
6. _____

lf
1. _____
2. _____

WRITE Write a sentence for each Core Word on a separate sheet of paper.

Spelling Words in Context

REAL-WORLD CONNECTION Write the Core Words that best complete the story. Use each word only once.

❖ Twister! ❖

A tornado is a fierce windstorm. It can blow a bicycle across a street like a _____ across a table. It can blow the _____ off a tree. It can pick up an animal, like a _____ or a _____, and carry it for miles. It can rip the roof off a house and _____ it through the air.

Don't let a tornado _____ you unprepared. If you are indoors, stay away from the windows. If you have time, _____ off the lights and appliances. Close the _____ on every door.

If you are outside, find a _____ and curl up in it. Don't _____ out until the tornado has passed. If you are in a car, get out and go to a safe place. A car is no _____ for a tornado.

Tornadoes can do a lot of damage. But if you're careful and you know what to do, you'll be safe. ❖

CONTEXT CLUES Write the Core Word that will complete each sentence.

1. I have a red _____ and brush.
2. The human hand has four fingers and a _____.
3. I only want _____ a sandwich today.
4. Can we make a _____ of cookies?

Unit 6 • Lesson 33

Building Spelling Vocabulary

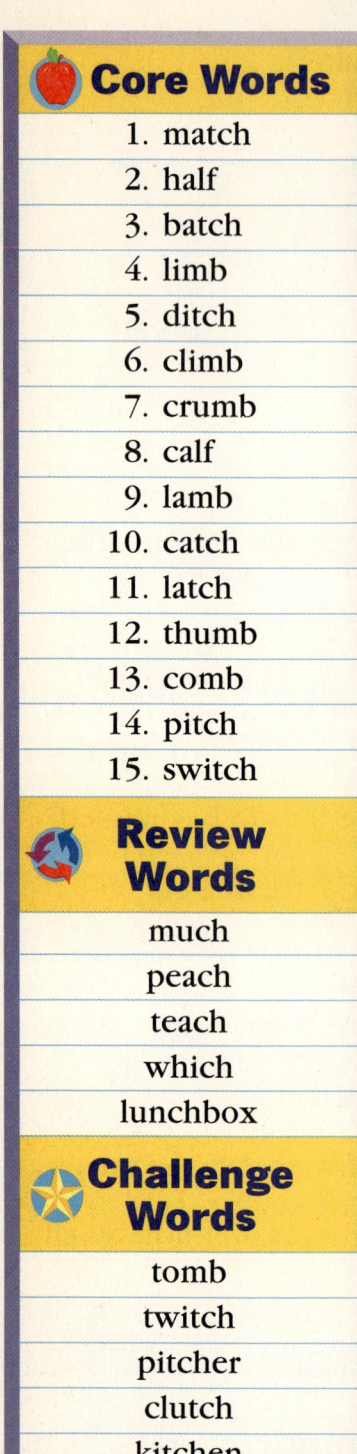

Core Words
1. match
2. half
3. batch
4. limb
5. ditch
6. climb
7. crumb
8. calf
9. lamb
10. catch
11. latch
12. thumb
13. comb
14. pitch
15. switch

Review Words
much
peach
teach
which
lunchbox

Challenge Words
tomb
twitch
pitcher
clutch
kitchen

WORD PARTS Use *tch*, *mb*, or *lf* to write the Core Words.

1. ba- _____
2. ca- _____
3. la- _____
4. ma- _____
5. di- _____
6. pi- _____
7. swi- _____
8. la- _____
9. li- _____
10. co- _____
11. cli- _____
12. cru- _____
13. thu- _____
14. ca- _____
15. ha- _____

LETTER CLUES Write the Review Words that have the same sounds as:

the /ch/ sound in *reach*

1. _____
2. _____
3. _____
4. _____

the /nch/ sound in *punch*

5. _____

WORD BUILDING Fill in the missing letters and write the Challenge Words.

1. to _ _ _____
2. clu _ _ _ _____
3. ki _ _ _ en _____
4. twi _ _ _ _____
5. pi _ _ _ er _____

142 Words with *lf*, *mb*, and *tch*

Proofreading and Writing

Proofreading Marks

- ◯ misspelling
- ∧ insert
- ⌒e delete
- ≡ make a capital letter
- / make a small letter
- ⊙ add a period

Practice Proofreading

Here is a draft of one student's postcard about a day on a farm. Find four misspelled Core Words. Circle them and write them correctly.

> In the morning I get dressed, brush my teeth, and coam my hair. I eat every crumm of my breakfast. Then I clime into a wagon and ride out to the field to pitch hay. I only work for haff a day. Then I go swimming or play catch.

1. _____
2. _____
3. _____
4. _____

Write on Your Own: Postcard

Plan to write a postcard to a friend about what you might do on a farm. Think about some of the things you might find on a farm, such as animals, crops, and haystacks. Choose and write at least four Core Words and other words to use in your postcard. Write your postcard on a separate sheet of paper, following the steps on page 159.

1. _____   4. _____
2. _____   5. _____
3. _____   6. _____

Now proofread your word list and postcard and correct any errors.

Unit 6 • Lesson 33

Sorting Spelling Patterns

34 Compound Words

Spelling Focus—Compound words are words that are made up of two words joined together.

SORT Write the Core Words that have the following endings.

Core Words

1. bedtime
2. sidewalk
3. rainbow
4. anything
5. playground
6. chalkboard
7. campfire
8. cardboard
9. underground
10. classroom
11. eyelash
12. horseback
13. lunchtime
14. spacewalk
15. spaceship

My Words

Core Word Sentences

My **bedtime** is eight p.m.
I slipped on the icy **sidewalk.**
See the colorful **rainbow.**
Can we do **anything** to help?
The **playground** is closed.
Erase the **chalkboard.**
The scouts lit the **campfire.**
The hat is in a **cardboard** box.
The **underground** train passed.
We learn in a **classroom.**
Her **eyelash** fell on her cheek.
We went **horseback** riding today.
Do you nap at **lunchtime?**
I would love to **spacewalk!**
The **spaceship** went to Mars.

-ground
1. _____
2. _____

-board
1. _____
2. _____

-walk
1. _____
2. _____

no common endings
1. _____
2. _____
3. _____
4. _____
5. _____
6. _____
7. _____

-time
1. _____
2. _____

WRITE Write a sentence for each Core Word on a separate sheet of paper.

Compound Words

Spelling Words in Context

 REAL-WORLD CONNECTION Write the Core Words that best complete the story. Use each word only once.

❖ Highs and Lows of Summer ❖

Are you looking for something really great to do this summer? Here are two places that kids love.

NASA Space Center is in Houston, Texas. Going inside the Center is almost like going over the _____. It's like another world. You can see a _____ and a lunar rover. And they're not _____ models. They're real! You can also go inside the Lunar Jumper. There's not much gravity in the Lunar Jumper. While walking inside, you can pretend to moonwalk or _____. Rocket Park is outside. It's like a _____, but better. As you walk along the _____, you can stop and see real rockets.

Carlsbad Caverns in New Mexico is another great place to visit. Here you go down instead of up. You walk through _____ caves. Sometimes it's so dark, you can't see _____. You can't even see your _____! At _____, you can stop in the underground cafeteria. After going through the caves, you can take a _____ ride or build a _____ at the campground.

You can learn a lot, even though neither place has a _____ or a _____. No matter which place you visit, you're sure to have fun. And you'll be tired by _____. ❖

Unit 6 • Lesson 34 145

Building Spelling Vocabulary

Core Words
1. bedtime
2. sidewalk
3. rainbow
4. anything
5. playground
6. chalkboard
7. campfire
8. cardboard
9. underground
10. classroom
11. eyelash
12. horseback
13. lunchtime
14. spacewalk
15. spaceship

Review Words
downtown
notebook
firefly
sunrise
grandmother

Challenge Words
grasshopper
stairway
scarecrow
cartwheel
touchdown

WORD PARTS Add these words to the numbered words to make the compound Core Words.

| walk | ground | ship | lash | fire | back |
| time | bow | thing | board | room | |

1. lunch _____
2. camp _____
3. eye _____
4. bed _____
5. space _____
6. rain _____
7. side _____
8. play _____
9. horse _____
10. under _____
11. space _____
12. any _____
13. card _____
14. chalk _____
15. class _____

WORD BUILDING Write the Review Word by joining two shorter words in each sentence.

1. Down at the library there is a map of the town.
   _____

2. It was grand of you to invite my mother.
   _____

3. Will the sun be shining when we rise tomorrow?
   _____

4. Did you find the note I left in your book?
   _____

5. The heat of the fire made the fly buzz.
   _____

SYLLABLES Write the Challenge Words and draw a line between the syllables.

1. _____   4. _____
2. _____   5. _____
3. _____

146 Compound Words

Proofreading and Writing

Proofreading Marks

◯ misspelling	≡ make a capital letter
∧ insert	/ make a small letter
ꝺ delete	⊙ add a period

Practice Proofreading

Here is a draft of one student's letter about life on another planet. Find four misspelled Core Words. Circle them and write them correctly.

> Evrybody wears travel packs on their backs so they can fly anywhere. Houses are made of strong cardbord that can be folded up and moved. Instead of using a chockboard in our clasroom, we use a giant computer screen.

1. _____
2. _____
3. _____
4. _____

Write on Your Own: Letter

Plan to write a letter to someone on Earth telling them about your life on another planet. Think about where you live and what you do. Choose and write at least four Core Words and other words that you will use in your letter. Write your letter on a separate sheet of paper, following the steps on page 159.

1. _____ 4. _____
2. _____ 5. _____
3. _____ 6. _____

Now proofread your word list and letter and correct any errors.

Unit 6 • Lesson 34   147

Sorting Spelling Patterns

35 Names of Months

Spelling Focus—The names of the months of the year are proper nouns. They have capital letters. Other words having to do with the calendar are not proper nouns. They do not have capital letters.

SORT Write the Core Words that fit the following categories.

Core Words

1. April
2. January
3. calendar
4. August
5. October
6. March
7. year
8. month
9. June
10. February
11. May
12. September
13. July
14. November
15. December

My Words

Core Word Sentences

March comes before **April**.
New Year's Day is **January** 1.
The **calendar** has dates.
My vacation is in **August**.
Halloween is **October** 31.
The end of winter is in **March**.
Fifty-two weeks are in a **year**.
Four weeks are in a **month**.
Graduation time is in **June**.
Valentine's Day is in **February**.
Memorial Day is in **May**.
School begins in **September**.
Independence Day is in **July**.
Thanksgiving is in **November**.
Christmas is **December** 25.

months of the year

1. _____
2. _____
3. _____
4. _____
5. _____
6. _____
7. _____
8. _____
9. _____
10. _____
11. _____
12. _____

words that are not proper nouns

1. _____
2. _____
3. _____

WRITE Write a sentence for each Core Word on a separate sheet of paper.

Spelling Words in Context

 REAL-WORLD CONNECTION Write the Core Words that best complete the story. Use each word only once.

❖ A New Year ❖

At the beginning of each new _____, we buy a _____ to help us keep track of the dates. The calendar lists every _____ in order from first to last.

The first month of the year is _____. Valentine's Day is celebrated in the second month, _____. The third month, when spring begins, is _____. On _____ Fools' Day, you can play a joke on a friend or family member. Mother's Day is in the month of _____. Father's Day and Flag Day are both in _____.

Independence Day comes on the fourth day of _____. The last full month of summer is _____. Fall begins in the month of _____. Halloween comes on the last day of _____. Thanksgiving is on the fourth Thursday of _____. The last month of the year, when winter begins, is _____. ❖

Unit 6 • Lesson 35

Building Spelling Vocabulary

Core Words
1. April
2. January
3. calendar
4. August
5. October
6. March
7. year
8. month
9. June
10. February
11. May
12. September
13. July
14. November
15. December

Review Words
die
trees
fall
spring
summer

Challenge Words
daily
seasons
twelve
weekly
winter

WORD ORIGINS These Latin word origins contain clues to the English words based on them. Write the Core Word that matches each word origin.

1. From *Iānus,* meaning "Janus." _____
2. From *septem,* meaning "seven." _____
3. From *octō,* meaning "eight." _____
4. From *novem,* meaning "nine." _____
5. From *decem,* meaning "ten." _____
6. From *Mārs,* meaning "Mars." _____
7. From *Aprīlis,* meaning "April." _____
8. From *Maia,* the name of a goddess. _____
9. From *Iūnō,* meaning "Juno." _____
10. From *Iūlius,* meaning "Julius." _____
11. From *Augustus,* the name of an emperor. _____

CHANGING LETTERS Write the Review Words formed by adding or changing one or more letters in each word.

1. pie _____   4. hall _____
2. simmer _____   5. bees _____
3. string _____

LETTER CLUES Fill in the missing letters to write each Challenge Word.

1. _ _ _ t _ _ _____
2. s _ _ s _ _ _ _____
3. _ _ el _ _ _____
4. _ ai _ _ _____
5. w _ _ k _ _ _____

150 Names of Months

Proofreading and Writing

Proofreading Marks

◯ misspelling   ≡ make a capital letter
∧ insert   / make a small letter
⌒e delete   ⊙ add a period

Practice Proofreading

Here is a draft of one student's list of important dates. Find four misspelled Core Words. Circle them and write them correctly.

My List of Important Dates
Febuary 2–Vacation begins
Aprel 28–Jen's birthday
Maye 13–Amy's party
June 2–Dan's driving lesson
Oktober 3–First day of new job
November 2–Pat and Julio's wedding

1. _____
2. _____
3. _____
4. _____

Write on Your Own: List of Dates

Plan to make a list of important dates that you would mark on your own calendar. Think about the month, date, and the reason why the date is important. Choose and write at least four Core Words and other words that you will use in your list. Write your list on a separate sheet of paper, following the steps on page 159.

1. _____ 4. _____
2. _____ 5. _____
3. _____ 6. _____

Now proofread your word list and list of dates and correct any errors.

Unit 6 • Lesson 35

36 Review for Lessons 31-35

Lesson 31

Lesson 31
- fort
- order
- tore
- burn
- hurry
- curb
- porch
- nurse
- forest
- hurt

🍎 **WORD SORT** Write two Core Words that spell the /ûr/ and the /or/ sounds for each pattern.

ur
1. _____
2. _____

or
3. _____
4. _____

🍎 **CONTEXT CLUES** Write a Core Word to complete each sentence. The missing word will rhyme with the underlined word.

5. If you ripped it again, you _____ more.

6. A little castle is a short _____.

🍎 **PHONETIC PATTERNS** Write the Core Word that matches each respelling.

7. /bûrn/ _____ 8. /nûrs/ _____

Lesson 32

Lesson 32
- know
- write
- kneel
- wrote
- knot
- wrist
- wrong
- knee
- knock
- knit

🍎 **WORD SORT** Write two Core Words that spell the /n/ and the /r/ sounds for each pattern.

kn
1. _____
2. _____

wr
3. _____
4. _____

🍎 **HOMOPHONES** Write Core Words to complete each sentence. The words will sound the same as the underlined words, but will have different spellings and meanings.

5. She wants to right a scary ghost story. _____

6. Mom tied a not in the string. _____

🍎 **SUFFIXES** Make these words show action in the past by adding the suffix -ed.

7. knock _____ 8. wrong _____

152 Lesson 36 Review

Review

Lesson 33

Lesson 33
- ditch
- switch
- comb
- latch
- half
- pitch
- limb
- calf
- batch
- thumb

🍎 **WORD SORT** Write two Core Words that spell the /f/, the /m/, and the /ch/ sounds for each pattern.

lf	mb	tch
1. _____	3. _____	5. _____
2. _____	4. _____	6. _____

🍎 **CLASSIFYING** Write the Core Word that fits each group.

7. cow, bull, _____
8. key, lock, _____
9. toe, finger, _____
10. quarter, third, _____

🍎 **LETTER CLUES** Fill in the missing letters and write the Core Words.

11. li _ _
12. swi _ _ _
13. ba _ _ _
14. di _ _ _

Lesson 34

Lesson 34
- cardboard
- campfire
- spacewalk
- bedtime
- rainbow
- anything
- spaceship
- sidewalk
- lunchtime
- eyelash

🍎 **WORD SORT** Write two compound Core Words that use each of these words.

time 1. _____   2. _____
walk 3. _____   4. _____

🍎 **RIDDLES** Write the Core Word that fits each clue.

5. Boxes are made of this. _____
6. This appears after it rains. _____

🍎 **WORD BUILDING** You can make a compound word by adding one word to another. Add the words *fire, thing, ship,* or *lash* to these words to make a Core Word.

7. eye _____
8. any _____
9. camp _____
10. space _____

Lesson 36 Review 153

Review

Lesson 35

Lesson 35
June
July
calendar
March
December
May
year
November
month
February

🍎 **WORD SORT** Write two Core Words for each category.

words ending in *-y*   words ending in *-ber*

1. _____   3. _____

2. _____   4. _____

🍎 **ANALOGIES** Write a Core Word to complete each analogy.

5. *Location* is to *map* as *date* is to _____.

6. *Day* is to *week* as *month* is to _____.

🍎 **WORD PARTS** Add the underlined word parts together to make Core Words. Some words will have to be capitalized.

7. <u>mo</u>nkey + te<u>nth</u> = _____

8. <u>j</u>uice + tu<u>ne</u> = _____

9. <u>mar</u>k + lu<u>nch</u> = _____

Spelling Strategy

THINK Look at the Core Word lists on pages 152–154. Choose one word from each list that is the hardest for you to spell. Write the word and a strategy to help you remember how to spell each word. For example: You'll find *rest* in the *forest*.

Words   Spelling Strategies

1. _____   _____

2. _____   _____

3. _____   _____

4. _____   _____

5. _____   _____

Review

Practice Prooofreding

Read the paragraph. Find eleven misspelled Core Words. Circle them and write them correctly.

Proofreading Marks	
◯	misspelling
∧	insert
ℯ	delete
≡	make a capital letter
/	make a small letter
⊙	add a period

    Kim rote a list of things she likes to do in the autumn months. in Setember, she likes to listen to the mermer of a faraway storme. In octobre, she likes to cach leaves as they fall on the sidwalk. In Novembur, she likes to clim the tree where the ren used to live She wonders if it will return in Aprill

1. _____
2. _____
3. _____
4. _____
5. _____
6. _____
7. _____
8. _____
9. _____
10. _____
11. _____

Now find two words that should begin with a capital letter and two places where a period should be added. Use the correct proofreading marks to show which letters should be capitals and where periods should be added.

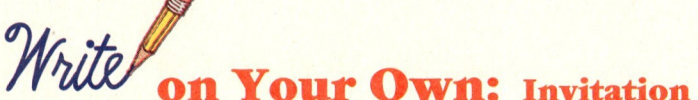 **on Your Own: Invitation**

Write an invitation to a friend for a party using at least six spelling words. First write the spelling words that you plan to use.

1. _____
2. _____
3. _____
4. _____
5. _____
6. _____

Now proofread your word list and invitation and correct any errors.

Lesson 36 Review   **155**

Review

SPELLING FUN Use Core Words from Lessons 31–35 to complete this puzzle.

Lesson 31
surprise
sport
nurse

Lesson 32
wrap
knew
wreck

Lesson 33
match
crumb
lamb

Lesson 34
anything
playground
campfire
horseback

Lesson 35
January
May

ACROSS
3. A clean plate, without a _____ on it
5. An athletic game
7. Use a saddle to ride this way.
8. Fifth month of the year
11. During recess we go to the _____.
13. He _____ the answer.
15. First month of the year

DOWN
1. You don't expect it.
2. Sounds the same as *rap*
4. A wrestling _____
6. Roast marshmallows over one.
9. A reckless driver might cause one.
10. Takes care of people

156 Lesson 36 Review

1 The *entry word* is the word you look up. Entry words are in bold type and are listed in alphabetical order. Sometimes there is more than one entry for a word. When this happens, each entry is numbered.

2 At the top of each dictionary page are two words called *guide words*. They are the first and last entry words appearing on that page. Guide words help you find an entry word quickly.

3 Words with more than one syllable are shown in parts. Spaces are used to show where words can be divided.

4 The *pronunciation* follows the entry word. It is given between two slashes. Special letters are used to show how to pronounce the word. A *pronunciation key* shows the sound for each special letter. The pronunciation key is found on each right-hand page of the dictionary.

5 An abbreviation for the *part of speech* of the entry word is given after the pronunciation. Some words can be more than one part of speech. If so, the dictionary may give a definition for each part of speech.

6 The dictionary also shows *irregular forms* of the entry word. If –*s, -es, -ed,* or –*ing* is simply added to the word, the dictionary does not list these regularly spelled forms.

7 One or more *definitions* are given for each entry word. If there is more than one definition, the definitions are numbered.

8 Sometimes the entry word is used in a *sample sentence or phrase* to help explain its meaning.

Speller Dictionary

adj.	adjective
adv.	adverb
conj.	conjunction
contr.	contraction
def.	definition
interj.	interjection
n.	noun
pl.	plural
prep.	preposition
pron.	pronoun
sing.	singular
v.	verb

••••• **A** •••••••••••••••••

ac count ant /ə koun′ tənt/ *n.* a person who takes care of financial records.

a cross /ə krôs′/ *adv.* from one side to the other. *We came across in a rowboat.* —*prep.* **1.** from one side to the other side of; over. **2.** on the other side of; beyond. *They live across the street from me.*

add /ad/ *v.* **1.** to find the sum of two or more numbers. **2.** to put in or on as something extra. *I like to add fruit to my yogurt.*

a fraid /ə frād′ / *adj.* **1.** feeling fear; frightened. **2.** feeling unhappy or sorry.

af ter /af′ tər/ *prep.* **1.** following in time. *After school, I walk home.* **2.** behind. *The twins walked after their mother.*

af ter noon /af tər nōōn′/ *n.* the part of day between noon and evening.

a gain /ə gen′/ *adv.* once more; another time. *I failed that test once, but I took it again and passed.*

age /āj/ *n., pl.* **ag es** time of life. *People can learn to swim even at a young age.* —*v.* **aged, ag ing** or **age ing.** to grow old.

air /âr/ *n.* **1.** the mixture of gases that surrounds Earth and forms its atmosphere. *Air is made up of nitrogen and oxygen and small amounts of other gases.* **2.** the open space above the earth; sky. **3.** fresh air. —*v.* **aired, air ing 1.** to let air through; freshen. **2.** to make known; express. *The workers aired their complaints.*

all /ôl/ *adj.* **1.** the whole of. **2.** every one. *Students from all the schools.* —*pron.* the whole amount or number. *All of us are going.* —*adv.* completely. *The work is all finished.* —*n.* everything that one has. *The team gave its all.*

al ler gist /al′ ər jist/ *n.* a doctor who treats allergies.

al ler gy /al′ ər jē/ *n.* an abnormal reaction of the body to a certain substance that is harmless to most people such as pollen or dust.

al loy /al′ oi, ə loi′/ *n.* a mixing of two or more metals or a metal and another substance. *Brass is an alloy of copper and zinc.*

al most /ôl′ mōst/ *adv.* very close to; nearly. *I am almost finished with the work.*

a loud /ə loud′ / *adv.* using the voice so as to be heard; out loud. *Students will read their reports aloud to the class.*

al ways /ôl′ wāz, ôl′ wēz/ *adv.* **1.** all the time; continuously. *There is always snow and ice at the North Pole.* **2.** every time; at all times. **3.** for all time; forever.

am ne sia /am nē′ zhə/ *n.* loss of memory.

an gle /ang′ gəl/ *n.* **1.** the figure formed by two lines that extend from one point. **2.** a corner. *The sculpture has many angles and curves.*

an y /en′ ē/ *adj.* **1.** one or some. *Sit in any chair.* **2.** every. *Any child can do this problem.* —*pron.* **1.** any one or ones. **2.** any quantity or part. —*adv.* to any extent.

an y thing /en′ ē thing/ *pron.* any thing; whatever. *I'll do anything you ask.* —*adv.* in any way; at all. *You aren't anything like your twin.*

ap pen dix /ə pen′ diks/ *n., pl.* **ap pen dixes** or **ap pen di ces** /ə pen′ də sēz′ / a section at the end of a book or other piece of writing.

ap ple /ap′ əl/ *n.* a round fruit with red, yellow, or green skin.

ap pren tice /ə pren′ tis/ *n.* a person who works for a skilled worker in order to learn a trade or art.

166 **Speller Dictionary**

approximation/balloonists

ap prox i ma tion /ə prok′ sə mā′ shən/ *n.* something that is nearly correct. *The figure 7,500,000 is an approximation of the population of New York City.*

A pril /ā′ prəl/ *n.* the fourth month of the year. April has 30 days.

A pril Fools' Day /ā′ prəl fōōlz dā/ *n.* a day when tricks are often played on people. It falls on April 1. Also, **All Fools' Day.**

Ar bor Day /är′ bər dā/ *n.* a day set aside for planting trees.

are /är/ *v.* a form of the present tense of *be* that is used with *you, we, they,* or the plural form of a noun.

aren't /ärnt, är′ ənt/ *contr.* shortened form of "are not." *Why aren't you going with us?*

art /ärt/ *n.* **1.** an activity by which one creates a work that has beauty or special meaning. **2.** the works created by this kind of activity. **3.** a skill, craft, or occupation that requires study, practice, or experience.

ask /ask/ *v.* **1.** to put a question about something; inquire. **2.** to put a question to. *I asked a police officer for directions.* **3.** to make a request. *May I ask for your help?*

as ter oids /as′ tə roidz/ *n.* plural of **as ter oid.** a small planet that revolves around the sun.

as trol o gy /ə strol′ ə jē/ *n.* the study of the influence that the stars and planets are supposed to have on people and events.

as tron o mer /ə stron′ ə mər/ *n.* a person who specializes in the science of the sun, moon, stars, and planets.

au di to ri um /ô di tôr′ ē əm/ *n.* a large room or building where a group of people can gather.

Au gust /ô′ gəst/ *n.* the eighth month of the year. August has 31 days.

aunt /ant, änt/ *n.* **1.** the sister of one's mother or father. **2.** the wife of one's uncle.

au thor /ô′ thər/ *n.* a person who has written a book, story, play, or article.

au tum nal /ô tum′ nəl/ *adj.* relating to or characteristic of autumn. *Apples are an autumnal fruit.*

a ware /ə wâr′/ *adj.* knowing or realizing; conscious. *We were not aware you were planning a party.*

a way /ə wā′/ *adv.* **1.** from this or that place. *The frightened rabbit hopped away.* **2.** at a distance. *They stood far away from us.* **3.** in another direction; aside. *I turned away to hide my tears.* **4.** from or out of one's possession or use. *Throw away that old coat.* **5.** at or to an end; out of existence. *The sound of footsteps faded away.* —*adj.* **1.** distant. **2.** absent; gone.

awe /ô/ *n.* great wonder, fear, and respect. *They read with awe that astronauts landed on the moon.*

aw ful /ô′ fəl/ *adj.* **1.** causing fear, dread, or awe; terrible. *The earthquake was an awful disaster.* **2.** very bad. **3.** very large, great.

ax le /ak′ səl/ *n.* a bar on which wheels turn. *The front axle of our car is broken.*

B

ba bies /bā′ bēs/ *n.* the plural of **baby.**

ba by /bā′ bē/ *n., pl.* **ba bies. 1.** a very young child; infant. **2.** the youngest person in a family or group. **3.** a person who acts in a childish way. —*v.* **ba bied, ba by ing.** to treat like a baby. *My parents babied me when I was sick.* —*adj.* **1.** of or for a baby. **2.** very young. *Cubs are baby bears.*

bal ance /ba′ ləns/ *v.* **bal anced, bal anc ing.** to put or keep in a steady position.

bald /bôld/ *adj.* **1.** having little or no hair on the head. **2.** without a natural covering. *The bald hilltop had no trees or shrubs.*

bal loon ists /bə lōō′ nists/ *n.* people who operate or ride in balloons.

/a/	at
/ā/	late
/â/	care
/ä/	father
/e/	set
/ē/	me
/i/	it
/ī/	kite
/o/	ox
/ō/	rose
/ô/	brought raw
/oi/	coin
/ŏŏ/	book
/ōō/	too
/or/	form
/ou/	out
/u/	up
/yōō/	cube
/ûr/	turn germ learn firm work
/ə/	about chicken pencil cannon circus
/ch/	chair
/hw/	which
/ng/	ring
/sh/	shop
/th/	thin
/ᴛʜ/	there
/zh/	treasure

Speller Dictionary **167**

bare /bâr/ *adj.*, **bar er, bar est.**
1. without covering or clothing; naked.
2. empty. *After we took the books out, the shelves were bare.* —*v.* **bared, bar ing.** to uncover. *The cat bared its claws.*

batch /bach/ *n., pl.* **batch es.** bread, cookies or rolls baked at the same time. *The batch of rolls was hot from the oven.*

bat ting /bat′ ing/ *v.* a form of **bat**, to hit with a stick. *He was batting the ball.*

bear /bâr/ *n.* a large, heavy animal with shaggy fur. The black bear, brown bear, grizzly bear, and polar bear are types of bears. —*v.* **bore, borne,** or **born, bear ing.** 1. to hold up; support or carry. 2. to produce offspring. 3. to put up with patiently.

beast /bēst/ *n.* an animal with four feet. *The lion is a beast that lives in Africa.*

be cause /bi kôz′ / *conj.* for the reason that. *You're cold because you did not wear your sweater.*

bed time /bed′ tīm/ *n.* the time to go to bed. *I am sleepy at bedtime.*

been /bin/ *v.* past participle of *be*. *I have been visiting my grandparents for a week.*

be fore /bi for′/ *prep.* 1. in front of; ahead of. 2. in the presence of. *The criminals stood before the judge.* —*adv.* 1. at an earlier time; previously. 2. in front of; in advance. —*conj.* 1. earlier than the time when. *It grew dark before the children finished.* 2. rather than; sooner than. *I would beg before I would steal.*

be gin /bi gin′ / *v.* **be gan, be gun, be gin ning.** 1. to do the first part of something; make a start. 2. to come into being; start.

bend /bend/ *v.* **bent, bend ing.** 1. to change the shape of something by making it curved or crooked. *We bent pieces of wire to make hooks.* 2. to move the top part of the body forward and down; stoop; bow.
—*n.* something bent. *The campers' tent is just beyond the bend in the trail.*

ber ries /ber′ ēz/ *n.* the plural of **berry**.

ber ry /ber′ ē/ *n., pl.* **ber ries.** a small, juicy, fleshy fruit that has one or more seeds.

best /best/ *adj.* 1. of the highest quality; better than all others. 2. most preferred; most suitable. —*adv.* 1. with the most success or effectiveness. *I work best when I work by myself.* 2. most. *I like all fruits, but I like peaches best.*
—*n.* something or someone of the highest quality. —*v.* to do better than; defeat. *Our chess team bested their chess team.*

bet ter /bet′ ər/ *adj.* 1. of higher quality. *These are better pants than those torn ones.* 2. more preferred; more suitable. *A firm mattress is better for your back.* 3. improved in health. —*adv.* 1. with more success or effectiveness. *Cactuses grow better in dry soil.* 2. to a higher degree; more.
—*v.* 1. to make better; improve. *You can better your piano playing if you practice.* 2. to do better than; outdo.

be tween /bi twēn′/ *adv.* in the space or time separating two things. *A sandwich is two pieces of bread with a filling between.* —*prep.* 1. in the space or time separating. 2. joining; connecting. *There is a bridge between the island and the mainland.* 3. involving; among. *A quarrel broke out between two students.* 4. by the combined action of. *Between us, we can clean our room in an hour.*

bi an nu al /bī an′ yōō əl/ *adj.* happening twice a year.

bi cy cle /bī′ si kəl/ *n.* a light vehicle with two wheels, one behind the other. It has handlebars and uses pedals to turn the wheels.
—*v.* **bi cy cled, bi cy cling.** to ride a bicycle.

adj.	adjective
adv.	adverb
conj.	conjunction
contr.	contraction
def.	definition
interj.	interjection
n.	noun
pl.	plural
prep.	preposition
pron.	pronoun
sing.	singular
v.	verb

bird /bûrd/ *n.* an animal that has wings, two legs, and a body covered with feathers. Birds have a backbone, are warm-blooded, and lay eggs.

birth day /bûrth′ dā/ *n.* **1.** the day on which a person is born. **2.** the return each year of this day.

bite /bīt/ *v.* **bit, bit ten** or **bit, bit ing.** **1.** to seize, cut into, or pierce with the teeth. *The child bit off a piece of carrot.* **2.** to wound with teeth, fangs, or a stinger. —*n.* **1.** a seizing or cutting into something with the teeth. **2.** a wound made by biting. **3.** a piece bitten off. *Do you want a bite of my apple?*

bi ting /bī′ ting/ *v.* a form of **bite**. It is used with a helping verb. *She was biting some corn.*

blaze /blāz/ *n.* **1.** a bright flame; a glowing fire. **2.** a bright light. **3.** a bright display. *The circus parade was a blaze of color.* **4.** a mark made on a tree or rock to show a trail or boundary. —*v.* **blazed, blaz ing.** **1.** to burn brightly. **2.** to shine brightly. **3.** to show a trail or boundary by putting marks on trees or rocks. *The hikers will blaze a trail in the woods.*

blush /blush/ *v.* **blushed.** to get a red face. *The shy boy blushed when he met people.* —*n., pl.* **blush es.** becoming red in the face because of shame or embarrassment. *I listened with a blush as my parents corrected me.*

boil /boil/ *v.* to heat something until it is very hot and bubbling.

bomb /bom/ a hollow case filled with something that can explode. It is used as a weapon.

booth /bōōth/ *n.* a stand at a fair or market where things are sold.

Bos ton Tea Par ty /bôs′ tən tē pär′ tē/ *n.* a raid on British ships in Boston Harbor on December 16, 1773, in which American colonists threw chests of tea overboard as a protest against British taxation on tea.

bot tle /bot′ əl/ *n.* a container, usually made of glass or plastic, which holds liquids. —*v.* **bot tled, bot tling.** to put in bottles. *That company bottles soft drinks.*

bound /bound/ *adj.* **1.** fastened; tied. **2.** certain; sure. **3.** going or intending to go; headed. *The train is bound for New York.* —*v.* **1.** past tense and past participle of *bind*, to tie together; fasten. *We bound the carton of books with rope.* **2.** to form the boundary of. **3.** to leap; spring; jump. —*n.* **1.** a line that marks the farthest edge; boundary. **2.** a long or high leap. *With one bound, the deer crossed the stream.*

boy /boi/ *n.* a very young male child.

brain storm /brān′ storm/ *n.* a sudden, bright idea; inspiration. *I tried for hours to find an answer to our problem, and then I had a brainstorm.*

brand /brand/ *n.* **1.** a kind or make of something. **2.** a mark made on the skin of cattle or other animals. **3.** a mark of disgrace. *In former times a brand was burned on the skin of criminals.* —*v.* **1.** to mark with a brand. **2.** to call by a bad or shameful name. *I didn't want to be branded as a coward.*

brawl /brôl/ *n.* a noisy fight. —*v.* **brawled, brawl ing.** to fight noisily.

bread /bred/ *n.* **1.** a food made by mixing flour or meal with water or milk, and then baking it in an oven. **2.** the food and other things needed for a person to live. *We earn our daily bread by working.*

brick /brik/ *n.* a block of clay baked in a kiln or in the sun.

bright /brīt/ *adj.* **1.** giving much light. **2.** clear; strong. *Paint the chair bright red.* **3.** smart; clever.

broil /broil/ *v.* **broiled, broil ing.** **1.** to cook over an open fire or under the flame in the broiler of a stove. **2.** to be

/a/	at
/ā/	late
/â/	care
/ä/	father
/e/	set
/ē/	me
/i/	it
/ī/	kite
/o/	ox
/ō/	rose
/ô/	brought, raw
/oi/	coin
/ŏŏ/	book
/ōō/	too
/or/	form
/ou/	out
/u/	up
/yōō/	cube
/ûr/	turn, germ, learn, firm, work
/ə/	about, chicken, pencil, cannon, circus
/ch/	chair
/hw/	which
/ng/	ring
/sh/	shop
/th/	thin
/th̸/	there
/zh/	treasure

Speller Dictionary 169

broom/capital

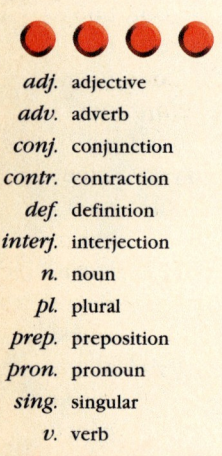

adj.	adjective
adv.	adverb
conj.	conjunction
contr.	contraction
def.	definition
interj.	interjection
n.	noun
pl.	plural
prep.	preposition
pron.	pronoun
sing.	singular
v.	verb

or make very hot. *The hot sun broiled us.*

broom /broŏm, broŏm/ *n.* **1.** a brush with a long handle, used for sweeping. **2.** a bush that has long, thin branches, small leaves, and usually yellow flowers.

broth er /brəth′ ər/ *n.* son of the same parents.

brown /broun/ *n.* a dark color like that of chocolate or cocoa. —*adj.* having the color brown. —*v.* to make or become brown. *Brown the onions in a frying pan.*

bub ble /bub′ əl/ *n.* a small, round body of air or other gas, usually in or on the surface of a liquid. *There are bubbles in soda water.* —*v.* **bub bled, bub bling.** to form bubbles.

bun nies /bun′ ēz/ *n.* the plural of **bunny.**

bun ny /bun′ ē/ *n., pl.* **bun nies.** a small animal with long ears, a short tail, and soft fur; rabbit.

bur glar /bûr′ glər/ *n.* a person who breaks into a place to steal something.

burn /bûrn/ *v.* **burned** or **burnt, burn ing. 1.** to set on fire; be on fire. **2.** to injure by fire, heat, or certain rays, like those of the sun. *Be careful not to burn your hand on the hot stove.* **3.** to use as fuel to make light or heat. —*n.* an injury caused by fire or heat.

but ter /but′ ər/ *n.* **1.** a solid, yellowish fat used as a spread for bread and in cooking. **2.** a spread that is like butter. —*v.* to spread with butter.

but ter fly /but′ ər flī/ *n., pl.* **but ter flies.** an insect with a thin body and four large, often brightly colored wings.

buy /bī/ *v.* **bought, buy ing.** to get something by paying money for it; purchase. —*n.* something offered for sale at a low price; bargain.

buzz /buz/ *n., pl.* **buzz es.** a low, humming sound. —*v.* **buzzed,**

buzz ing. 1. to make the low, humming sound that a bee makes. *The fly buzzed in my ear.* **2.** to fly an airplane low over something.

by /bī/ *prep.* **1.** close to; beside. *There is a small table by my bed.* **2.** up to and beyond; past. *The express train went by our house.* **3.** through the action of. *This book was written by a famous author.* —*adv.* **1.** near. *I just stood by and watched.* **2.** past. *Years went by.*

•••C•••••••••••

ca boose /kə boŏs′/ *n.* a railroad car at the end of a freight train.

cage /kāj/ *n., pl.* **cag es.** a place closed in by bars. Some animals are kept in a cage.

cal en dar /kal′ ən dər/ *n.* **1.** a chart showing the days, weeks, and months of a year. **2.** a schedule of events that will take place.

calf /kaf/ *n., pl.* **calves. 1.** the young of cattle and related animals. **2.** a young seal, elephant, or whale. **3.** leather that is made from the skin or hide of a calf.

camp fire /kamp′ fīr/ *n.* an outdoor fire that is used for cooking or keeping warm in a camp.

can dle /kan′ dəl/ *n.* a stick of wax or tallow with a string inside it.

can dy /kan′ dē/ *n., pl.* **can dies.** a sweet food made of sugar or syrup with flavoring, nuts, or fruit. —*v.* **can died, can dy ing.** to cover or cook with sugar.

cane /kān/ *n.* a stick or staff, usually made of wood.

can't /kant/ *contr.* shortened form of "can not." *He can't swim.*

can teens /kan tēnz′/ *n.* small metal containers for carrying liquid to drink.

cap i tal /kap′ i təl/ *n.* **1.** a city or town where the government of a country or state is located. *Washington, D.C., is the capital of the United States.*

Speller Dictionary

2. the large form of a letter of the alphabet.

cap i tol /kap′ i təl/ *n.* **1.** the building in which a state legislature meets. **2. Capitol** the building in which the U.S. Congress meets in Washington, D.C.

card board /kärd′ bord/ *n.* a heavy, stiff paper. Cardboard is used to make boxes and posters. —*adj.* made of cardboard.

care ta ker /kâr′ tā′ kər/ *n.* a person who takes care of something or someone. *The park's caretaker mows the grass.*

cart wheel /kärt′ hwēl, kärt′ wēl/ *n.* **1.** the wheel of a cart. **2.** a kind of jump from one's feet to one's hands and back again.

cas sette /kə set′/ *n.* a tape to place in a tape recorder or player. *We listened to one of our music cassettes.*

catch /kach/ *n.* **1.** the act of catching something. **2.** something that holds or fastens. **3.** something that is caught. —*v.* **caught, catch ing. 1.** to take or get hold of something that or someone who is moving. **2.** to become hooked or fastened. **3.** to get; receive. *Dress warmly or you will catch a cold.* **4.** to come upon suddenly or unexpectedly; surprise or discover. *They were caught in the act of stealing.*

caught /kôt/ *v.* past tense and past participle of **catch.** *I caught the butterfly in a net.* See **catch.**

cause /kôz/ *n.* **1.** a person or thing that makes something happen. *The hurricane was the cause of great damage to the town.* —*v.* **caused, caus ing.** to make something happen; result in.

cel e brate /sel′ ə brāt/ *v.* **cel e brat ed, cel e brat ing.** to observe a special day, like a holiday, in a way that makes it different from other days.

cell /sel/ *n.* **1.** a small, plain room in a prison, convent, or monastery. **2.** the very small, basic unit of living matter. **3.** a device that changes chemical or solar energy into electrical energy.

cel lar /sel′ ər/ *n.* a room or group of rooms built underground.

cent /sent/ *n.* a coin of the U.S. and Canada. One hundred cents is equal to one dollar.

cen tral /sen′ trəl/ *adj.* **1.** in, at, or near the center or middle. **2.** very important; main; chief. *They both work in the bank's central office.*

cen tu ry /sen′ chə rē/ *n., pl.* **cen tur ies.** a period of one hundred years.

cer tain /sûr′ tən/ *adj.* **1.** sure; positive. **2.** known but not named; some; particular. *Certain animals hunt for food at night.*

chair /châr/ *n.* **1.** a piece of furniture for one person to sit on. **2.** a chairperson of a department or committee.

chair per son /châr′ pûr′ sən/ *n.* a person who leads a meeting, department, or committee.

chalk board /chôk′ bord/ *n.* a hard, smooth board that is made to be written or drawn on with chalk; blackboard.

change /chānj/ *n.* **1.** the act or result of making something different. *We made a change in our plans.* **2.** something that can be put in place of another. *Bring a change of clothing on the camping trip.* **3.** the money that is given back when the amount paid is more than the amount owed. —*v.* **1.** to make or become different. **2.** to replace with another or others; exchange. **3.** to put on other clothes.

chem i cal /kem′ i kəl/ *n.* a substance made by or used in chemistry. *Ammonia is a chemical used for cleaning.*

chew /choo/ *v.* **1.** to crush and grind something with the teeth. **2.** to make by chewing. *The puppy chewed a hole in the slipper.*

/a/	at
/ā/	late
/â/	care
/ä/	father
/e/	set
/ē/	me
/i/	it
/ī/	kite
/o/	ox
/ō/	rose
/ô/	brought raw
/oi/	coin
/oo/	book
/oo/	too
/or/	form
/ou/	out
/u/	up
/yoo/	cube
/ûr/	turn germ learn firm work
/ə/	about chicken pencil cannon circus
/ch/	chair
/hw/	which
/ng/	ring
/sh/	shop
/th/	thin
/th/	there
/zh/	treasure

child/cloud

child /chīld/ *n., pl.* **chil dren. 1.** a son or daughter. **2.** a young boy or girl. *That is a good book for a child of ten.* **3.** a baby; infant.

chil dren /chil′ drən/ *n.* the plural of **child.**

choice /chois/ *n.* **1.** the act or result of choosing. **2.** the chance to choose. *We were given a choice between going to the movies and visiting the zoo.* —*adj.,* **choic er, choic est.** of very good quality; excellent.

choke /chōk/ *v.* **choked, chok ing. 1.** to stop or hold back the breathing of by squeezing or blocking the windpipe. **2.** to make or become unable to breathe easily. **3.** to block or clog; fill up. *Grease choked the kitchen drain.* **4.** to keep from growing or progressing normally. *Weeds choked the flowers in the garden.*

choose /chōōz/ *v.* **chose, cho sen, choos ing. 1.** to decide to take one or more from all that are available; pick. **2.** to decide or prefer to do something.

chose /chōz/ *v.* past tense of **choose.** See **choose.**

Christ mas /kris′ məs/ *n.* the yearly celebration of the birth of Jesus. It falls on December 25.

cir cus /sûr′ kəs/ *n., pl.* **cir cus es.** a show with trained animals and acrobats, clowns, and other people who entertain.

cit ies /sit′ ēz/ *n.* the plural of **city.**

cit y /sit′ ē/ *n., pl.* **cit ies.** a large area where many people live and work. A city is larger than a town.

Civ il War /siv′ əl wôr/ *n.* **1.** the war between the northern and southern states of the United States that occurred between 1861 and 1865. **2. civ il war** a war between two opposing groups or sections within a country.

clam ber /klam′ bər/ *v.* **clam bered, clam ber ing.** to climb by using both the hands and the feet. *We clambered slowly up the dunes behind the beach.*

class room /klas′ rōōm, klas′ rŏŏm/ *n.* a room in which classes are held.

claw /klô/ *n.* a sharp nail on a bird or animal's foot.

clean /klēn/ *v.* to make clean. —*adj.* **1.** free from dirt. **2.** honorable or fair. *The coach wants our team to always play clean football.* **3.** complete; thorough. *The dog seized the hamburger and made a clean escape.* —*adv.* completely. *The arrow went clean through the target.*

cliff /klif/ *n.* a high, steep face of rock or earth. *From the edge of the cliff, we could see the beach far below.*

climb /klīm/ *v.* **1.** to move upward or in some other direction over, across, or through something, using the hands and feet. **2.** to grow upward or upward on. *The ivy climbed the side of the house.* —*n.* **1.** the act of climbing. **2.** a place to be climbed. *That mountain is a difficult climb.*

clock /klok/ *n.* a device used for measuring and showing the time. —*v.* to find out the speed of something by using a device to measure time. *We clocked the runners with a stopwatch.*

close[1] /klōz/ *n.* end; finish. *At the close of the day, we all went home.* —*v.* **1.** to shut. **2.** to bring or come together. *The dog's teeth closed on the bone.* **3.** to bring or come to an end.

close[2] /klōs/ *adj.,* **clos er, clos est. 1.** with little space or time between; near. *Our house is close to the school.* **2.** having affection for each other; intimate. **3.** without fresh air; stuffy. **4.** nearly even; almost equal. *It was a close race.* **5.** careful; thorough. *Pay close attention.* —*adv.* in a close position or way. *Your car is parked too close to the curb.*

cloud /kloud/ *n.* **1.** a gray or white mass of tiny drops of water or bits of

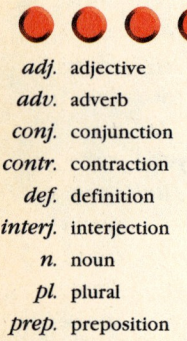

adj.	adjective
adv.	adverb
conj.	conjunction
contr.	contraction
def.	definition
interj.	interjection
n.	noun
pl.	plural
prep.	preposition
pron.	pronoun
sing.	singular
v.	verb

172 **Speller Dictionary**

clown/couldn't

ice floating in the sky. **2.** something like a cloud. *A cloud of birds filled the sky.* —*v.* **1.** to cover with a cloud or clouds. **2.** to become cloudy.

clown /kloun/ *n.* a person who makes people laugh by playing tricks or doing stunts. —*v.* to act like a clown. *Don't clown around so much.*

clutch /kluch/ *v.* **1.** to grasp tightly. **2.** to try to grasp or seize. —*n., pl.* **clutch es. 1.** a tight grasp. **2.** a device in a machine that connects or disconnects the motor.

coal /kōl/ *n., pl.* **coal. 1.** a black mineral that is burned as a fuel to heat buildings or make electricity. **2.** a piece of glowing or burned wood. —*adj.* pertaining to coal.

coas tal plain /kōst′ əl plān/ *n.* a low land along a coast.

coil /koil/ *v.* to wind around in a curl. *Snakes sometimes coil their bodies when they sleep.* —*n.* an object that is wound up in a curl. *A spring is a coil.*

coin /koin/ *n.* a piece of metal used as money. —*v.* **1.** to make money by stamping metal. **2.** to invent. *If you coined a new word, do you think other people would begin to use it?*

cold /kōld/ *adj.* **cold er, cold est. 1.** having a low temperature; not warm. **2.** feeling a lack of warmth; chilly. *The children were cold after playing outside in the snow.* **3.** not friendly or kind. —*n.* **1.** a lack of warmth or heat. *The cold made my teeth chatter.* **2.** a common sickness that causes sneezing, coughing, and a running or stuffy nose.

col lo quy /kol′ ə kwē/ *n., pl.* **col lo quies.** a serious discussion.

col or /kul′ ər/ *n.* **1.** a quality of light as we see it with our eyes. *The color of grass is green.* **2.** the coloring of the skin. *I see you have a healthy color now that you are well again.* —*v.* to give color to.

Co lum bus Day /kə lum′ bəs dā/ *n.* a legal holiday celebrated annually to commemorate the discovery of America by Christopher Columbus on October 12, 1492. This holiday is now celebrated on the second Monday in October. —*adj.* pertaining to Columbus Day.

comb /kōm/ *n.* **1.** a piece of plastic, metal, or other material that has a row of teeth and is used to smooth or arrange hair. **2.** a fleshy red crest on the head of chickens and other birds. —*v.* **1.** to arrange or smooth with a comb. **2.** to search thoroughly in. *The police combed the woods.*

com e dy /kom′ i dē/ *n., pl.* **comedies.** a story that has a happy ending.

com pass /kum′ pəs/ *n., pl.* **com pas ses.** an instrument for showing directions. A compass has a magnetic needle that points north.

cone /kōn/ *n.* **1.** a shape that is round on the bottom and comes to a point at the top. **2.** a cone-shaped holder for ice cream, made of cookie dough. **3.** a rounded, seed-bearing structure found on pine and other evergreen trees.

Con gress /kong′ gris/ *n.* **1.** a branch of the government of the United States that makes laws. **2. con gress** *pl.* **con gres ses.** the law-making body of a country.

cop per /kop′ ər/ *n.* **1.** a reddish metallic element. **2.** a reddish brown color. —*adj.* made of copper.

cor ner /kor′ nər/ *n.* **1.** the place or point where two lines or surfaces come together. **2.** the place where two streets come together. —*adj.* at or near a corner. —*v.* to force or drive into a dangerous or difficult place or position. *The dog cornered the cat.*

cor ri dor /kor′ i dər/ *n.* a long hallway.

could /koŏd/ *v.* was able to. *He could run a mile in seven minutes.*

could n't /koŏd′ ənt/ *contr.* shortened form of "could not." *The little child couldn't reach the high shelf.*

/a/	at
/ā/	late
/â/	care
/ä/	father
/e/	set
/ē/	me
/i/	it
/ī/	kite
/o/	ox
/ō/	rose
/ô/	brought
	raw
/oi/	coin
/ŏŏ/	book
/ōō/	too
/or/	form
/ou/	out
/u/	up
/yōō/	cube
/ûr/	turn
	germ
	learn
	firm
	work
/ə/	about
	chicken
	pencil
	cannon
	circus
/ch/	chair
/hw/	which
/ng/	ring
/sh/	shop
/th/	thin
/th̸/	there
/zh/	treasure

Speller Dictionary

could 've /ko͝od' əv/ *contr.* shortened form of "could have." *I wish she could've gone with us.*

coun cil /koun' səl/ *n.* a group of people who meet to discuss a problem or other matter.

count /kount/ *n.* **1.** the act of counting. **2.** the number of things there are when you add them up; total. **3.** a European nobleman. —*v.* **1.** to find out how many of something there are; add up. **2.** to say or write down numbers in order. **3.** to include or be included when things are added.

count er clock wise /koun' tər klok' wīz/ *n.* in the direction opposite to the direction in which the hands of a clock move.

coun try /kun' trē/ *n., pl.* **coun tries.** **1.** any area of land; region. **2.** an area of land that has boundaries and has a government that is shared by all the people; nation. —*adj.* having to do with land outside of cities or towns; rural. *We drove along narrow country roads.*

craft /kraft/ *n,. pl.* **crafts.** **1.** a special skill that a person has. **2.** a trade or work that needs special skill. *Woodworking is a craft that takes years to master.* **3.** a boat, ship or aircraft. *That boat is a private craft.*

crash /krash/ *n., pl.* **crash es.** **1.** a sudden loud noise like something breaking or smashing. **2.** a violent collision. **3.** a sudden ruin or failure in business. *Much money was lost in the crash of the stock market.* —*v.* **1.** to make a sudden loud noise. **2.** to collide violently.

crawl /krôl/ *n.* **1.** a very slow movement. **2.** a fast swimming stroke. —*v.* **1.** to move very slowly. *Babies crawl by moving on their hands and knees.* **2.** to be covered, or feel as if covered, with crawling things.

cray on /krā' on, krā' ən/ *n.* a colored stick made of wax material used for drawing or writing. —*v.* to use crayons to draw or color.

creek /krēk, krik/ *n.* a small stream.

crop /krop/ *n.* **1.** plants that are grown to be used as food or to be sold for profit. **2.** the total amount of a plant grown as a crop that is gathered; harvest. **3.** a group of persons or things that come at the same time. *There was a large crop of new students at school this fall.* —*v.* **cropped, crop ping.** to cut or bite off the top part of something. *The deer cropped the bushes behind our house.*

crowd /kroud/ *n.* a large number of people gathered together. —*v.* **1.** to put or force too many people or things into too small a space. **2.** to gather closely or in large numbers. **3.** to move by pushing or shoving.

crown /kroun/ *n.* a head cover that is worn by a king or queen. *The king's crown was made of gold.* —*v.* to put a crown on someone's head to make him or her a king or queen. *The old king will step down and will crown his son.*

crumb /krum/ *n.* a tiny piece of bread, cake, cracker, or cookie.

crust /krust/ *n.* **1.** the hard, crisp outside part of bread, rolls, or other food. **2.** any hard outside part or coating. —*v.* to cover or become covered with a crust. —**crust y**, *adj.*

curb /kûrb/ *n.* the edge of the sidewalk that curves down to the street. *Park the car close to the curb.*

cut ting /kut' ing/ *v.* a form of **cut**, to make a part, or open with a knife or other sharp object. *She was cutting the meat into pieces.*

D

dai ly /dā' lē/ *adj.* happening or appearing each day. *Our class has a daily math lesson.* —*adv.* every day. *I brush my teeth daily.*

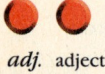

adj.	adjective
adv.	adverb
conj.	conjunction
contr.	contraction
def.	definition
interj.	interjection
n.	noun
pl.	plural
prep.	preposition
pron.	pronoun
sing.	singular
v.	verb

dance /dans/ *v.* **danced, danc ing.** to move to music. —*n.* a party where people gather to dance. *The band played at the dance.*

dare /dâr/ *v.* **dared, dar ing.** to invite to be brave enough to try. *I dare you to jump over that fence.*

dark /därk/ *adj.* **1.** having little or no light. **2.** black or brown rather than light in color. —*n.* **1.** a lack of light. **2.** night or nightfall; the end of daylight.

dawn /dôn/ *n.* **1.** the first light that appears in the morning; daybreak. **2.** the beginning or first sign. —*v.* **1.** to begin to get light in the morning. **2.** to begin to be clear or understood. *It dawned on us that we were being teased.*

day break /dā′ brāk/ *n.* the time each morning when light first appears; dawn.

days /dāz/ *n.* the plural of *day*. *Days are made up of 24 hours. There are seven days in a week.*

dead /ded/ *n.* **1.** people who are no longer living. **2.** the time of greatest darkness or coldness. *A noise woke me up in the dead of night.* —*adj.* **1.** no longer living or having life. **2.** not having life. **3.** without power, activity, or interest. *I can't make a phone call because the telephone is dead.* **4.** complete; total. *When the curtain rose in the theater, there was dead silence.* **5.** sure or certain; exact. *Try to hit the target at dead center.* —*adv.* **1.** completely. **2.** directly; straight. *The exit from the highway is dead ahead.*

deal /dēl/ *n.* **1.** a bargain or agreement; a business transaction **2.** a large amount or quantity. *My cousin spends a great deal of time making furniture.* —*v.* **dealt, deal ing. 1.** to act on or be concerned with. *I'm looking for a book that deals with dogs.* **2.** to act or behave. *The principal dealt harshly with the fighting students.* **3.** to conduct business; trade. **4.** to give or deliver. *Whose turn is it to deal the cards?*

dec ade /dek′ ād/ *n.* ten years.

De cem ber /di sem′ bər/ *n.* the twelfth and last month of the year. *December has 31 days.*

deck /dek/ *n.* **1.** a floor with no roof. *We like to sun on the deck near the pool.* **2.** a platform or other flat surface serving as a floor or level in a boat or ship.

de clare /di klâr′/ *v.* **de clared, de claring. 1.** to announce or make something known. *The two countries declared war.* **2.** to say strongly and firmly. *They declared that they were right.*

de gree /di grē′/ *n.* a unit for measuring temperature. *A person's normal body temperature is 98.6 degrees.*

des ert /dez′ ərt/ *n.* a hot, dry sandy area of land with few or no plants growing on it.

desk /desk/ *n.* a piece of furniture with a flat or sloping top.

de stroy /di stroi′/ *v.* to ruin completely; wreck. *The earthquake destroyed the city.*

dew /dōō, dyōō/ *n.* moisture from the air that forms drops on cool surfaces. *There was dew on the grass.*

did n't /did′ ənt/ *contr.* shortened form of "did not." *I didn't do my homework.*

die /dī/ *v.* **died, dy ing.** to stop living. *Many plants die in the winter.*

dif fer ence /dif′ ər əns, dif′ rəns/ *n.* the state or quality of being unlike or different. *Do you notice a difference in how people talk?* **2.** a way of being unlike or different. *One of the differences between alligators and crocodiles is that crocodiles have longer heads.* **3.** the amount by which one quantity is greater or less than another. *The difference between 16 and 12 is 4.*

dig it /dij′ it/ *n.* one of the numerals 0, 1, 2, 3, 4, 5, 6, 7, 8, 9.

/a/	at
/ā/	late
/â/	care
/ä/	father
/e/	set
/ē/	me
/i/	it
/ī/	kite
/o/	ox
/ō/	rose
/ô/	brought raw
/oi/	coin
/o͝o/	book
/o͞o/	too
/or/	form
/ou/	out
/u/	up
/yo͞o/	cube
/ûr/	turn germ learn firm work
/ə/	about chicken pencil cannon circus
/ch/	chair
/hw/	which
/ng/	ring
/sh/	shop
/th/	thin
/th̷/	there
/zh/	treasure

Speller Dictionary 175

din ner /din′ ər/ *n.* **1.** the main meal of the day. **2.** a formal meal in honor of some person or event.

dirt /dûrt/ *n.* **1.** mud, dust, or other material that makes something unclean. **2.** loose earth or soil.

dis tres sing /dis tres′ sing/ *adj.* causing pain and upset. *The news about your accident is very distressing.*

ditch /dich/ *n., pl.* **ditch es.** a long, narrow hole dug in the ground and used to drain water.

dive /dīv/ *v.* **dived** or **dove, dived, div ing. 1.** to plunge headfirst into water. **2.** to plunge downward quickly and at a steep angle. *The plane lost power and dived sharply.* —*n.* **1.** a headfirst plunge into water. *It's not safe to do a dive from the rocks into the lake.* **2.** a quick, steep plunge. *The plane went into a dive.*

div ing /dīv′ ing/ *v.* a form of **dive**. It is used with a helping word.

does /duz/ *v.* a form of *do.* I do; he or she *does. He does the dishes.*

does n't /duz′ ənt/ *contr.* shortened form of "does not." *The cup doesn't hold much milk.*

dog /dôg/ *n.* an animal related to coyotes, wolves, and foxes which makes a barking noise. —*v.* **dogged, dog ging.** to follow closely in the way a hunting dog would.

doll /dol/ *n.* a toy that looks like a baby, a child, or a grown-up.

dol lar /dol′ ər/ *n.* a unit of money in the United States and in Canada which is worth one hundred cents.

done /dun/ *v.* past participle of *do. The carpenters have done a very good job on our new kitchen.* —*adj.* cooked. *When the meat is done, we can start our dinner.*

don key /dong′ kē/ *n.* an animal that looks like a small horse.

don't /dōnt/ *contr.* shortened form of "do not." *Please don't tell anyone else the secret.*

door /dor/ *n.* a movable object that is used to open or close an entrance in something.

dou ble /dub′ əl/ *adj.* **1.** twice as many or as much. **2.** having or made up of two parts. *People stood in a double line.* —*adv.* two instead of one; in pairs. —*n.* **1.** something that is twice as much. **2.** a person or thing that is very much or just like another. *The actor used a double to do the dangerous stunts.* —*v.* **dou bled, dou bling. 1.** to make or become twice as many or as much. **2.** to bend, fold, or turn over or back. **3.** to serve a second purpose. *The sofa doubles as a bed.*

down /doun/ *n.* **1.** one of the chances that a football team gets to move the ball 10 yards. **2.** fine, soft feathers. —*adv.* **1.** from a higher to a lower place. **2.** to or in a lower position, level, or condition. **3.** to a calmer condition. *The noisy crowd quieted down.* —*v.* **1.** to bring or put down. **2.** to swallow quickly. —*prep.* from a higher to a lower place; along, through, or into. *We rolled down the hillside.*

down town /doun′ toun′/ *adv.* to or in the main part or business district of a town. *We went downtown.* —*adj.* going to or located in the main part or business district of a town. *The downtown stores.*

draft /draft/ *n.* **1.** a current of air in an enclosed space. *I could feel a cold draft from the open window.* **2.** a sketch, plan, or rough copy of something written. —*v.* to make a sketch, plan, or rough copy of something. —*adj.* used for pulling loads. *Elephants are used as draft animals in some countries.*

draw /drô/ *n.* **1.** the act of drawing. **2.** a game or contest that ends with an even score or no winner; tie. —*v.* **drew, drawn, draw ing. 1.** to move by pulling; haul. **2.** to take out; to bring out. *The nurse carefully drew the splinter from my foot.* **3.** to

adj.	adjective
adv.	adverb
conj.	conjunction
contr.	contraction
def.	definition
interj.	interjection
n.	noun
pl.	plural
prep.	preposition
pron.	pronoun
sing.	singular
v.	verb

make a mark or picture with lines, using a pencil, crayon, or other writing tool.

drawn /drôn/ *v.* past participle of **draw.** *The artist has drawn many sketches of the church.* See **draw.**

drift /drift/ *v.* **1.** to move because of a current of air or water. *We stopped rowing and let our boat drift downstream.* **2.** to pile up in masses from the action of the wind. *The snow drifted to 6 feet.* —*n.* **1.** movement caused by a current of air or water. *Scientists measured the drift of the glacier.* **2.** something that has been moved along or piled up by air or water currents.

drow sy /drou′ zē/ *adj.*, **drow si er, drow si est.** half asleep; sleepy. *I felt drowsy after dinner and decided to take a nap.*

drum /drum/ *n.* a musical instrument you beat to make a sound. —*v.* **drummed, drum ming.** to beat a drum. *She can drum faster than her brother.*

due /dōō, dyōō/ *n.* **1.** something that is owed. **2. dues.** a fee that a person pays to a club for being a member. —*adj.* **1.** owed or owing. **2.** expected or supposed to arrive or be ready. *The train is due at noon.* —*adv.* straight, directly. *The explorers walked due west toward the setting sun.*

dump /dump/ *n.* a place where garbage and trash are dumped. —*v.* to drop, unload, or empty.

dune /dōōn, dyōōn/ *n.* a mound or ridge of sand that has been piled up by the wind.

dusk /dusk/ *n.* the time of day just before the sun goes down; twilight. —**dusk y,** *adj.*

du ty /dōō′ tē, dyōō′ tē/ *n., pl.* **du ties. 1.** something that a person is supposed to do. **2.** a tax paid on goods that are brought into or taken out of a country.

E

each /ēch/ *adj.* every one of two or more things or persons thought of as individuals or one at a time. *Each player gets a turn.* —*pron.* every individual person or thing in a group. *The farmer gave each of us a ride on the horse.* —*adv.* for each one. *These apples are a quarter each.*

eas y /ē′ zē/ *adj.*, **eas i er, eas i est. 1.** needing only a little work. *The job of mowing the lawn was easy.* **2.** without pain, trouble, or worry. *They hope to have an easy life if their business is successful.* **3.** not strict or difficult to please. *We have an easy science teacher.*

egg /eg/ *n.* a container for the developing young of a bird or animal.

eld er ly /el′ dər lē/ *adj.* rather old. *Our elderly neighbor plans to retire.*

em boss /em bôs′/ *v.* **em bossed, em boss ing.** to decorate with a raised design. *My parents' stationery is embossed with their initials.*

en dan ger /en dān′ jər/ *v.* **en dan gered, en dan ger ing.** to expose to danger. **en dan gered** /en dān′ jərd/ *adj.* in danger of becoming extinct. *The whooping crane is an endangered species.*

en gine /en′ jin/ *n.* a machine that uses energy to run other machines.

en gi neer /en jə nîr′/ *n.* a person who is trained in engineering. *An engineer may plan and design bridges, roads, or airplanes.*

en joy /en joi′/ *v.* **en joyed, en joy ing. 1.** to get joy or pleasure from; be happy with. *I enjoy playing baseball and football.* **2.** to have a good time. *We all enjoyed ourselves at the movies.*

e qual /ē′ kwəl/ *adj.* the same in amount, size, value, or quality. *Four quarts equal one gallon.*

e qui lat er al /ē′ kwi lat′ ər əl/ *adj.* having all sides the same length.

/a/	at
/ā/	late
/â/	care
/ä/	father
/e/	set
/ē/	me
/i/	it
/ī/	kite
/o/	ox
/ō/	rose
/ô/	brought, raw
/oi/	coin
/ŏŏ/	book
/ōō/	too
/or/	form
/ou/	out
/u/	up
/yōō/	cube
/ûr/	turn, germ, learn, firm, work
/ə/	about, chicken, pencil, cannon, circus
/ch/	chair
/hw/	which
/ng/	ring
/sh/	shop
/th/	thin
/th/	there
/zh/	treasure

e qui nox /ē′ kwə noks′/ *n.* one of the two days of the year when daytime and nighttime are equal in length all over the earth.

e ter ni ty /i tûr′ ni tē/ *n.* time without beginning or end; all time. *Will those mountains last for eternity?*

eve ning /ēv′ ning/ *n.* the late afternoon and early nighttime. —*adj.* relating to or occurring in the evening. *We eat our evening meal at seven o'clock.*

eve ry /ev′ rē/ *adj.* each person or thing of all the people or things that are part of a group. *Every student in the class is here today.*

ex haus tion /eg zôs′ chən/ *n.* the condition of being very tired. *The runner's exhaustion was caused by a seven-mile run.*

ex port /ek spôrt′, ek′ spôrt′/ *v.* to send goods to other countries to be sold or traded. *Brazil exports coffee to the United States.*

eye lash /ī′ lash/ *n., pl.* **eye lash es.** one of the short hairs growing on the edge of the eyelid.

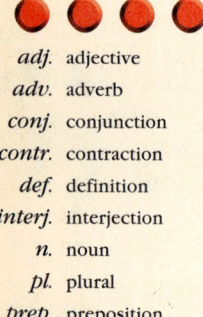

adj. adjective
adv. adverb
conj. conjunction
contr. contraction
def. definition
interj. interjection
n. noun
pl. plural
prep. preposition
pron. pronoun
sing. singular
v. verb

F

face /fās/ *n.* **1.** the front of the head. **2.** a look on the face; expression. **3.** the front, main, or outward part of something. —*v.* **faced, fac ing. 1.** to have or turn the face toward. **2.** to deal with firmly and courageously.

fail /fāl/ *v.* **1.** to not succeed in doing or getting something. **2.** to get too low a grade in a test or course of study; not pass. **3.** to be of no use or help to; disappoint. *Their friends failed them when they refused to keep their promise.* **4.** to not be enough; run out. *The water supply failed during the emergency.* **5.** to become weaker in strength or health. *My cat's eyesight is beginning to fail.* **6.** to not do; neglect. *If you fail to* answer when your name is called, you will be marked absent.

fair /fâr/ *adj.* **1.** not in favor of any one more than another or others; just. **2.** according to the rules. **3.** neither too good nor too bad; average. *The performance was only fair.* **4.** pleasing to the eye; attractive. **5.** sunny, not cloudy. —*n.* **1.** a public showing of farm products. **2.** any large showing of products or objects.

fall /fôl/ *v.* **fell, fall en, fall ing. 1.** to come down from a higher place; drop. **2.** to take place; happen. *Christmas falls on December 25.* —*n.* **1.** a coming down from a higher place. **2.** the season of the year coming between summer and winter; autumn.

fam i ly /fam′ ə lē, fam′ lē/ *n., pl.* **fam i lies. 1.** a group of people who are related and who live together, including parents, children, and sometimes other relatives. **2.** the children of a father and mother. **3.** a group of related animals or plants.

fare /fâr/ *n.* **1.** the cost of a ride on a bus, train, airplane, ship, or taxi. *The bus driver collected the fares.* **2.** a passenger who pays a fare. —*v.* **fared, far ing.** to get along; do. *Are you faring well at your new school?*

fa ther /fä′ t͟hər/ *n.* a man who has children.

Fa ther's Day /fä′ t͟hərz dā/ *n.* a day set aside in honor of fathers, celebrated each year on the third Sunday in June.

fawn /fôn/ *n.* a baby deer.

Feb ru ar y /feb′ rōō er′ ē, feb′ yōō er′ ē/ *n., pl.* **Feb ru ar ies.** the second month of the year. February has 28 days except in a leap year, when it has 29.

fence /fens/ *n.* **1.** a structure that is used to surround, protect, or mark off an area. **2.** a person who buys and sells stolen goods. —*v.* **fenced, fenc ing. 1.** to put a fence around. **2.** to fight with a sword or foil; take part in the sport of fencing.

fen nel /fen′ əl/ *n.* an edible plant with bright green leaves and yellow flowers.

fetch /fech/ *v.* **fetched, fetch ing.** to go after and bring back.

film /film/ *n.* **1.** a piece of radiation-sensitive cellulose for taking pictures **2.** a movie. *We saw a film about space travel.* —*v.* to make a movie of. *She wants to film the sun coming up tomorrow.*

fin ish /fin′ ish/ *n., pl.* **fin ish es. 1.** the last part of something; end. **2.** the surface of something. *The table has a shiny finish.* —*v.* **1.** to bring to an end; come to the end of; complete. **2.** to use up completely. **3.** to treat the surface of in some way. *I used clear varnish to finish the cabinet.*

fire fly /fīr′ flī/ *n., pl.* **fire flies.** a small bug that gives off light when it flies at night.

fire truck /fīr′ truk/ *n.* a truck that is used to help firefighters put out fires.

first /fûrst/ *adj.* before all others. —*adv.* **1.** before all others. **2.** for the first time. —*n.* **1.** a person or thing that is first. *This invention is the first of its kind.* **2.** the beginning.

Flag Day /flag dā/ *n.* the anniversary of the day in 1777 when the Stars and Stripes was made the official flag of the United States. It falls on June 14.

flame /flām/ *n.* **1.** one of the streams of light given off by a fire. **2.** gas or vapor that has been set on fire to give off light or heat. **3.** the condition of burning. *The house burst into flame.* —*v.* **flamed, flam ing. 1.** to burn with flames; blaze. **2.** to light up or glow. *The fighter's eyes flamed with anger.*

flap jack /flap′ jak/ *n.* a word sometimes used for *pancake,* a flat, thin cake made of batter.

flew /flōō/ *v.* past tense of **fly. 1.** to move through the air with wings. *The bird flew away as soon as it saw the cat creeping toward it.* **2.** to pass, move, or be propelled through the air by wind or other force.

flock /flok/ *n.* **1.** a group of animals of one kind that is herded or gathered together. **2.** a large number or group. —*v.* to move or gather in crowds.

flow chart /flō′ chart/ *n.* a step-by-step diagram.

flow er /flou′ ər/ *n.* **1.** the part of a plant that makes seeds; blossom. **2.** a plant grown for its showy, sometimes brightly colored petals. —*v.* to produce flowers; blossom. *Cherry trees flower in the early spring.*

flute /flōōt/ *n.* a long, thin, musical instrument played by blowing across a hole at one end. —*v.* **flut ed, flut ing.** to play the flute. —*adj.* **flut ed** marked with grooves.

fog /fôg, fog/ *n.* **1.** a cloud of small drops of water close to the earth's surface. **2.** a state of confusion; daze. —*v.* **fogged, fog ging.** to cover or become covered with fog.

food /fōōd/ *n.* something that is eaten or taken in by people, animals, or plants that keeps them alive and helps them grow; nourishment.

for est /for′ ist, fôr′ ist/ *n.* many trees and plants covering a large area of land; woods.

fort /fort/ *n.* a strong place or building where soldiers live. It is kept safe from enemies.

fos sil /fos′ əl/ *n.* the hardened remains or traces of an animal or plant that lived long ago. *We found fossils of ancient leaves in rock.*

four /for/ *n.* one more than three; 4.

foy er /foi′ ər/ *n.* an entrance or lobby.

Fri day /frī′ dē, frī′ dā/ *n.* the sixth day of the week.

friend /frend/ *n.* **1.** a person whom one knows well and likes. **2.** a person who supports or favors something. *The governor is a friend of public education.*

/a/	at
/ā/	late
/â/	care
/ä/	father
/e/	set
/ē/	me
/i/	it
/ī/	kite
/o/	ox
/ō/	rose
/ô/	brought raw
/oi/	coin
/ŏŏ/	book
/ōō/	too
/or/	form
/ou/	out
/u/	up
/yōō/	cube
/ûr/	turn germ learn firm work
/ə/	about chicken pencil cannon circus
/ch/	chair
/hw/	which
/ng/	ring
/sh/	shop
/th/	thin
/th/	there
/zh/	treasure

fright/glide

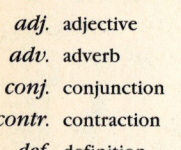

adj.	adjective
adv.	adverb
conj.	conjunction
contr.	contraction
def.	definition
interj.	interjection
n.	noun
pl.	plural
prep.	preposition
pron.	pronoun
sing.	singular
v.	verb

fright /frīt/ *n.* **1.** a sudden fear or alarm. **2.** a person or thing that is ugly or shocking. *You were a fright in the witch costume that you wore to the party.*

fringe /frinj/ *n., pl.* **fring es 1.** a border of hanging threads or cords. *The bedspread has a fringe around the edge.* **2.** anything like a fringe.

frog /frôg, frog/ *n.* a small animal with moist skin, webbed feet, and no tail.

frost /frôst/ *n.* **1.** tiny ice crystals that form on a surface when water vapor in the air freezes. *There was frost on the windowpane this morning.* **2.** very cold weather during which the temperature is below freezing. —*v.* **1.** to cover with frost. **2.** to cover with frosting or something like frosting.

frown /froun/ *n.* a wrinkling of the forehead. —*v.* **1.** to wrinkle the forehead in thought, anger, or worry. *The captain frowned at the bad news.* **2.** to look with anger or disapproval.

froze /frōz/ *v.* past tense of **freeze. 1.** to harden because of cold. **2.** to stop movement. **3.** to be or become very cold.

full /fŏŏl/ *adj.* **1.** holding as much or as many as possible. **2.** having or containing a large number or quantity. *We had a house full of guests for the party.* —*adv.* completely; entirely. *I filled the pitcher full with lemonade.*

fu ture /fyōō′ chər/ *adj.* happening in the time after the present; coming. —*n.* **1.** the time that is to come. **2.** another word for future tense.

G

games /gāmz/ *n.* things done for fun. *Tag and hide-and-go-seek are two games that we play at lunchtime.*

gen er al /jen′ ər əl/ *adj.* **1.** for all; for the whole. *A general meeting of the club was held.* **2.** by all or many; among all or many. *There was a general panic during the storm.* **3.** not concerned with details. *The president spoke in a general way.* —*n.* an armed forces officer of the highest rank.

gen tle /jen′ təl/ *adj.,* **gen tler, gen tlest. 1.** mild and kindly. **2.** soft or low. **3.** easy to handle; tame. *The child rode a gentle horse.*

gent ly /jent′ lē/ *adv.* in a gentle way. *The snow fell gently.*

germ /jûrm/ *n., pl.* **gcrms.** a tiny particle that can cause disease. *Viruses and bacteria are germs.*

gi ant /jī′ ənt/ *n., pl.* **giants. 1.** an imaginary creature that looks like a huge person. **2.** a person or thing that is very large, powerful, or important. *That doctor is a giant in her field.* —*adj.* very large.

gift /gift/ *n.* **1.** something given; present. **2.** talent; ability. *That student has a gift for acting.*

give /giv/ *n.* the quality of being able to bend without breaking or yielding to pressure. *A hard mattress has very little give.* —*v.* **gave, giv en, giv ing. 1.** to hand, pass, present, or grant. **2.** to make or do; bring about; cause. **3.** to produce. *Both cows and goats give milk.* **4.** to break down; yield. *If the dam gives, the town will be flooded.*

glare /glâr/ *n.* **1.** a strong, unpleasant light. **2.** an angry look or stare. —*v.* **glared, glar ing. 1.** to shine with a strong, unpleasant light. **2.** to give an angry look.

glass /glas/ *n., pl.* **glass es. 1.** a hard, clear material that breaks easily. **2.** a container made of glass that is used for drinking. **3. glasses.** a pair of lenses made of glass, used to help a person see better; eyeglasses.

glide /glīd/ *n.* the act of gliding. —*v.* **glid ed, glid ing. 1.** to move smoothly along without any effort. **2.** to fly or

180 Speller Dictionary

descend slowly without using a motor for power. *The hawk glided over the field looking for food.*

goal /gōl/ *n.* **1.** something that a person wants and tries to become or do; aim; purpose. **2.** a place in certain games where players must get the ball or puck in order to score. **3.** the point or points made by getting the ball or puck into such a place.

goat /gōt/ *n., pl.* **goats** or **goat.** an animal that is related to the sheep. They are raised in many parts of the world for their milk, hair, meat, and skin.

gold en /gōlʹ dən/ *adj.* **1.** made of or containing gold. **2.** having the color or shine of gold; bright or shining. *The field of golden wheat swayed in the wind.* **3.** very good or valuable; excellent.

gold en rod /gōlʹ dən rod/ *n.* a tall plant that has long stalks of yellow flowers.

gold rush /gōld rush/ *n.* a sudden rush of people to an area where gold has been discovered.

gown /goun/ *n.* a woman's dress. *She wore a beautiful, long gown.*

grand fa ther /grandʹ fä ŧhər/ *n.* the father of one's father or mother.

grand moth er /grandʹ muŧh ər/ *n.* the mother of one's mother or father.

grass hop per /grasʹ hop ər/ *n.* an insect that has long, powerful legs which it uses for jumping. It also has wings and eats grasses and crops.

grav i ty /gravʹ i tē/ *n., pl.* **grav i ties.** the force that pulls things toward the center of the earth. The pull of gravity on an object causes the object to have weight.

grew /grōō/ *v.* past tense of **grow,** to become bigger; increase. *They grew tomatoes on their farm.*

grip /grip/ *n.* **1.** a firm hold; tight grasp. **2.** firm control or power. *The city was in the grip of a heavy snowstorm.* **3.** a part by which something is held; handle. —*v.* **gripped, grip ping. 1.** to take hold of firmly and tightly. *He gripped the edge of the cliff with all his might.* **2.** to attract and keep the interest of. *That novel really gripped us.*

grouch /grouch/ *n., pl.* **grouch es.** a person who is often cross and has a bad temper. —**grouch y,** *adj.*

Ground hog Day /groundʹ hogʹ dā/ *n.* February 2. On this day, the groundhog is supposed to come out of its hole. If it sees its own shadow, there will be six more weeks of winter. If it doesn't see its shadow, spring will come soon.

growl /groul/ *n.* a deep, harsh, rumbling sound made in the throat. —*v.* to make a deep, harsh, rumbling sound in the throat. *The bear growled when we got close to its cage.*

gruff /gruf/ *adj.* **1.** rough to hear. *He has a gruff voice.* **2.** unfriendly. *The angry man was gruff to the clerk.*

guess /ges/ *v.* to have an idea, think, believe, when you do not know for sure. *Can you guess what is in the large blue box?* —*n.* an opinion formed without having enough knowledge or facts to be sure. *My guess is that it will rain tomorrow.*

gull /gul/ *n.* a white and gray bird. Gulls live on or near the water.

gup pies /gupʹ ēz/ *n.* the plural of *guppy.*

gup py /gupʹ ē/ *n.* a very small fish with bright colors. *We keep our guppy in a fishbowl.*

gym /jim/ *n., pl.* **gyms 1.** a room or building for physical exercise; gymnasium. **2.** a course in physical education that is given in a school or college.

gyp sy /jipʹ sē/ *n., pl.* **gyp sies,** (sometimes **Gyp sy**). a person belonging to a group of people who came to Europe from India long ago. Gypsies are a wandering people, and they now live scattered throughout the world.

/a/	at
/ā/	late
/â/	care
/ä/	father
/e/	set
/ē/	me
/i/	it
/ī/	kite
/o/	ox
/ō/	rose
/ô/	brought raw
/oi/	coin
/ŏŏ/	book
/ōō/	too
/or/	form
/ou/	out
/u/	up
/yōō/	cube
/ûr/	turn germ learn firm work
/ə/	about chicken pencil cannon circus
/ch/	chair
/hw/	which
/ng/	ring
/sh/	shop
/th/	thin
/ŧh/	there
/zh/	treasure

H

hab i tat /hab′ i tat/ *n.* the place where an animal or plant naturally lives and grows. *The natural habitat of fish is water.*

had n't /had′ nt/ *contr.* shortened form of "had not." *We hadn't seen that movie before Friday night.*

hair /hâr/ *n.* **1.** a very thin, threadlike growth on the skin of people and animals. **2.** a mass of such growths. *My friend's hair is brown and wavy.*

half /haf/ *n., pl.* **halves. 1.** one of two equal parts of something. *A pint is half of a quart.* **2.** either of two time periods in certain sports. —*adj.* being one of two equal parts. —*adv.* **1.** to the extent of one half. **2.** partly; somewhat. *I was half asleep during the movie.*

Hal low een /hal ə wēn′/ *n.* a holiday on October 31 that is celebrated by dressing up in costumes, collecting treats, and playing tricks. *adj.* pertaining to Halloween.

ham burg er /ham′ bûr gər/ *n.* **1.** ground beef. **2.** a rounded, flat portion of ground beef.

ham mer /ham′ ər/ *n.* **1.** a tool with a heavy metal head on a handle. *A hammer is used for driving nails.* **2.** anything that is like a hammer in shape or use. —*v.* **1.** to strike again and again; pound. *I hammered in the last nail.* **2.** to pound into shape with a hammer.

hand /hand/ *n.* **1.** the end part of the arm from the wrist down in humans and some other animals. **2.** a member of a group or crew; laborer. **3.** a round of applause; clapping. —*v.* to give or pass with the hand. *Please hand me the pepper.*

han dle /han′ dəl/ *n.* the part of an object that is made to be grasped by the hand. —*v.* **han dled, han dling. 1.** to touch or hold with the hand. **2.** to manage, control, or deal with. *The teacher handled the problem well.*

Ha nuk kah /hä′ nə kə/ Also **Cha nu kah.** *n.* a Jewish holiday commemorating the rededication of the Temple of Jerusalem after the victory of Judas Maccabeus over the king of ancient Syria in 165 B.C. It is celebrated by lighting candles on eight successive nights.

hard /härd/ *adj.* **1.** solid and firm to the touch; not soft. **2.** needing or using much effort. **3.** having great force or strength. —*adv.* with effort or energy. **2.** with force or strength. **3.** with difficulty. *The runner was breathing hard.*

has n't /haz′ nt/ *contr.* shortened form of "has not." *Who hasn't read this book?*

hat box /hat′ boks/ *n., pl.* **hat box es.** a box in which to keep a hat. *Mr. Drew carries his brown hat in a hatbox.*

hatch /hach/ *v.* **hatched, hatch ing.** to come from an egg. *The chicks hatched by pecking through their shells.*

haul /hôl/ *n.* **1.** the act of hauling. **2.** something that is gotten by catching or winning. —*v.* **1.** to pull or move with force; drag. **2.** to carry; transport. *Railroads haul freight across the country.*

haunt ed /hôn′ tid/ *adj.* visited by ghosts; scary. *The empty old house looked haunted.*

have /hav/ *v.* **had, hav ing. 1.** to own; possess. *Everyone in my family has straight black hair.* **2.** to consist of; contain. **3.** to hold in the mind. **4.** to carry on; engage in. *We had a discussion in class.* **5.** to experience. *Have a good time!* **6.** to give birth to. **7.** to be forced or obligated. *I have to be home by five o'clock.* **8.** to permit; allow. *I wanted to keep snakes as pets, but my parents wouldn't have it.* **9.** also used as an auxiliary verb to show that the action of the main verb is finished. *We have done all of our homework.*

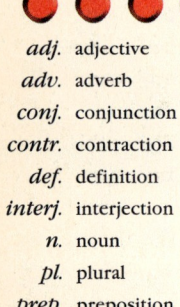

adj.	adjective
adv.	adverb
conj.	conjunction
contr.	contraction
def.	definition
interj.	interjection
n.	noun
pl.	plural
prep.	preposition
pron.	pronoun
sing.	singular
v.	verb

have n't /hav′ ənt/ *contr.* shortened form of "have not." *I haven't been to a dance yet.*

hawk /hôk/ *n.* a strong bird that can kill other birds and small animals.

head /hed/ *n.* 1. the top part of the human body or any animal body. 2. the top or front part of something. *Hit the nail on the head.* 3. a firm, rounded cluster of leaves or flowers. *Please buy a head of lettuce.* 4. a person who is above others in rank; chief. *He is the head of the company.* *pl. for definitions 5 and 6.* **head.** 5. a single person or animal. *The cowhands rounded up forty head of cattle.* 6. mental ability. *You have a good head for figures.* —*v.* 1. to be or go to the top or front of; lead. 2. to be in charge of. *Our best writer heads the school newspaper.* 3. to direct or move in a direction. *We head for the beach on hot days.* —*adj.* top, chief, or front. *My cousin is the head lifeguard at the pool.*

he'd /hēd/ *contr.* 1. shortened form of "he had." 2. shortened form of "he would."

hef ty /hef′ tē/ *adj.*, **hef ti er, hef ti est.** 1. big and strong; muscular. 2. heavy; weighty.

held /held/ *v.* past tense and past participle of *hold*.

he'll /hēl/ *contr.* shortened form of "he will" or "he shall."

here's /hirz/ *contr.* shortened form of "here is." *Here's the book I was telling you about.*

he's /hēz/ *contr.* shortened form of "he is" or "he has."

hide /hīd/ *n.* the skin of an animal. *Leather is made from hides.* —*v.* **hid, hid den** or **hid, hid ing.** 1. to put or keep out of sight. 2. to keep secret. *The lost children tried to hide their fears from each other.*

hid ing /hī′ ding/ *v.* a form of **hide.** It is used with a helping word. *We were hiding in the barn.* See **hide.**

high /hī/ *n.* 1. a high place or point. *The temperature today reached a new high for the year.* 2. the arrangement of gears in an automobile, bicycle, or other vehicle that gives the greatest speed. —*adj.* 1. tall. 2. at a great distance from the ground. 3. above or more important than the others. *A general has a high rank in the army.* 4. noble or lofty. *Their high ideals made them refuse a reward.* —*adv.* at or to a high place. *The hikers climbed high up the hill.*

hike /hīk/ *v.* **hiked, hik ing.** to take a long walk. —*n.* a long walk. *We took a long hike in the woods.*

hik ing /hī′ king/ *v.* a form of **hike.** It is used with a helping word. *She was hiking by the stream.* See **hike.** —*n.* the act of taking a long walk or march.

hill /hil/ *n.* 1. a raised, rounded part of the earth's surface. 2. a small heap or mound. *Ants have made hills in our backyard.*

hinge /hinj/ *n., pl.* **hinges** a joint on which a door, gate, or lid moves back and forth or up and down. *The hinges on the old door squeak.* —*v.* **hinged, hing ing.** 1. to put hinges on; attach by hinges. 2. to depend. *The team's chances hinge on the next two games.*

hob bies /hob′ ēz/ *n.* plural of **hobby.**

hob by /hob′ ē/ *n., pl.* **hob bies.** something done regularly in one's spare time for pleasure.

hog /hôg, hog/ *n.* a fully grown pig.

hoist /hoist/ *v.* to lift or pull up.

hole /hōl/ *n.* 1. a hollow place in something solid. 2. an opening through something. *I wore a hole in my sweater.*

hol i days /hol′ ə dāz/ *n.* Days when people don't have to work or go to school.

horn /horn/ *n.* 1. a hard, pointed growth on the head of some animals that have hooves. 2. something that looks like the horn of an animal. 3. a

/a/	at
/ā/	late
/â/	care
/ä/	father
/e/	set
/ē/	me
/i/	it
/ī/	kite
/o/	ox
/ō/	rose
/ô/	brought raw
/oi/	coin
/o͝o/	book
/o͞o/	too
/or/	form
/ou/	out
/u/	up
/yo͞o/	cube
/ûr/	turn germ learn firm work
/ə/	about chicken pencil cannon circus
/ch/	chair
/hw/	which
/ng/	ring
/sh/	shop
/th/	thin
/t͟h/	there
/zh/	treasure

brass musical instrument. 4. a device used to make a loud warning sound.

horse /hors/ *n.* 1. a large animal with four legs, hooves, and a long, flowing mane and tail. 2. any mammal belonging to the horse family that includes horses, zebras, and asses. 3. a frame with legs used to hold things like wood being sawed.

horse back /hors′ bak/ *n.* the back of a horse. *Riders on horseback.* —*adv.* on the back of a horse. *Some of us are going to ride horseback.*

hos tile /hos′ təl/ *adj.* feeling or showing hatred or dislike. *After the fight, the students gave each other hostile looks.*

hot dog /hot dog/ *n.* a long, thin sausage; frankfurter.

house¹ /hous/ *n.* 1. a building in which people live; home. 2. the people who live in a house. 3. any building used for a special purpose.

house² /houz/ *v.* **housed, hous ing.** to give a place to live or stay. *We housed our friends until their new home was ready.*

how's /houz/ *contr.* shortened form of "how is." *How's your team doing this year?*

huge /hyo͞oj/ *adj.,* **hug er, hug est.** great in size or amount; very big; enormous.

hu mane /hyo͞o mān′/ *adj.* having sympathy for others; wanting to prevent pain.

hur ri cane /hûr′ i kān/ *n.* a storm with very strong winds and heavy rain.

hur ry /hûr′ ē/ *v.* **hur ried, hur ry ing.** to move faster than is usual; rush. —*n., pl.* **hur ries.** 1. the act of moving very quickly. 2. the wish or need to act or move very quickly. *The children were in a hurry to go outside and play.*

hurt /hûrt/ *v.* **hurt, hurt ing.** 1. to cause pain or injury. *It hurt my feelings when my classmates laughed at me.* 2. to be painful. *My knee hurts* because I twisted it. —*n.* a pain or injury. —*adj.* to be injured.

I

I'd /īd/ *contr.* 1. shortened form of "I had." 2. shortened form of "I would."

I'll /īl/ *contr.* 1. shortened form of "I shall." 2. shortened form of "I will."

I'm /īm/ *contr.* shortened form of "I am." *I'm happy to see you.*

i mag ine /i maj′ in/ *v.* **i mag ined, i mag in ing.** to picture a person or thing in the mind. *Try to imagine a dragon breathing fire.*

im mune /i myo͞on′/ *adj.* protected from a disease. *The doctor gave me a vaccination that made me immune to measles.*

im port /im pôrt′/ *v.* **im port ed, im port ing.** to buy goods from another country. *The United States imports tea from India.*

In de pend ence Day /in di pen′ dəns dā/ *n.* a holiday observed on July 4, commemorating the adoption of the Declaration of Independence on July 4, 1776. Also, **Fourth of July.**

in e qual i ty /in′ i kwol′ i tē/ *n.* the condition of not being equal. *Often there is an inequality between what we hope for and what we get.*

in fin i ty /in fin′ i tē/ *n., pl.* **in fin i ties.** 1. something that is endless, such as space or time. 2. an indefinitely large amount or number: *an infinity of details.*

in sen si tive /in sen′ si tiv/ *adj.* lacking feeling, sensitivity, or perception. *The banker is a cruel and insensitive person.*

is n't /iz′ ənt/ *contr.* shortened form of "is not." *Our dog isn't a puppy anymore.*

it'll /it′ əl/ *contr.* 1. shortened form of "it shall." 2. shortened form of "it will."

it's /its/ *contr.* 1. shortened form of "it has." 2. shortened form of "it is."

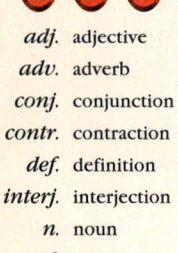

adj. adjective
adv. adverb
conj. conjunction
contr. contraction
def. definition
interj. interjection
n. noun
pl. plural
prep. preposition
pron. pronoun
sing. singular
v. verb

I've/knight

I've /īv/ *contr.* shortened form of "I have."

J

jam /jam/ *n.* a sweet spread made from fruit.

Jan u ar y /jan′ yo͞o âr ē/ *n., pl.* **Jan u ar ies.** the first month of the year. January has 31 days.

jeep /jēp/ *n.* a small, powerful automobile that moves easily over poor, rough roads.

jin gle /jing′ gəl/ *v.* **jin gled, jin gling.** to make or cause to make a tinkling or ringing sound. —*n.* **1.** a tinkling or ringing sound. **2.** a light, short tune that is easy to remember.

jog /jog/ *v.* **jogged, jog ging.** to run or move at a slow, steady pace. —*n.* a slow, steady pace.

join /join/ *v.* **joined, join ing 1.** to put or fasten together so as to become one. **2.** to become a member of. **3.** to get together with. *Our friends joined us at our table.* **4.** to take part with others.

ju li enne /jo͞o lē en′/ *adj.* cut into thin strips. *I like julienne carrots.*

Ju ly /jyo͞o lī′/ *n., pl.* **Ju lies.** the seventh month of the year. July has 31 days.

jump /jump/ *v.* **1.** to use a push from one's feet to move through or into the air. **2.** to move or get up suddenly. **3.** to increase or rise in a quick or unexpected way. *The price of gasoline jumped.* —*n.* **1.** the act of jumping. **2.** the distance covered by jumping. **3.** a sudden move or start.

June /jo͞on/ *n.* the sixth month of the year. June has 30 days.

June teenth /jo͞on′ tēnth/ *n.* a summer celebration in Texas. *Are you going to the Juneteenth concert?*

jun gle /jung′ gəl/ *n.* tropical land that has many trees, plants, and wild animals. *It is hot in the jungle.* —*adj.* pertaining to the jungle.

just /just/ *adj.* fair and right; honest. —*adv.* **1.** not more or less than; exactly. **2.** a little while ago. *I just saw your parents.* **3.** no more than; only. *It's just a scratch.*

K

keep /kēp/ *n.* food and a place to live. *When the children grew up, they all started earning their own keep.* —*v.* **kept, keep ing. 1.** to continue to have, hold, or do. *Keep mixing the batter until it is smooth.* **2.** to continue or cause to continue in a certain place or condition; stay or cause to stay. *The teacher asked the class to keep quiet.* **3.** to store or put. **4.** to hold back or stop. *The cold weather may keep the plants from budding.* **5.** to take care of. *That farmer keeps a big herd of cows.*

kiss /kis/ *n., pl.* **kiss es.** a touch with the lips as a sign of greeting or affection. —*v.* to touch with the lips as a sign of greeting or affection.

kitch en /kich′ ən/ *n.* a room or place where food is cooked.

knap sack /nap′ sak′/ *n.* a bag made for carrying clothes, equipment, or other supplies on the back.

knave /nāv/ *n.* a lying, disloyal person; scoundrel.

knee /nē/ *n.* the part in the middle of the leg that bends.

kneel /nēl/ *v.* **knelt** or **kneeled, kneel ing.** to go down on a bent knee or knees. *The knights and ladies kneeled before the royal couple.*

knew /no͞o, nyo͞o/ *v.* past tense of **know.** *Who knew the answer to the question?* See **know.**

knife /nīf/ *n., pl.* **knives. 1.** a tool that is used in cutting. **2.** the part of a tool or machine that cuts; blade. —*v.* **knifed, knif ing.** to cut or stab with a knife.

knight /nīt/ *n.* **1.** a soldier in the Middle Ages who gave his loyalty to a king or lord. **2.** a man who holds this

/a/ at
/ā/ late
/â/ care
/ä/ father
/e/ set
/ē/ me
/i/ it
/ī/ kite
/o/ ox
/ō/ rose
/ô/ brought raw
/oi/ coin
/o͝o/ book
/o͞o/ too
/or/ form
/ou/ out
/u/ up
/yo͞o/ cube
/ûr/ turn germ learn firm work
/ə/ about chicken pencil cannon circus
/ch/ chair
/hw/ which
/ng/ ring
/sh/ shop
/th/ thin
/t͟h/ there
/zh/ treasure

knit/less

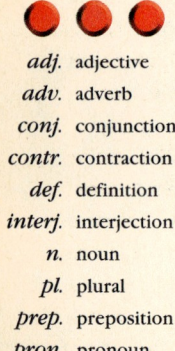

adj.	adjective
adv.	adverb
conj.	conjunction
contr.	contraction
def.	definition
interj.	interjection
n.	noun
pl.	plural
prep.	preposition
pron.	pronoun
sing.	singular
v.	verb

title today as an honor for service to his country. —*v.* to raise to the rank of knight. *The king knighted two soldiers.*

knit /nit/ *v.* **knit ted, knit ting.** to join wool closely together with two needles. *You knit lovely sweaters.* —*adj.* made of knit cloth. *She wore a knit sweater to school.*

knock /nok/ *v.* **knocked 1.** to strike with a sharp, hard blow; hit. **2.** to push or cause to fall. —*n.* **1.** a sharp, hard blow; hit. *The player got a knock on the head.* **2.** a pounding or rattling noise. *engine knock.*

knot /not/ *n.* **1.** the place where pieces of thread, string, or cord are tied around each other. **2.** a tangle or lump. *There were knots in the dog's coat.* **3.** a unit of speed on water —*v.* **knot ted, knot ting.** to tie or tangle in or with a knot or knots. *I knotted the string.*

know /nō/ *v.* **knew, known, know ing. 1.** to understand clearly; be certain of the facts or truth of. **2.** to be acquainted or familiar with. **3.** to have skill or experience with. *That student knows how to type very well.*

knowl edge /nol′ ij/ *n.* an understanding that is gained through experience or study. *I have no knowledge of Dutch.*

known /nōn/ *v.* past participle of **know.** *A great deal is known about the effects of pollution.* See **know.**

Kwan za /kwän′ zə/ *n.* an annual festival, originally an African harvest festival, celebrated by some Americans in December.

• • • L • • • • • • • • • • • • • • • •

La bor Day /lā′ bər dā/ *n.* a legal holiday in honor of working people, observed in the United States on the first Monday in September.

lad der /lad′ ər/ *n.* a device made of two long side pieces joined together by short pieces called rungs, which are used as steps.

lair /lâr/ *n.* place where a wild animal lives or rests; den.

lamb /lam/ *n.* **1.** a young sheep. **2.** the meat from a lamb.

lamp /lamp/ *n.* a device that produces light. Some lamps use electric light bulbs; others burn oil, kerosene, or gas to give light.

lam prey /lam′ prē/ *n., pl.* **lam preys.** any of a group of fish that look like eels.

land form /land′ form/ *n.* a feature on the surface of the earth, such as a valley or mountain range.

large /lärj/ *adj.,* **larg er, larg est.** big in size or amount. *That large house has twenty rooms.*

latch /lach/ *n., pl.* **latch es.** a small piece of metal or wood for holding a door, window, or gate closed. —*v.* to fasten or close the latch of something.

law /lô/ *n.* **1.** a rule made by a government for all the people in a town, state, or country. **2.** a set or system of such rules. *The law of the United States is based on the system used in England.* **3.** the profession of a lawyer. **4.** any rule or custom. *This book covers the laws of English grammar.*

left /left/ *v.* past tense and past participle of *leave. I left my books at home.* —*adj.* on or toward the side of the body that is to the west when one faces north. *Walk on the left side of the road.* —*n.* the left side or direction. *My sister was seated on my left.*

lend /lend/ *v.* **lent, lend ing. 1.** to let a person have or use something for a while. **2.** to provide; give. *Bright lights lend excitement.*

less /les/ *n.* a smaller amount or quantity. —*adj.* not as much. *I have less work to do today than I had yesterday.* —*adv.* to a smaller extent. —*prep.* minus. *10 less 7 is 3.*

186 Speller Dictionary

let's/loud

let's /lets/ *contr.* shortened form of "let us." *Let's go for a walk.*

let ter /let′ ər/ *n.* **1.** a mark that stands for a spoken sound. *The word "run" has three letters.* **2.** a written message.

li brar i an /lī brâr′ ē ən/ *n.* a person who is in charge of or works in a library.

li brar y /lī′ brâr ē/ *n., pl.* **li brar ies.** **1.** a collection of books, magazines, and newspapers. **2.** a room or building for such a collection.

lift /lift/ *v.* to take or raise up. —*n.* a free ride. *The truck driver gave me a lift into town.*

light /līt/ *adj.* **1.** having little weight; not heavy. **2.** not great in amount or force. *A light rain fell.* **3.** easy to do or bear. *We did some light cleaning in the living room.* **4.** moving easily; graceful; nimble. **5.** happy; cheerful. **6.** amusing; not serious. **7.** bright; not dark. **8.** pale in color. —*n.* **1.** the form of energy that makes it possible for us to see. **2.** something that gives off brightness. **3.** something used to set fire to something else. **4.** the time of day when the sun first shines. **5.** knowledge; understanding. —*v.* **light ed** or **lit, light ing.** **1.** to burn or cause to burn. **2.** to cause to give off light. **3.** to give brightness to. **4.** to show the way by means of light or lights.

lily /lil′ ē/ *n., pl.* **lil ies.** a large, showy flower that is shaped like a trumpet. *The lily grows from a bulb.*

limb /lim/ *n.* **1.** a part of the body of an animal or human other than the head or torso **2.** a large branch.

lime light /līm′ līt/ *n.* center of interest. *The election campaign put the candidate's family in the limelight.*

Lin coln's Birth day /ling′ kənz bərth′ dā/ *n.* a holiday on February 12 for Abraham Lincoln's birthday.

line /līn/ *n.* **1.** a long, thin mark or stroke. **2.** anything like a line. *Your forehead is full of lines.* **3.** a limit or boundary; edge. **4.** a number of persons or things arranged one after the other; row. **5.** a short letter, note, or verse. **6.** a cord or cable used for a special purpose. *We hung the wash on the line to dry.* **7. lines.** the words spoken by a person in a play. —*v.* **lined, lin ing.** **1.** to mark or cover with lines. **2.** to form a line along. *Trees line the edge of the road.* **3.** to cover the inside of. *The tailor lined the wool suit with silk.*

lit tle /lit′ əl/ *n.* **1.** a small amount. *I ate only a little because I wasn't hungry.* **2.** a short time or distance. *Step back a little.* —*adj.,* **less** or **less er** or **lit tler, least,** or **lit tlest. 1.** small in size or amount. **2.** short in time or distance. —*adv.* **less, least.** not much; slightly. *Snow is little seen in warm, dry places.*

lob by /lob′ ē/ *n., pl.* **lob bies. 1.** a hall or room at the entrance to a building. **2.** a person or group that tries to convince legislators to vote in a certain way. —*v.* **lob bied, lob by ing.** to try to convince legislators to vote in a certain way. *A group of citizens lobbied against the bill to build a new highway.*

log /lôg, log/ *n.* **1.** a piece of a tree cut with the bark still on. **2.** the record of the voyage of a ship or the flight of an airplane. —*v.* **logged, log ging. 1.** to cut down trees in a forest and shape them into logs. **2.** to make a record.

loose /lo͞os/ *v.* **loosed, loos ing. 1.** to set free; let go. **2.** to make or become less tight; loosen or unfasten. —*adj.* **1.** not fastened or attached firmly. **2.** free. *The canary is loose in the house.* **3.** not tight. *My friend wears a loose jacket.*

loud /loud/ *adj.* **1.** having a strong sound; not quiet. *The jet plane made a loud noise.* **2.** too bright; gaudy. *Do you really want to wear that loud tie?* —*adv.* in a loud way.

/a/ at
/ā/ late
/â/ care
/ä/ father
/e/ set
/ē/ me
/i/ it
/ī/ kite
/o/ ox
/ō/ rose
/ô/ brought raw
/oi/ coin
/o͝o/ book
/o͞o/ too
/or/ form
/ou/ out
/u/ up
/yo͞o/ cube
/ûr/ turn
    germ
    learn
    firm
    work
/ə/ about
    chicken
    pencil
    cannon
    circus
/ch/ chair
/hw/ which
/ng/ ring
/sh/ shop
/th/ thin
/t͟h/ there
/zh/ treasure

Speller Dictionary 187

loyal /loi′ əl/ *adj.* having or showing strong and lasting affection and support for someone or something. *The old friends were loyal to each other.*

lu nar /lōō′ nər/ *adj.* of or having to do with the moon. *The astronauts brought back lunar rocks for study.*

lunch box /lunch′ boks/ *n., pl.* **lunch box es.** a small box in which to keep and carry one's lunch.

lunch time /lunch′ tīm/ *n.* time of day to eat lunch.

M

mag ic /maj′ ik/ *n.* **1.** the power to control forces of nature and events by using special charms or spells. **2.** the art or skill of doing tricks to entertain people. —*adj.* using magic; done by or seeming to be done by magic.

mail /māl/ *n.* **1.** letters, cards, and packages that are sent or received through a post office. **2.** the system by which mail is sent, moved, or delivered. —*v.* to send by mail.

main /mān/ *adj.* the most important; the largest; chief. *The main street goes through the center of town.* —*adv.* **main ly.**

make /māk/ *v.* **made, mak ing. 1.** to form or bring into being; to construct. **2.** to cause to be, become, or happen. *The smell of food made me hungry.* **3.** to cause or force to do. *A funny movie always makes me laugh.* **4.** to earn. *I made ten dollars a day.* —*n.* the style or type of something that is sold; brand.

mak ing /mā′ king/ *v.* form of **make.** It is used with a helping word. *They are making a meal.* See **make.**

man y /men′ ē/ *n.* a large number. —*adj.,* **more, most.** made up of a large number. —*pron.* a large number of people or things. *Many were late for school today.*

mar ble /mär′ bəl/ *n., pl.* **marbles. 1.** a type of smooth, mottled stone often used in building and sculpture. **2.** a small, hard ball of glass used in games. —*adj.* pertaining to marble (in meaning).

March /märch/ *n.* the third month of the year. March has 31 days.

Mar di Gras /mär′ dē grä/ *n.* a celebration held on the last day before Lent, marked by parades and festivities.

mare /mâr/ *n.* a female horse.

Mar tin Lu ther King Day /mär′ tən lōō′ thər king dā/ *n.* a holiday observed on the third Monday in January to celebrate the birthday of Martin Luther King, Jr., the black civil rights leader.

match /mach/ *n., pl.* **match es. 1.** a person or thing that is suitable with or very much like another. **2.** a game or contest. **3.** a short, thin piece of wood or cardboard used to start a fire. —*v.* **matched, match ing. 1.** to be suitable with, equal to, or like something. **2.** to find or bring together things that are exactly alike.

math /math/ *n.* the study of numbers.

May /mā/ *n.* the fifth month of the year. May has 31 days.

meal /mēl/ *n.* **1.** grain or other food that has been ground. *I mixed corn meal into the batter.* **2.** the food served or eaten at one time. *Breakfast is an important meal.*

Me mo ri al Day /mə mor′ ē əl dā/ *n.* a legal holiday in memory of members of the military killed in all American wars. It was originally celebrated on May 30, and is now usually celebrated on the last Monday in May. Also, **Decoration Day.**

mem o rize /mem′ ə rīz′/ *v.* to learn by heart. *I memorized the poem by repeating it over and over.*

mess /mes/ *n., pl.* **mess es.** a group of things that is not neat or clean. *Fred had to clean the mess in his room.*

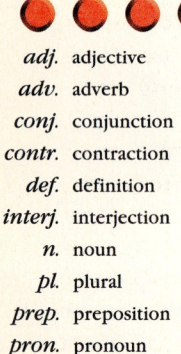

adj. adjective
adv. adverb
conj. conjunction
contr. contraction
def. definition
interj. interjection
n. noun
pl. plural
prep. preposition
pron. pronoun
sing. singular
v. verb

me te or oids /mē′ tē ə roidz′/ *n.* particles of matter from space before they enter Earth's atmosphere.

mice /mīs/ *n.* the plural of *mouse.*

mid night /mid′ nīt/ *n.* twelve o'clock at night.

mil li sec ond /mil′ ə sek′ ənd/ *n.* 1/1,000 of a second.

miss /mis/ *n., pl.* **miss es 1.** a failure to hit or reach something. **2.** a title for a girl or for a woman who is not married. —*v.* **1.** to fail to do something attempted or planned; fail to get, reach, hit, meet, find, or catch. *We missed the bus.* **2.** to notice or feel the absence or loss of a person or thing. *I missed her when she was away.*

mitt /mit/ *n.* a big glove used to protect the hand.

mo las ses /mə las′ iz/ *n.* a sweet, thick, yellowish brown syrup that is made from sugarcane.

mold /mōld/ *n.* **1.** a hollow form that is made in a special shape for liquid or soft material to be poured into it. **2.** a furry-looking covering of fungus that grows on food and damp surfaces. —*v.* **1.** to make into a special shape; form. **2.** to influence and give form to. *Our parents help mold our habits.* **3.** to become covered with mold.

mo men tar i ly /mō′ mən ter′ ə lē/ *adv.* for a moment. *Our train was momentarily delayed.*

Mon day /mun′ dē, mun′ dā/ *n.* the second day of the week.

month /munth/ *n.* one of twelve groups of days that make up a year. Each month has 28 to 31 days.

moon /mo͞on/ *n.* **1.** a heavenly body that revolves around Earth from west to east once every 29½ days. **2.** a satellite of any planet.

mopped /mopt/ *v.* past tense and past participle of **mop,** to wash with a mop. *She mopped the floor.*

more /mor/ *adj.* **1.** greater in number, amount, or degree. *A gallon is more than a quart.* **2.** additional; further. —*adv.* **1.** to a greater amount or degree. **2.** in addition; again. —*n.* an extra amount. *Our dogs always want more to eat.*

morn ing /mor′ ning/ *n.* the early part of the day, ending at noon.

moss /mos/ *n., pl.* **moss es.** a small green plant that grows in groups to form a soft, thick mat on the ground, on rocks, or on trees. —**moss y,** *adj.*

moth /môth/ *n.* an insect that looks like a butterfly, has a thick body, and eats holes in fabrics.

moth er /muth′ ər/ *n.* the female parent; Mom.

Moth er's Day /muth′ ərz dā/ *n.* a day set aside in honor of mothers, observed annually on the second Sunday of May.

mo tion /mō′ shən/ *n.* the act of moving; movement. *The car suddenly went into motion.* —*v.* to show or signal by a movement of the hand or head. *Can you motion the boat to come closer?*

moun tain /moun′ tən/ *n.* a mass of land that rises very high above the surrounding area.

Mount E ver est /mount ev′ ûr′ est/ *n.* name of the world's highest mountain. *The climbers reached the top of Mount Everest.*

mouse /mous/ *n., pl.* **mice. 1.** a small, furry animal with a pointed nose, small ears, and a long, thin tail. **2.** a small instrument that can be connected to a computer to move the cursor on a monitor.

mouth [1] /mouth/ *n., pl.* **mouths.** /mouthz/ **1.** the opening through which people and animals take in food. **2.** any opening that is like a mouth. *We entered the mouth of the cave.*

mouth [2] /mouth/ *v.* to say or repeat in an insincere way.

move /mo͞ov/ *v.* **moved, mov ing. 1.** to change the place or direction of something. **2.** to put in motion. **3.** to

/a/	at
/ā/	late
/â/	care
/ä/	father
/e/	set
/ē/	me
/i/	it
/ī/	kite
/o/	ox
/ō/	rose
/ô/	brought raw
/oi/	coin
/o͝o/	book
/o͞o/	too
/or/	form
/ou/	out
/u/	up
/yo͞o/	cube
/ûr/	turn germ learn firm work
/ə/	about chicken pencil cannon circus
/ch/	chair
/hw/	which
/ng/	ring
/sh/	shop
/th/	thin
/th/	there
/zh/	treasure

Speller Dictionary

change location of home or business. *She will move from Houston to Boston.* **4.** to stir a person's feelings.

mov ie /moo′ vē/ *n.* a film; motion picture.

much /much/ *adj.* **more, most.** great in amount or degree. *We had too much rain.* —*adv.* **more, most.** to a great degree; very. *I was very much upset.* —*n.* a great amount. *Much has been written about the Civil War.*

mul ti pli er /mul′ tə plī′ ər/ *n.* a number that tells how many times to multiply another number. *If you multiply 2 times 4, the multiplier is 2.*

mur mur /mûr′ mər/ *n., pl.* **mur murs.** a soft, low sound. *I heard the murmur of people's voices.* —*v.* to make a soft, low sound. *Did you hear the car murmur?*

N

nar row /nar′ ō/ *adj.* **1.** not wide or broad. **2.** limited or small. *People with narrow minds don't like new ideas.* —*v.* to make or become narrow. *The workers narrowed the sidewalk.*

naugh ty /nô′ tē/ *adj.*, **naugh ti er, naugh ti est.** behaving badly; mischievous or disobedient. *The teacher made us stay after school because we were naughty today.*

neat /nēt/ *adj.*, **neat er, neat est.** **1.** clean and orderly; tidy. *You have neat handwriting.* **2.** having or showing care for keeping things in order. *My cousin is neater than I am and has a tidy room.* **3.** done in a clever way. *We learned a neat trick.*

nee dle /nē′ dəl/ *n.* **1.** a thin, pointed instrument with a hole in one end for thread. **2.** a pointer on a compass or dial. **3.** a sharp, thin, hollow tube that is used to put fluid into or take fluid out of the body. —*v.* **nee dled, nee dling.** to annoy or tease. *My friends needled me about my new haircut.*

need n't /nē′ dənt/ *contr.* shortened form of "need not." *You needn't hurry, because we have plenty of time.*

neigh bor hood /nā′ bər hood/ *n.* **1.** a small area or district in a town or city where people live. **2.** the people living in the same area or district.

new /noo, nyoo/ *adj.* **1.** having existed only a short time; recently grown or made. **2.** not yet familiar or experienced. **3.** not yet used or worn. *Do you like my new shoes?* **4.** coming or beginning again.

New Year's Day /noo yērz dā/ *n.* a holiday that celebrates the first day of the year, January 1.

nice /nīs/ *adj.*, **nic er, nic est.** **1.** pleasant or agreeable. **2.** kind and thoughtful. *It was nice of you to ask us to the party.* **3.** having or showing good manners; polite.

night /nīt/ *n.* **1.** the time when it is dark; time between the setting and rising of the sun. **2.** the darkness of night. **3.** the beginning of night; nightfall.

noise /noiz/ *n.* **1.** a sound that is loud and harsh. **2.** any sound.

nois y /noi′ zē/ *adj.*, **nois i er, nois i est.** making much noise.

noon /noon/ *n.* twelve o'clock in the daytime; the middle of the day.

note book /nōt′ book/ *n.* a book with blank pages for notes.

noth ing /nuth′ ing/ *n.* **1.** no thing; not anything. **2.** a person or thing that is of no importance. *One dollar is nothing to a rich person.* **3.** zero. —*adv.* in no way; not at all. *You look nothing like your parents.*

No vem ber /nō vem′ bər/ *n.* the eleventh month of the year. *November has 30 days.*

now /nou/ *adv.* **1.** at this time; at this moment. **2.** without delay; immediately. **3.** under the present conditions or circumstances. —*conj.*

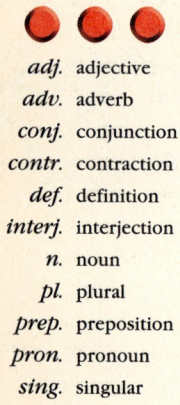

adj.	adjective
adv.	adverb
conj.	conjunction
contr.	contraction
def.	definition
interj.	interjection
n.	noun
pl.	plural
prep.	preposition
pron.	pronoun
sing.	singular
v.	verb

since. *Now that the rain has stopped, the game can continue.* —*n.* the present time. —*interj.* a word used to express warning, sympathy, or disapproval.

nurse /nûrs/ *n.* **1.** a person who is trained to take care of sick people and to teach people how to stay healthy. **2.** a person who is hired to take care of children. —*v.* **nursed, nurs ing. 1.** to take care of. **2.** to feed a baby or young animal from a nipple. **3.** to treat with care.

O

o be di ent /o bē′ dē ənt/ *adj.* tending or willing to do what one is told. *The obedient children went to bed.*

Oc to ber /ok tō′ bər/ *n.* the tenth month of the year. October has 31 days.

odd /od/ *adj.* **1.** different from the usual or normal; strange; peculiar. **2.** happening or appearing now and then; occasional. *I do odd jobs after school.* **3.** any whole number not exactly divisible by two. *Five and seven are odd numbers.*

of fer /ô′ fər/ *v.* **1.** to present to be accepted or turned down. *They offered some suggestions for the party.* **2.** to show a desire to do or give something; volunteer. *My friend offered to help me wash the car.* —*n.* **1.** the act of offering. **2.** something offered. *The salesman turned down our offer.*

oil /oil/ *n.* **1.** any one of a large group of substances that are greasy and will dissolve in alcohol but not in water. **2.** a liquid that is found beneath the earth's surface; petroleum. —*v.* to cover, polish, or supply with oil. *I helped oil the furniture.*

old /ōld/ *adj.* **old er, old est. 1.** not young; aged. **2.** of age. *The girl is five years old.*

o mis sion /ō mish′ ən/ *n.* the act or state of being left out.

once /wuns/ *adv.* **1.** one time. **2.** in a time now past; before. *Parents were once children.* —*n.* one single time. *May I borrow your bicycle just this once?* —*conj.* as soon as; when. *The game is easy, once you learn the rules.*

on ly /ōn′ lē/ *adj.* **1.** alone of its kind; solitary. *My friend is an only child.* **2.** best of all. *You are the only singer for the role.* —*adv.* **1.** no more than. **2.** no one or nothing other than. —*conj.* except that; but. *I would have gone to the park, only it was raining.*

or der /or′ dər/ *n., pl.* **or ders. 1.** a command to do something. **2.** the way in which things are arranged. **3.** a condition in which laws or rules are obeyed. —*v.* **1.** to tell to do something; give an order to. **2.** to ask for.

oth er /uth′ r/ *adj.* **1.** different from the one or ones already mentioned. *If you can't help me, maybe some other person can.* **2.** remaining. *The other guests haven't arrived yet.* **3.** more, extra, or further. *I have no other gloves.* —*pron.* **1.** a different or additional person or thing. **2.** the remaining one. —*adv.* in a different way; otherwise.

over /ō′ vər/ *adv.* **1.** above. *A plane flew over our house.* **2.** across a space. *Toby walked over to meet us.* —*adj.* finished. *School is over at 3 o'clock.*

oys ter /oi′ stər/ *n.* an animal that has a soft body and a rough, hinged shell.

P

page /pāj/ *n., pl.* **pag es.** one side of a sheet of paper in a book.

pag eant /paj′ ənt/ *n.* a colorful celebration for an important event.

par al lel /par′ ə ləl′/ *adj.* being the same distance apart at all points. *Parallel lines never meet each other. The rails of a railroad track are parallel.*

/a/	at
/ā/	late
/â/	care
/ä/	father
/e/	set
/ē/	me
/i/	it
/ī/	kite
/o/	ox
/ō/	rose
/ô/	brought raw
/oi/	coin
/o͝o/	book
/o͞o/	too
/or/	form
/ou/	out
/u/	up
/yo͞o/	cube
/ûr/	turn germ learn firm work
/ə/	about chicken pencil cannon circus
/ch/	chair
/hw/	which
/ng/	ring
/sh/	shop
/th/	thin
/th̸/	there
/zh/	treasure

Speller Dictionary

parallelogram/pitcher

par al lel o gram /par′ ə ləl′ ə gram/ *n.* a flat figure with four sides. The opposite sides of a parallelogram are both equal in length and parallel.

par a site /par′ ə sīt/ *n.* an animal or plant that lives on or in another animal or plant.

park /pärk/ *n.* **1.** a piece of land, often having benches, trees, paths, and playgrounds, used by people for enjoyment and recreation. **2.** a large area of land that is left in its natural state by the government. —*v.* to leave an automobile or other vehicle in one place for a time. *We parked the car.*

paste /pāst/ *n.* something that makes papers stick together. —*v.* **past ed, past ing.** to make papers stick together with paste. *I will paste a picture into this book.*

path /path/ *n.* **1.** a trail or way for walking. *We had to shovel a path through the snow to our garage.* **2.** the line along which a person or thing moves. *The scientist traced the path of the comet.*

pause /pôz/ *n.* a short stop or rest. *After a pause because of rain, the game continued.* —*v.* to stop for a short time.

peace /pēs/ *n.* **1.** freedom from fighting or conflict. **2.** a lack of noise or disorder; quiet or calm. *My grandparents love the peace and quiet of the country.*

peach /pēch/ *n., pl.* **peach es.** a round, sweet fruit with a big pit inside. A peach is pink and yellow.

pear /pâr/ *n.* a sweet fruit, round at one end, and smaller toward the other end. Pears are usually yellow.

peb ble /peb′ əl/ *n.* a small stone.

pen cil /pen′ səl/ *n.* a long, thin tool for writing or drawing. —*v.* **pen ciled, pen cil ing.** to write, draw, or mark with a pencil.

pen nies /pen′ ēz/ *n.* the plural of **penny.**

pen ny /pen′ ē/ *n., pl.* **pen nies. 1.** a coin that is worth one cent. One hundred pennies equal one dollar. **2.** a British coin. One hundred pennies equal one pound.

peo ple /pē′ pəl/ *n., pl.* **peo ple** or **peo ples** (*for definition 2*). **1.** men, women, and children; persons. **2.** all of the persons making up a nation, race, tribe, or group. **3.** family; relatives. —*v.* **peo pled, peo pling.** to fill with people; inhabit. *A great number of human beings people the earth.*

pick /pik/ *n.* **1.** the best one or ones. **2.** an act of choosing; selection. *Take your pick of the books on the table.* **3.** a small thin piece of plastic or other material used to pluck the strings of a guitar or other instrument. **4.** a tool with a wooden handle and a metal head that is pointed at one end or both. Also called a **pick ax**. **5.** a pointed tool. —*v.* **1.** to take from a number offered; select or choose. **2.** to gather with the fingers. **3.** to remove with the fingers or something pointed. *Our dog loves to pick the meat off a bone.* **4.** to pull at and let go; pluck. **5.** to cause on purpose. *The bully picked a fight with me after school.*

piece /pēs/ *n.* **1.** a part that has been broken, cut, or torn from something, fragment. **2.** one of a group or set of similar things. *We're missing two chess pieces.* —*v.* **pieced, piec ing.** to join the parts or pieces of.

pi geon /pij′ ən/ *n.* a bird that has a plump body, a small head, and thick, soft feathers; dove.

pipe /pīp/ *n.* a tube through which things flow. A pipe can carry water or air from one place to another. *She blew air into the bubble pipe.*

pitch /pich/ *v.* **1.** to throw or toss. *We watched the farmer pitch grain into the barn.* **2.** to play the position of pitcher.

pitch er /pich′ ər/ *n.* **1.** a baseball player who throws the ball to the batter. **2.** a

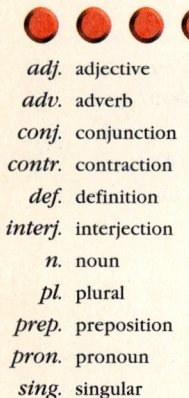

adj. adjective
adv. adverb
conj. conjunction
contr. contraction
def. definition
interj. interjection
n. noun
pl. plural
prep. preposition
pron. pronoun
sing. singular
v. verb

Speller Dictionary

container with a handle and a lip or spout. A pitcher is used for holding and pouring liquids.

place /plās/ *n.* **1.** a part of space; location; area. **2.** a home. **3.** a space or seat for a person. —*v.* **placed, plac ing. 1.** to put or be in a particular spot or location. **2.** to identify by connecting with the correct time and location. *I can't place you.* **to take place.** to happen, occur.

plan /plan/ *n.* **1.** a way of doing something that has been thought out ahead of time. **2.** something that a person intends to do. **3.** a drawing that shows how the parts of something are arranged. —*v.* **planned, plan ning. 1.** to think out a way of doing something ahead of time. **2.** to have an intention; intend. **3.** to make a drawing of.

plant /plant/ *n.* **1.** a living thing that, unlike animals, stays in one place, makes its own food, and has rigid cell walls. **2.** a building or group of buildings containing equipment used in making something. *A power plant produces electricity.* —*v.* **1.** to set or place in the ground so that it will take root and grow. **2.** to place or set firmly in position. —*adj.* pertaining to plants.

plate /plāt/ *n.* **1.** a flat or shallow dish. **2.** a flat, thin piece of metal. *Modern warships are covered with plates of steel.* **3.** a piece of metal on which something is or can be engraved. —*v.* **plat ed, plat ing.** to cover with a coat of silver, gold, or other metal.

play /plā/ *n.* **1.** activity that is done for fun or pleasure; sport. **2.** a move or turn in a game. *The quarterback made a great play.* **3.** a story that is written to be acted out on stage. —*v.* **1** to do something for fun or pleasure. **2.** to be in or have a game. **3.** to compete against in a game. *Our team played the champions in a chess tournament.* **4.** to make or cause to make music or other sounds. *I'm learning to play the piano.*

play ground /plā′ ground/ *n.* an outdoor area where children play.

please /plēz/ *v.* **pleased, pleas ing. 1.** to give pleasure to. *Breakfast in bed pleased my mother.* **2.** to want or prefer. *The children may buy whatever they please.* **3.** to be so kind as to. *Please give me some more beans.*

plumb /plum/ *n.* a weight at the end of a line used to measure how deep something is.

plunge /plunj/ *v.* **plunged, plung ing. 1.** to put in suddenly. *I plunged my hand into the water.* **2.** to dive or fall suddenly. *The swimmer plunged into the water.* —*n.* the act of plunging. *The campers enjoy an early morning plunge in the lake.*

point /point/ *n.* **1.** a fine, sharp end. **2.** the main idea, purpose. *What is the point of the joke?* —*v.* **point ed, point ing. 1.** to show where something is by aiming a finger or other thing at it. **2.** to aim; direct. *I pointed the telescope at the moon.*

poi son /poi′ zən/ *n.* a drug or other substance that harms or kills by chemical action. —*v.* **1.** to give poison to. **2.** to put poison in. **3.** to have a bad effect on. *The gossip poisoned their minds with lies.*

po lice /pə lēs′/ *n.* a group of persons given power by a government to keep order and enforce the law. —*v.* **po liced, po lic ing.** to keep order in.

pond /pond/ *n.* a body of water surrounded by land.

po nies /pō′ nēz/ *n.* the plural of **pony.**

po ny /pō′ nē/ *n., pl.* **po nies.** a small kind of horse.

pool /pool/ *n.* **1.** a game played with hard balls and a stick called a cue. **2.** an arrangement in which a number of people share something. **3.** a tank of water to swim in, indoors

/a/	at
/ā/	late
/â/	care
/ä/	father
/e/	set
/ē/	me
/i/	it
/ī/	kite
/o/	ox
/ō/	rose
/ô/	brought raw
/oi/	coin
/o͝o/	book
/o͞o/	too
/or/	form
/ou/	out
/u/	up
/yo͞o/	cube
/ûr/	turn germ learn firm work
/ə/	about chicken pencil cannon circus
/ch/	chair
/hw/	which
/ng/	ring
/sh/	shop
/th/	thin
/t͟h/	there
/zh/	treasure

porch/queen

or outdoors. **4.** a small body of still water. **5.** a small amount of any liquid. —*v.* to put into a common fund or group effort. *The children pooled their money.*

porch /porch/ *n., pl.* **porch es.** an area with a roof built onto the outside of a house by a door.

por poise /por′ pəs/ *n.* an animal that lives in the sea. The porpoise is a mammal and is related to the dolphin and whale.

pot ter /pot′ ər/ *n.* a person who makes pots, bowls, dishes, and other things from clay.

pouch /pouch/ *n., pl.* **pouch es.** a bag; sack. *The mail carrier took the letters out of a pouch.*

prat tle /prat′ əl/ *v.* **prat tled, prat tling.** to talk childishly or foolishly; babble.

press /pres/ *n., pl.* **press es. 1.** a pushing on something. *A press of the button started the elevator.* **2.** a machine for printing things; printing press. —*v.* **1.** to use force on something; push. **2.** to iron. *The tailor pressed the pants.*

prize /prīz/ *n.* something that is won in a contest or game. —*adj.* that has won or is good enough to win a prize. *He raised a prize calf for the fair.* —*v.* **prized, priz ing.** to think very highly of. *I prize this fossil because I found it myself.*

prized /prīzd/ *v.* past tense and past participle of **prize.** See **prize.**

proc ess /pros′ es/ *n.* a series of steps that are done in making something. *The process of making bread is simple but takes time.*

proud /proud/ *adj.* **1.** having a strong sense of satisfaction in a person or thing. *I am proud of the bookcase I made.* **2.** having self-respect.

prove /prōōv/ *v.* **proved, proved** or **prov en, prov ing.** to show that something is true. *Columbus wanted to prove that the world was round.*

pub lish /pub′ lish/ *v.* **pub lished, pub lish ing.** to put together books and magazines. *Dad's company is publishing a new comic book!*

pud dle /pud′ əl/ *n.* a small pool of water or other liquid that is not very deep.

pull /pŏŏl/ *n.* **1.** the work done or the force used in moving something by pulling it. **2.** the act of pulling something. —*v.* **1.** to grab or hold something and move it forward or toward oneself. **2.** to remove or tear out something. *The dentist had to pull my tooth.*

pul ley /pŏŏl′ ē/ *n., pl.* **pulleys.** a wheel with a groove around it that a rope or chain can be pulled over.

pup pies /pup′ ēz/ *n.* the plural of *puppy.*

pup py /pup′ ē/ *n., pl.* **pup pies.** a young dog.

puz zle /puz′ əl/ *n.* **1.** something that confuses. **2.** a toy, game, or object that presents a problem to solve. —*v.* **puz zled, puz zling. 1.** to confuse or be hard to understand. **2.** to think hard in order to answer or solve something. *I puzzled over the last question.* —*adj.* pertaining to a puzzle.

Q

quail /kwāl/ *n., pl.* **quails** or **quail.** a fat, wild bird. *People hunt quail for food.* —*adj.* pertaining to quail.

quar ter /kwor′ tər/ *n.* **1.** one of four equal parts. **2.** a coin of the U.S. and Canada equal to twenty-five cents or 1/4 of a dollar. **3.** the moment at the end of each fourth of an hour. —*v.* **1.** to divide into four equal units. **2.** to give a place to live.

quar tet /kwor′ tet/ *n.* a group of four singers or musicians performing together.

queen /kwēn/ *n.* **1.** the wife or widow of a king. **2.** a woman who rules a

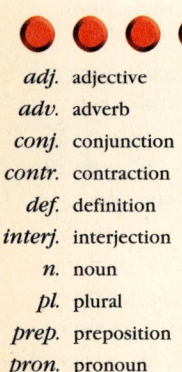

adj.	adjective
adv.	adverb
conj.	conjunction
contr.	contraction
def.	definition
interj.	interjection
n.	noun
pl.	plural
prep.	preposition
pron.	pronoun
sing.	singular
v.	verb

kingdom. **3.** a woman or thing that is beautiful or important. *Some people call that singer the queen of jazz.*

ques tion /kwes′ chən/ *n.* **1.** something asked in order to get an answer or find out something. **2.** a matter to be talked over. *The meeting dealt with the question of who would be the next president of the club.* —*v.* **1.** to ask questions of or about. **2.** to express doubt about.

quick /kwik/ *adj.* **1.** done or happening in a short time; fast. **2.** thinking, learning, or reacting easily and rapidly. *The child has a quick mind.*

qui et /kwī′ it/ *adj.* **1.** making little or no noise; without noise. **2.** with little or no disturbance or motion; not busy; peaceful. —*n.* the condition of being quiet. —*v.* to make or become quiet.

qui et ly /kwī′ ət lē/ *adv.* in a quiet way. *He walked quietly into the room so that no one heard him.*

quilt /kwilt/ *n.* a cover for a bed. It is two layers of cloth with something soft inside.

quit /kwit/ *v.* **quit** or **quit ted, quit ting. 1.** to stop doing something. **2.** to go away from; leave. *I may quit my job.* **3.** to give up or stop trying.

quite /kwīt/ *adv.* **1.** very much or completely. **2.** really; actually. *Climbing the mountain was quite an achievement.*

R

race /rās/ *n.* **1.** a contest to find out who is fastest. **2.** any contest. —*v.* **raced, rac ing. 1.** to take part in a contest of speed; be in a race against. **2.** to move or go very fast.

raft /raft/ *n.* a kind of flat boat made of logs or boards that have been fastened together.

rain bow /rān′ bō/ *n.* a curve of colored light seen in the sky when the sun shines through tiny drops of water in the air.

raise /rāz/ *n.* an increase in amount. —*v.* **raised, rais ing. 1.** to move or cause to move to a higher position, place, degree, or amount. **2.** to cause to rise or appear. *The bee sting raised a bump on the child's arm.* **3.** to gather together to collect. *The town raised money to build a new school.* **4.** to take care of and help to grow. *My parents raised four children.* **5.** to stir up; bring about. *Someone was raising a commotion in the hall.*

range /rānj/ *n., pl.* **ranges. 1.** the distance or extent between certain limits. **2.** the distance or area over which something can travel or extend. **3.** a large area of land on which livestock roam and graze. *The cowhands rounded up the cattle on the open range.* **4.** a row or series, especially of mountains. —*v.* **ranged, rang ing. 1.** to go between certain limits. *The class's scores on the math test ranged from 82 to 97.* **2.** to wander or roam.

rare /râr/ *adj.,* **rar er, rar est. 1.** not often happening, seen, or found. **2.** unusually fine; excellent. *The cliffs have a rare beauty.* **3.** cooked for only a short time. *Do you like your hamburgers rare?*

rasp ber ries /raz′ ber ēz/ *n.,* plural of **rasp ber ry.** a small, sweet fruit of a prickly plant.

re call /ri kôl′/ *v.* **recalled, recalling. 1.** to bring back to mind; remember. *Your face is familiar, but I don't recall your name.* **2.** to take or order back. *The auto maker recalled the defective cars.*

re cy cle /rē sī′ kel/ *v.* **re cy cled, re cy cling.** make available for reuse or renewal. *All the people in our town are recycling paper, plastic, and glass.*

re group /rē groop′/ *v.* to again form a group or unit. *Our club will regroup tomorrow.*

/a/ at
/ā/ late
/â/ care
/ä/ father
/e/ set
/ē/ me
/i/ it
/ī/ kite
/o/ ox
/ō/ rose
/ô/ brought
    raw
/oi/ coin
/o͝o/ book
/o͞o/ too
/or/ form
/ou/ out
/u/ up
/yo͞o/ cube
/ûr/ turn
    germ
    learn
    firm
    work
/ə/ about
    chicken
    pencil
    cannon
    circus
/ch/ chair
/hw/ which
/ng/ ring
/sh/ shop
/th/ thin
/t͟h/ there
/zh/ treasure

re turn /ri tûrn′/ v. **1.** to come or go back. **2.** to happen or take place again. *Winter returns every year.* **3.** to give or put back in the same way. —n. **1.** the act of returning. **2.** an amount of money made as a profit. *The returns from the cake sale were pleasing.*

re view /ri vyōō′/ v. to study, go over, or examine again. *I reviewed my notes.*

rice /rīs/ n. a grain that grows in warm, wet places. Rice is eaten by many people in the world.

right /rīt/ adj. **1.** correct or true; free from mistakes. **2.** just, moral, or good. **3.** on or toward the side of the body that is to the east when one is facing north. **4.** proper; suitable. —n. **1.** something that is just, moral, or good. **2.** a just, moral, or lawful claim. *Every citizen is guaranteed the right to free speech.* —adv. **1.** correctly. **2.** according to what is just, moral, or good. **3.** in a proper way; suitable. —v. to make good, just, or correct. *I righted the wrong.*

risk /risk/ n. a chance of loss or harm; danger. —v. to put in danger of loss or harm. *My parents risked losing money when they bought a store.*

road /rōd/ n. **1.** a strip of pavement or cleared ground that people or vehicles use to go from one place to another. **2.** a way for going or moving toward something wanted. *Many people helped him on his road to fame.*

roam /rōm/ v. **roamed, roaming.** to go around without any particular place to go; wander. *We roamed through the woods.*

Rome /rōm/ n. the capital of Italy, in the central part of the country.

root /rōot, rŏot/ n. **1.** the part of the plant that grows into the ground. **2.** a part where something begins; origin. —v. **1.** to develop roots and begin to grow. **2.** to fix or establish firmly. **3.** to dig in the earth with the snout. *The pig rooted about for food.* **4.** to search for something; rummage. **5.** to support a team or a person in a contest.

rot /rot/ v. **rot ted, rot ting.** to spoil; become bad. *Fruit rots if it is out too long.*

roy al /roi′ əl/ adj. **1.** of or having to do with the king or queen or their family. **2.** suitable for or like a king or queen or their family. *We were given a royal welcome.*

rub ber /rub′ ər/ n. **1.** a strong, elastic, waterproof substance that comes from the milky liquid in certain tropical trees. **2.** a short boot or overshoe that protects shoes from water.

rub ble /rub′ əl/ n. rough, broken pieces of stone, rock, or other solid material.

ruth less /rōoth′ lis/ adj. not having pity or mercy. *The dictator was a ruthless ruler.*

S

sack /sak/ n. a large bag that is made of coarse, strong material. —v. to steal all the valuable things from a town or city that has been captured in a war.

safe /sāf/ adj., **saf er, saf est.** free from harm or danger. *The baby was safe in his mother's arms.* —n. a place for keeping things safe.

said /sed/ v. past tense and past participle of **say.** *I said that I would like some more fruit.*

sail /sāl/ v. to move on the water in a boat. *They sail on the lake.*

sale /sāl/ n. **1.** an act of selling. *A clerk makes many sales.* **2.** the offering or selling of something for less than it usually costs. *This store is having a big sale.* **on sale** selling at a very low price. *The toy once sold for five dollars. Now it is on sale for two dollars.*

adj.	adjective
adv.	adverb
conj.	conjunction
contr.	contraction
def.	definition
interj.	interjection
n.	noun
pl.	plural
prep.	preposition
pron.	pronoun
sing.	singular
v.	verb

Sat ur day /sat′ ər dē, sat′ ər dā/ *n.* the seventh day of the week.

sauce /sôs/ *n.* **1.** a liquid or creamy mixture served with food. **2.** a food consisting of fruit that has been stewed.

sau sage /sô′ sij/ *n.* finely chopped meat that is mixed with spices. It is often stuffed into a thin case.

saw /sô/ *n.* a tool or machine that has a sharp metal blade with teeth. It is used for cutting wood, metal, or other hard materials. —*v.* **sawed, sawed** or **sawn, saw ing. 1.** to cut or be cut with a saw. *He will saw the wood for the clubhouse.* **2.** past tense of **see**, to look at with the eyes; view. *I see better with glasses. Who saw the helicopter?*

scare crow /skâr′ krō/ *n.* a figure of a person used to scare crows and other birds away from crops.

scat ter /skat′ ər/ *v.* **1.** to spread or throw about in various places. *The wind scattered the leaves all over the yard.* **2.** to cause to separate and go in different directions. *Loud thunder scattered the cattle.*

sca venge /skav′ ənj/ *v.* **scav enged. 1.** to find or collect by searching. **2.** to search (something) for material that can be used.

sca ven ger /skav′ ən jər/ *n.* a person who searches through trash for things that can be used or sold to others.

scent /sent/ *n.* **1.** a smell. **2.** the trail by which someone or something can be traced or found. —*v.* to sense by or as if by the sense of smell. *The dogs scented the rabbit.*

school /skōōl/ *n.* **1.** a place for teaching and learning. **2.** the students, teachers, and other people who work at such a place. **3.** the process of being educated at a school. —*v.* to train or teach. *Doctors must school themselves to handle emergencies.*

scold /skōld/ *v.* to find fault with; speak sharply to. *The teacher scolded the student.*

scoop /skōōp/ *n.* **1.** small shovel or cup-shaped utensil. *She dug a hole in the sand with a scoop.* **2.** the amount taken up in a scoop. —*v.* **1.** to gather with a sweeping motion. **2.** to dig out with a scoop. *He scooped up all the weeds in his yard.*

score /skor/ *v.* **scored, scor ing. 1.** to make a point or points in a game or test. **2.** to keep a record of points made or assign points in a game or test. **3.** to achieve or win. *You scored a great success by winning all three races.* —*n.* **1.** the points or a record of the points made in a game or on a test. **2.** a set or group of twenty. **3.** written or printed music. *She studied the score before the recital.*

scout /skout/ *n.* **1.** a person or thing sent out to gather and bring back information, such as a soldier, ship, or aircraft sent out during wartime to gather information about the enemy. **2.** a person who belongs to a scouting organization. —*v.* to look around for something. *We will scout the town for a good place to eat.*

scrub /skrub/ *v.* to rub hard to wash or clean. *His hands were so dirty, he had to scrub them.*

sea /sē/ *n.* **1.** the large body of salt water that covers almost three fourths of the earth's surface; ocean. **2.** a large part of this body of salt water, usually partly enclosed by land.

seam /sēm/ *n.* **1.** a line formed by sewing together the edges of two or more pieces of material. **2.** any mark or line like a seam.

sea sons /sē′ znz/ *n.* The four seasons of the year are winter, spring, summer, and fall.

sea son al /sē′ zə nəl/ *adj.* happening at a certain season. *The blooming of flowers is a seasonal event.*

/a/	at
/ā/	late
/â/	care
/ä/	father
/e/	set
/ē/	me
/i/	it
/ī/	kite
/o/	ox
/ō/	rose
/ô/	brought, raw
/oi/	coin
/ŏŏ/	book
/ōō/	too
/or/	form
/ou/	out
/u/	up
/yōō/	cube
/ûr/	turn, germ, learn, firm, work
/ə/	about, chicken, pencil, cannon, circus
/ch/	chair
/hw/	which
/ng/	ring
/sh/	shop
/th/	thin
/th/	there
/zh/	treasure

seed /sēd/ *n., pl.* **seeds** or **seed. 1.** the part of a flowering plant from which a new plant will grow. **2.** the source or cause of something. *A lack of sleep was the seed of my bad mood.* —*v.* **1.** to plant land with seeds. **2.** to take seeds out of. *The cook seeded the watermelon.*

seem /sēm/ *v.* **1.** to appear to be. *That book seems easy to read.* **2.** to appear to oneself. *I seem to have forgotten your name.*

seen /sēn/ *v.* past participle of **see.**

send /send/ *v.* **sent, send ing. 1.** to cause to go from one place to another. **2.** to cause to go, come, or be. *Send a reply to the letter.*

sent /sent/ *v.* past tense and past participle of **send.** *I sent a package to my neighbors.* See **send.**

sen tence /sen′ təns/ *n.* **1.** a group of words that gives a complete thought. **2.** a punishment for crime set by a court. —*v.* **sen tenced, sen tenc ing.** to set the punishment of. *The judge sentenced her to ten days in jail.*

Sep tem ber /sep tem′ bər/ *n.* the ninth month of the year. September has 30 days.

ser vice /sûr′ vis/ *n., pl.* **services. 1.** use or help. *"How may I be of service to you?" said the salesperson.* **2.** a system or way of giving something. *The service in this restaurant is very slow.*

set tle ment /set′ əl mənt/ *n.* **1.** a small village or group of houses. *During the 1800s, pioneers built many settlements in the American West.* **2.** a colony. *Part of Canada was once a French settlement.*

sev en /sev′ ən/ *n. and adj.* one more than six; 7.

sew /sō/ *v.* **sewed, sewed** or **sewn, sew ing.** to make, fasten, or close things with a needle and thread. *Sew the button on your shirt.*

shake /shāk/ *v.* **shook, shak en, shak ing. 1.** to move quickly up and down, back and forth, or from side to side. *Shake the bottle to mix the salad dressing.* **2.** to remove or throw by moving up and down or from side to side. *The dog shook the water from its coat.* —*n.* the act of shaking. *The child scared the dog away with a shake of a big stick.*

sha king /shāk′ ing/ *v.* a form of **shake.** It is used with a helping word. *She was shaking the tree to make the ripe apples fall down.* See **shake.**

sham poo /sham pōō′/ *n.* **1.** a special soap used to wash hair, rugs, or furniture coverings. **2.** an act of washing with shampoo. —*v.* to wash hair, rugs, or furniture coverings with a special soap.

shan't /shant/ *contr.* shortened form of "shall not."

share /shâr/ *n.* **1.** the part that is given or belongs to one person. *My share of the bill came to three dollars.* **2.** one of the equal parts into which the ownership of a company or business is divided. —*v.* **shared, shar ing. 1.** to use with another or others. *Two of us shared a tent.* **2.** to divide into portions and give to others as well as to oneself. *I shared my sandwich.* **3.** to have a share; take part.

share hold er /shâr′ hōl dər/ *n.* another word for stockholder; someone who owns part of a corporation.

sharp /shärp/ *adj.* **1.** having an edge or point that cuts or pierces easily. **2.** having a pointed end, not rounded. **3.** harsh or biting. *The strong cheese had a sharp taste.* —*adv.* **1.** at the moment that is mentioned and not any other. *We must leave at ten o'clock sharp.* **2.** in a sharp manner. —*n.* a tone or note in music that is one half note above its natural pitch.

she /shē/ *pron.* a female person or animal that is being talked about. —*n.* a female person or animal. *Is the puppy a she or a he?*

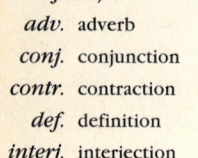

adj.	adjective
adv.	adverb
conj.	conjunction
contr.	contraction
def.	definition
interj.	interjection
n.	noun
pl.	plural
prep.	preposition
pron.	pronoun
sing.	singular
v.	verb

she'd /shēd/ *contr.* **1.** shortened form of "she had." **2.** shortened form of "she would."

she'll /shēl/ *contr.* **1.** shortened form of "she will." **2.** shortened form of "she shall."

she's /shēz/ *contr.* **1.** shortened form of "she is." *She's late this morning.* **2.** shortened form of "she has." *She's been doing her homework.*

shine /shīn/ *v.* **shone** or **shined, shin ing. 1.** to give or reflect light. *The stars shine at night.* **2.** to be or make bright. *Their faces shone with happiness.* —*n.* **1.** light or brightness. *The silver has a nice shine.* **2.** the act of polishing.

shin ing /shīn′ ing/ *v.* a form of **shine.** It is used with a helping word. *The sun was shining.* See **shine.**

shirt /shûrt/ *n.* a piece of clothing worn on the upper part of the body, often having a collar, sleeves, and buttoned front.

shoe /sho͞o/ *n.* an outer covering for the foot.

shoot /sho͞ot/ *n.* a new or young plant or stem; sprout. —*v.* **shot, shoot ing. 1.** to hit with a bullet, arrow, or the like. **2.** to move or cause to move fast. **3.** to come forth; sprout; grow. *The bean plants are shooting up from the ground.* **4.** to cause a weapon to send forth bullets, arrows, or the like; fire. **5.** to photograph or film, as for television or a motion picture.

short /shôrt/ *adj.* **1.** not long or tall. **2.** not having or being enough. —*adv.* **1.** in a sudden or unexpected way; suddenly. *The horse stopped short.* **2.** not quite up to. —*n.* **1.** a short circuit. **2. shorts.** pants that are worn above the knee.

shot /shot/ *v.* the past tense and past participle of *shoot.* See **shoot.** —*n.* **1.** a tiny ball that comes out of a fired gun. *The shot hit the target.* **2.** an injection given with a needle or syringe. **3.** an aim or stroke in certain games.

should /sho͝od/ *v.* ought to. *You should do your homework.*

should n't /sho͝od′ ənt/ *contr.* shortened form of "should not." *You shouldn't play in the street.*

should 've /sho͝od′ əv/ *contr.* shortened form of "should have." *I really should've gone with you.*

shout /shout/ *n.* a loud call; yell. *I gave a shout when I found the lost puppy.* —*v.* to call loudly; yell.

shrewd ness /shro͞od′ nes/ *n.* cleverness or skillfulness. *The boys' shrewdness helped them escape safely.*

shut /shut/ *v.* **shut, shut ting. 1.** to move something so as to block or cover up an entrance or opening; close. **2.** to become closed. **3.** to confine. *The dog was shut inside.*

shut tle /shut′ əl/ *n.* a device on a loom. It carries yarn back and forth through the yarn strung on the loom.

sick /sik/ *adj.* **1.** suffering from a disease or having poor health; ill. **2.** having to do with sickness or illness. **3.** upset; disturbed.

side walk /sīd′ wôk/ *n.* a path by a side of a street or road where people can walk.

sigh /sī/ *n.* the act or sound of sighing. —*v.* **1.** to make a long, deep breathing sound because of sadness, tiredness, or relief. **2.** to make a sound like this. *The wind sighed through the trees.*

sight /sīt/ *n.* **1.** the power or ability to see. **2.** the act of seeing. *I recognized you at first sight.* **3.** the range or distance a person can see. **4.** the presence of something in the range that a person can see. *The sight of strangers frightened the baby.* **5.** something that is unpleasant, funny, or odd to look at. *You're a sight in that hat.* —*v.* to see with the eyes. *The hawk sighted its prey down in the valley.*

since /sins/ *adv.* **1.** from a particular time in the past until now. **2.** at some time between a particular time in the

/a/	at
/ā/	late
/â/	care
/ä/	father
/e/	set
/ē/	me
/i/	it
/ī/	kite
/o/	ox
/ō/	rose
/ô/	brought raw
/oi/	coin
/o͝o/	book
/o͞o/	too
/or/	form
/ou/	out
/u/	up
/yo͞o/	cube
/ûr/	turn germ learn firm work
/ə/	about chicken pencil cannon circus
/ch/	chair
/hw/	which
/ng/	ring
/sh/	shop
/th/	thin
/th/	there
/zh/	treasure

sinew/soft

past until now. **3.** before now; ago. *Our neighbors have long since moved away.* —*prep.* during the time after. *My parents had been gone since noon.* —*conj.* **1.** during the period after. *I haven't seen the twins since March.* **2.** for the reason that; because.

sin ew /sin′ yōō/ *n.* a strong cord or band of tissue that joins a muscle to a bone; a tendon. The sinews make it possible for the muscles to move an arm, leg, or other part of the body.

sin gle /sing′ gəl/ *adj.* **1.** only one. **2.** to be used by one person only. *The traveler asked for a single room at the hotel.* —*n.* a hit in baseball or softball that allows the batter to reach first base safely. —*v.* **sin gled, sin gling. 1.** to pick or choose from others. *They singled out the black cat as their favorite.* **2.** to hit a single in a baseball or softball game.

sink /singk/ *v.* **sank** or **sunk, sunk** or **sunk en, sink ing. 1.** to go down or cause to go down partly or completely below a surface. **2.** to become less. **3.** to go or cause to go through or into deeply. *The rain sank into the soil.* —*n.* a basin of metal, porcelain, or other material that is used to hold water.

sir loin /sûr′ loin/ *n.* a cut of beef from the upper part of the loin.

sis ter /sis′ tər/ *n.* the daughter of the same parents or parent.

six /siks/ *n.,* and *adj., pl.* **six es.** one more than five; 6.

skate /skāt/ *n.* **1.** a special shoe with a metal runner attached to the sole; ice skate. **2.** a special shoe with small wheels attached to the sole; roller skate. —*v.* **skat ed, skat ing.** to glide on skates. **skat ed** /skāt′ ed/ *v.* past tense and past participle of **skate**.

skat ing /skāt′ ing/ *v.* a form of **skate**. It is used with a helping word. *We were skating in the park.* See **skate.** —*adj.* pertaining to skating.

slip pers /slip′ ərz/ *n.* the plural of *slipper.* Low shoes that slip on the feet. *He walks around the house in slippers.*

small /smôl/ *n.* a narrow part. *Don't strain the small of your back while lifting the package.* —*adj.* **1.** not large; little. *A mouse is a small animal.* **2.** not important. *We had a small problem trying to decide who should drive.*

smell /smel/ *n.* **1.** the sense by which odors are recognized. **2.** an odor or scent. *I love the smell of the sea.* —*v.* **smelled** or **smelt, smell ing. 1.** to sense an odor by using the nose. **2.** to test or sample by smelling; sniff.

smile /smīl/ *n.* an expression of the face that is made by turning up the corners of the mouth. —*v.* **smiled, smil ing.** to have or give a smile. *The children smiled when they saw the clown.*

smil ing /smīl′ ing/ *v.* a form of **smile**. It is used with a helping word. *The happy baby is smiling.* See **smile.**

snatch /snach/ *v.* to grab suddenly or quickly.

so /sō/ *adv.* **1.** to this or that extent. *It was so cold that we stayed indoors.* **2.** very. *I am so glad.* —*adj.* true. —*conj.* for the purpose that. *Please turn off the lights so I can go to sleep.* —*pron.* **1.** more or less. **2.** the same. *That is a lazy dog and will always be so.* —*interj.* used to express or introduce another thought.

soap /sōp/ *n.* a substance used for washing and cleaning. —*v.* to rub or cover with soap.

soc cer /sok′ ər/ *n.* a game in which two teams of eleven try to move a round ball into a goal by striking it with any part of their bodies except the hands and arms.

sock /sok/ *n.* a knitted or woven cloth covering for the foot and the lower leg.

soft /sôft/ *adj.* **soft er, soft est. 1.** easy to shape; not hard. *The soft clay was*

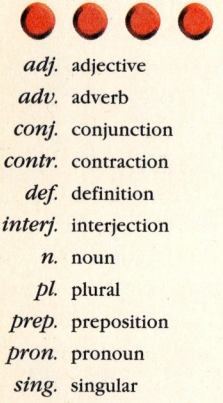

adj.	adjective
adv.	adverb
conj.	conjunction
contr.	contraction
def.	definition
interj.	interjection
n.	noun
pl.	plural
prep.	preposition
pron.	pronoun
sing.	singular
v.	verb

Speller Dictionary

easy to mold. **2.** smooth to the touch; not rough. **3.** gentle, not harsh or sharp. *The soft breeze felt warm.*

soil /soil/ *n.* **1.** the top part of the ground in which plants grow; dirt; earth. **2.** a country or land. *The U.S. has fought in many wars on foreign soil.* —*v.* to make or become dirty. *White clothes soil easily.*

sold /sōld/ *v.* past tense and past participle of **sell,** to give in exchange for money. *He sold the book for two dollars.*

some /sum/ *adj.* **1.** being one or ones not named or known. *Some birds cannot fly.* **2.** being of a number or amount that is not stated. *Have some dessert.* —*pron.* a number or amount that is not stated. *Please eat some of the salad.* —*adv.* approximately; about. *The club has some forty members.*

son /sun/ *n.* a male offspring or adopted child.

soon /sōōn/ *adv.* **1.** in a short time. **2.** before the expected time; early. **3.** without a delay; quickly.

sound /sound/ *adj.* **1.** strong and healthy. **2.** free from any damage, flaw, decay, or weakness. **3.** based on facts, truth, or good sense; sensible. —*adv.* deeply and completely. *The baby is sound asleep.* —*n.* **1.** what can be heard. **2.** one of the noises that make up human speech. —*v.* **1.** to make or cause to make a noise. **2.** to seem to be.

south /south/ *n.* **1.** the direction to the right when you face east. **2.** any region or place that is in this direction. —*adj.* and —*adv.* toward the south. *Many birds travel south in the winter.* **3. South.** the southern region of the U.S.

space ship /spās′ ship/ *n.* something in which people travel to go to outer space.

space walk /spās′ wôk/ *v.* to make movements in outer space outside a spacecraft.

spade /spād/ *n.* a tool used to dig. *Barbara used a spade to dig holes for her new spring plants.*

spare /spâr/ *v.* **spared, spar ing. 1.** to not hurt or injure; show mercy to. **2.** to give or get along without. *Can you spare a dollar?* **3.** to have remaining as extra or not used. —*adj.,* **spar er, spar est. 1.** more than is needed; extra. **2.** small in amount or quantity. —*n.* **1.** one or an amount of something that is extra. **2.** the knocking down of all the pins in bowling with two rolls of the ball.

speed /spēd/ *n.* **1.** quick or fast motion. **2.** the rate of motion. *He drove the car at a speed of forty miles per hour.* —*v.* **sped** or **speed ed, speed ing. 1.** to go or cause to go quickly or rapidly. **2.** to drive faster than is safe or lawful.

spell /spel/ *n.* **1.** a word or words supposed to have magic power. **2.** the power to attract or delight greatly. *It was hard to resist the spell of the beautiful music.* **3.** a period of time. *Sit and rest for a short spell.* —*v.* **spelled** or **spelt, spell ing. 1.** to take a person's place at doing something for a time. *If you're tired, I'll spell you at mowing the lawn.* **2.** to write or say the letters of a word in the right order. **3.** to mean. *The player's injury spelled defeat for the team.*

spent /spent/ *v.* past tense and past participle of **spend,** to pay money. —*adj.* worn-out; exhausted. *a spent runner.*

sphere /sfir/ *n.* a round body like a ball. All the points on the surface of a sphere are the same distance from its center.

spill /spil/ *n.* **1.** an act or instance of spilling or the amount spilled. **2.** a tumble or fall. —*v.* **spilled** or **spilt, spill ing. 1.** to make or let something fall, run out, or flow. *The child spilled milk on the tablecloth.* **2.** to fall or flow

/a/	at
/ā/	late
/â/	care
/ä/	father
/e/	set
/ē/	me
/i/	it
/ī/	kite
/o/	ox
/ō/	rose
/ô/	brought raw
/oi/	coin
/ŏŏ/	book
/ōō/	too
/or/	form
/ou/	out
/u/	up
/yōō/	cube
/ûr/	turn germ learn firm work
/ə/	about chicken pencil cannon circus
/ch/	chair
/hw/	which
/ng/	ring
/sh/	shop
/th/	thin
/ŧh/	there
/zh/	treasure

out. *The words spilled from his mouth with great emotion.*

spin /spin/ *v.* **spun, spin ning. 1.** to turn around quickly. **2.** to make thin fibers into thread. **3.** to feel dizzy. —*n.* **1.** a quick, turning motion. **2.** a quick ride. *I took a spin on my bicycle.*

splash /splash/ *v.* **splashed, splash ing. 1.** to throw water or other liquid about. **2.** to fall, strike, or move with the throwing about of water. *The diver splashed into the pool.* —*n.* **1.** the act or sound of throwing water about. **2.** a spot of water or other liquid, or a spot of color. *The black horse had a splash of white on its nose.*

splat ter /splat′ ər/ *v.* another word for *spatter,* to scatter in or splash with small drops or bits.

splen did /splen′ did/ *adj.* **1.** very beautiful or magnificent. **2.** very good; excellent.

splint /splint/ *n.* an arrangement of plastic or wood that keeps something in place. *She wore a splint around her broken finger.*

splin ter /splin′ tər/ *n.* a thin, sharp piece broken off from something hard or brittle. —*v.* to break into thin, sharp pieces.

split /split/ *v.* **split, split ting.** to break into parts. *He split the wood with an ax.*

splurge /splûrj/ *v.* **splurged, splurg ing.** to spend money with no attention to cost; to spend too much money.

spoil /spoil/ *n.* property that has been seized by force. *The soldiers carried away jewels and other spoils from the conquered city.* —*v.* to become so bad it cannot be eaten. *The meat will spoil.* —*v.* **spoiled** or **spoilt, spoil ing.** to damage or hurt in some way.

spoke /spōk/ *n.* one of the rods or bars that connect the rim of a wheel to a hub. —*v.* past tense of **speak,** to use or utter words; talk. *I spoke to them yesterday.*

sponge /spunj/ *n.* **1.** a simple water animal that has a body that is full of holes and absorbs water easily. **2.** a cleaning pad that looks like the skeleton of a sponge colony. —*v.* **sponged, spong ing.** to clean with a sponge. *We sponged the dirty walls.*

sport /sport/ *n., pl.* **sports. 1.** a game in which a person is physically active and often is competing with someone else. **2.** amusement; fun. *They collect butterflies for sport.* —*v.* to amuse oneself; play. *We watched the colts sporting in the field.*

spot /spot/ *n.* **1.** a mark or stain left by dirt, food, or other matter. **2.** a mark or area on something that is different from the rest. **3.** a place. —*v.* **spot ted, spot ting. 1.** to mark or be marked with a stain or blot. **2.** to see; recognize. *I spotted you in the crowd.*

spray /sprā/ *n.* the water that goes through the air in little drops. *A spray came out of the hose.* —*v.* to sprinkle liquid on. —**spray er,** *n.*

spread /spred/ *v.* **spread, spread ing. 1.** to open wide or stretch out. **2.** to put or make a thin layer or covering on. *I spread peanut butter on my toast.* **3.** to scatter or reach out over an area; extend. *The fire spread through the house.* —*n.* **1.** the act of spreading. **2.** the amount or extent to which something opens wide. *The spread of the robin's wings was 15 inches.* **3.** a bedcover.

spring /spring/ *v.* **sprang** or **sprung, sprung, spring ing. 1.** to move forward or jump up quickly; leap. **2.** to come or appear suddenly. *The words sprang from my lips.* —*n.* **1.** a jump or leap. **2.** the season of the year that comes between winter and summer. **3.** a spiral-shaped piece of metal that regains its shape after being compressed.

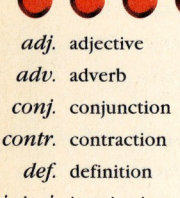

adj.	adjective
adv.	adverb
conj.	conjunction
contr.	contraction
def.	definition
interj.	interjection
n.	noun
pl.	plural
prep.	preposition
pron.	pronoun
sing.	singular
v.	verb

sprin kle /spring′ kəl/ v. **1.** to scatter something in small drops or bits. *We sprinkled sugar on the cookies.* **2.** to scatter small drops of liquid on; to rain gently. —n. **1.** a light rain. **2.** a small quantity of something; sprinkling.

sprock et /sprok′ it/ n. a part on a wheel that engages a chain.

sprout /sprout/ n. a young shoot from a seed or plant. *The sprouts grew into new leaves.* —v. to begin to grow. *The garden vegetables began to sprout.*

spruce /sproos/ n. a tree with cones and short leaves shaped like needles. —v. to fix up or make better-looking.

spy /spī/ n., pl. **spies.** a person who watches others secretly. —v. **spied, spy ing. 1.** to watch others secretly; act as a spy. **2.** to catch sight of; spot. *The sailor spied a ship on the horizon.*

square /skwâr/ n. **1.** a figure having four sides that are all the same length and four right angles. **2.** something having the shape of a square. **3.** an open space in a city or town. —adj., **squar er, squar est. 1.** having four sides that are all the same length and four right angles. **2.** shaped somewhat like a cube. **3.** forming a right angle. *This desk has square corners.* —v. **squared, squar ing. 1.** to make into the form of a right angle. **2.** to mark in a square or squares. —adv. **square ly** directly and firmly. *The truck hit the car squarely.*

squash /skwosh/ n. **1.** any of several vegetables of various shapes that grow on vines. Squashes are usually yellow, orange, or green. **2.** a game somewhat like tennis and handball. —v. **1.** to squeeze or press into a soft or flat mass; crush. **2.** to force or squeeze into a small area.

squawk /skwok/ n. **1.** a shrill, harsh cry, such as one made by a frightened chicken. **2.** a complaint. —v. to make such a sound or complaint.

squeak /skwēk/ n. a short, thin, high sound or cry. *We heard the squeak of the rusty hinges.* —v. to make a short, thin, high sound or cry. *The mouse squeaked.*

squeal /skwēl/ v. to make a loud, shrill cry or sound. *The child squealed with delight.* —n. a loud, shrill cry or sound. *There was a squeal of brakes.*

squeeze /skwēz/ v. **1.** to press hard. *Squeeze the tube of toothpaste.* **2.** to get by squeezing or by putting on pressure. **3.** to force by pushing or shoving. *The rabbit could barely squeeze through the opening.* —n. the act of squeezing.

squid /skwid/ n., pl. **squids** or **squid.** a sea animal that has ten long arms.

squig gle /skwig′ əl/ n. a wavy or twisting line; wriggly mark or twist. *I made squiggles in my pad.*

squint /skwint/ v. to partly close the eyes. *The bright sunlight made me squint.*

squir rel /skwûr′ əl/ n. a small animal with a long, bushy tail. Squirrels live in trees and feed mainly on nuts.

squirt /skwûrt/ v. **1.** to force liquid in a thin stream through a narrow opening. *The worker squirted oil on the rusty hinge.* **2.** to come out in a thin stream. *Ink squirted from the fountain pen.* —n. the act of squirting or the amount squirted.

stack /stak/ n. **1.** a large, neat pile of hay, straw, or grain. **2.** a number of things piled up one on top of the other; pile. —v. to pile or arrange in a stack.

stage /stāj/ n., pl. **stages. 1.** a raised platform on which people perform. **2.** a place where something important takes place. **3.** a single step, period, or degree in a process or development. *During the last stage of their journey, the explorers had very little food left.* —v. **staged, stag ing.** to plan, put on,

/a/	at
/ā/	late
/â/	care
/ä/	father
/e/	set
/ē/	me
/i/	it
/ī/	kite
/o/	ox
/ō/	rose
/ô/	brought raw
/oi/	coin
/o͝o/	book
/o͞o/	too
/or/	form
/ou/	out
/u/	up
/yo͞o/	cube
/ûr/	turn germ learn firm work
/ə/	about chicken pencil cannon circus
/ch/	chair
/hw/	which
/ng/	ring
/sh/	shop
/th/	thin
/th/	there
/zh/	treasure

or present. *The actors staged a wonderful production.*

stain /stān/ *n.* **1.** a mark or spot. **2.** a cause of shame or dishonor. *They vowed to wipe out the stain on their family's reputation.* **3.** a dye or other substance used to color something. —*v.* **1.** to spot or soil. **2.** to color with a dye or something like a dye. **3.** to bring shame or dishonor to.

stair /stâr/ *n.* **1. stairs.** a set of steps for going from one level or floor to another. **2.** a step in such a set.

stair way /stâr′ wā/ *n.* a staircase.

stamp /stamp/ *n.* **1.** a small piece of paper that is stuck on letters or packages to show that a mailing fee has been paid. **2.** a tool for cutting, shaping, or pressing a design, numbers, or letters on paper, wax, metal, or other material. *The librarian used a rubber stamp to put the date on the library card.* **3.** a bringing down of one's foot with force. —*v.* **1.** to bring down one's foot or feet with force. *The spoiled children stamped their feet in anger.* **2.** to mark with a tool that makes or prints a design, numbers, or letters. **3.** to put a postage stamp on.

stare /stâr/ *v.* **stared, star ing.** to look very hard or long with eyes wide open. —*n.* a long, fixed look with eyes wide open.

sta tion ar y /stā′ shə ner′ ē/ *adj.* not moving. *Traffic leaving the resort was nearly stationary.*

stay /stā/ *v.* **1.** to wait in one place; not leave; remain. **2.** to continue being. *We stayed friends for many years.* —*n.* a visit or stop. *After a brief stay at the seashore, they returned home.*

stew /stoo, styoo/ *v.* to cook by boiling slowly. *Stew the meat until it is done.* —*n.* the food cooked by boiling slowly. *The stew had chicken and beans in it.*

stew ard ess /styoo′ ər dis / *n., pl.* **stewardesses.** a woman who serves passengers on an airplane.

sting /sting/ *v.* **stung, sting ing. 1.** to prick or wound with a small, sharp point. **2.** to have or cause to have sharp, burning pain or hurt. —*n.* **1.** a sharp, pointed part of an insect or animal; stinger. **2.** a wound made by a stinger. **3.** a sharp, burning pain.

stitch /stich/ *n., pl.* **stitch es. 1.** one complete movement made with a needle and thread. **2.** any similar movement made with a needle and thread or yarn in knitting, crocheting, and embroidering. —*v.* to make, fasten, or mend with stitches; sew.

stock hold er /stok′ hōl′ dər/ *n.* a person who owns stock in a company or corporation; shareholder.

stock ing /stok′ ing/ *n.* a sheer, snug covering for the foot and leg.

store /stor/ *n.* **1.** a place where goods are sold. **2.** things put away for future use. *A store of firewood.* —*v.* **stored, stor ing.** to put away for future use.

storm /storm/ *n.* **1.** strong wind with heavy rain, hail, sleet, or snow. **2.** a sudden, strong outburst. *The baby's storm of tears made us worry.* —*v.* **1.** to blow hard with rain, hail, sleet, or snow. **2.** to rush with violence and anger. *After the argument, he stormed up the stairs.* **3.** to attack violently. *The army stormed the castle.*

sto ry /stor′ ē/ *n., pl.* **sto ries. 1.** an account of something that happened. **2.** an account made up to entertain people. **3.** a lie. **4.** a level or floor of a building.

sto ry tell er /stor′ ē tel′ ər/ *n.* a person who tells a story.

strad dle /strad′ əl/ *v.* **strad dled, strad dling. 1.** to sit, stand, or walk with one leg on each side of. *The cowboy straddled the horse.* **2.** to

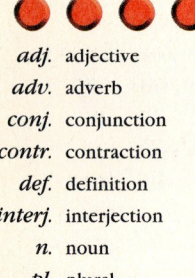

adj.	adjective
adv.	adverb
conj.	conjunction
contr.	contraction
def.	definition
interj.	interjection
n.	noun
pl.	plural
prep.	preposition
pron.	pronoun
sing.	singular
v.	verb

appear to favor both sides of an issue. —*n.* the act of straddling.

straight /strāt/ *adj.* **1.** not bent, curved, or crooked. **2.** in proper order. **3.** direct and truthful; honest; upright. —*adv.* **1.** in a straight way. **2.** without delay. *We went straight home from school.*

strain /strān/ *v.* **1.** to draw or pull tight; pull with force. **2.** to hurt or weaken by using too much or stretching too far. *I strained my eyes reading in dim light.* **3.** to use or drive to the utmost. *The porter strained every muscle to lift the heavy trunk.* —*n.* **1.** great force of weight. **2.** a hurt; injury. **3.** harmful pressure caused by worry or too much work; stress; tension. **4.** line of descent or ancestors. **5.** a characteristic or tendency that is inherited.

strange /strānj/ *adj.*, **strang er, strang est. 1.** odd or unusual. **2.** not familiar. *We heard a strange voice on the telephone.* **3.** ill at ease; uncomfortable.

strap /strap/ *n.* a long strip of leather, cloth, or other material used to hold things together or in place. —*v.* **strapped, strap ping.** to fasten or hold with a strap.

strat o sphere /strat′ ə sfir/ *n.* the layer of the earth's atmosphere that begins about 8 miles (13 kilometers) above the earth and ends about 30 miles (50 kilometers) above the earth.

stra tus /strā′ təs, strat′ əs/ *n., pl.* **stra ti** /strā′ tī, strat′ ī/ or **stra tus.** a low, grayish, watery cloud having a foggy appearance.

straw ber ry /strô′ ber ē, strô′ bə rē/ *n., pl.* **straw ber ries.** a sweet, red fruit of a plant that grows close to the ground.

streak /strēk/ *n.* **1.** a long, thin mark. *Streaks of lightning flashed across the sky.* **2.** a short period of time or brief series. *Our team's winning streak ended.* —*v.* **1.** to mark with streaks. **2.** to move at great speed.

stream /strēm/ *n.* **1.** a body of flowing water. **2.** a steady flow of movement. *A stream of people came out of the theater.* —*v.* **1.** to move steadily; flow. **2.** to wave or float. *The school banners streamed in the wind.*

street /strēt/ *n.* a public way in a town or city, often with sidewalks and buildings on both sides.

street light /strēt′ līt/ *n.* a light on a street or road.

strike /strīk/ *v.* **struck, struck** or **strick en, strik ing. 1.** to give a blow to; hit. **2.** to make an impression on. **3.** to set on fire by rubbing or hitting. *You must strike the match against the matchbook.* —*n.* **1.** the stopping of work. **2.** a sudden discovery. *The gold strike made them rich.* **3.** in baseball, a pitched ball that the batter swings at and misses or hits foul, or a pitched ball that passes through the strike zone.

string /string/ *n.* **1.** a thin line of twisted threads or wire. **2.** something like a string. *The violinist needs new strings for his violin.* **3. strings.** musical instruments with strings. —*v.* **strung, string ing. 1.** to put on a string. **2.** to provide with strings. *I strung my guitar.* **3.** to stretch from one place to another.

Stro ga noff /strō′ gə nôf′, strô′ —/ *n.* a dish usually of beef sliced and cooked with chopped onions, mushrooms, seasoning, and sour cream.

strong /strông/ *adj.* **1.** having much power, force, or energy; full of strength. *The strong winds damaged trees and buildings.* **2.** able to resist; firm. *The house has strong walls.*

stum ble /stum′ bəl/ *v.* **stum bled, stum bling. 1.** to lose one's balance; trip. **2.** to move or speak in a clumsy way. **3.** to discover by chance. *The detective stumbled on a clue.*

/a/	at
/ā/	late
/â/	care
/ä/	father
/e/	set
/ē/	me
/i/	it
/ī/	kite
/o/	ox
/ō/	rose
/ô/	brought raw
/oi/	coin
/o͝o/	book
/o͞o/	too
/or/	form
/ou/	out
/u/	up
/yo͞o/	cube
/ûr/	turn germ learn firm work
/ə/	about chicken pencil cannon circus
/ch/	chair
/hw/	which
/ng/	ring
/sh/	shop
/th/	thin
/th̷/	there
/zh/	treasure

sum /sum/ *n.* the number that results from adding two or more numbers together. *The sum of 6 plus 8 is 14.*

sum mer /sum′ ər/ *n.* the season of the year that comes between spring and autumn. —*v.* to spend the summer. *The family will summer in the mountains.*

Sun day /sun′ dē, sun′ dā/ *n.* the first day of the week.

sun rise /sun′ rīz/ *n.* the time of day when the sun first appears. *At sunrise, it becomes light outside.*

sun set /sun′ set/ *n.* the time of day when the sun last appears; the close of day. *At sunset, it becomes dark.*

sup per /sup′ ər/ *n.* the last meal of the day.

sur ger y /sûr′ jə rē/ *n.* an operation performed by a surgeon.

sur prise /sər prīz′, sûr prīz′/ *v.* **sur prised, sur pris ing. 1.** to cause to feel sudden wonder or amazement. **2.** to find suddenly and unexpectedly. *One morning we surprised two deer in our backyard.* —*n.* **1.** a feeling of wonder or amazement caused by something unexpected. **2.** something that causes surprise.

sweat er /swet′ ər/ *n.* a warm, knitted piece of clothing worn over the upper part of the body.

sweat shop /swet′ shop/ *n.* a place where people work long hours for little money.

swift /swift/ *adj.* **1.** moving or able to move very quickly. **2.** happening quickly; quick. *The frog made a swift leap.* —*n.* a bird with narrow wings and dark gray, brown, or bluish feathers.

switch /swich/ *n., pl.* **switch es. 1.** a long, thin stick or rod used for whipping. **2.** stroke or lash. *The cow brushed flies off with a switch of its tail.* **3.** a device used to open or close an electric circuit. —*v.* **1.** to strike with a switch. **2.** to move or swing with a quick motion. *The cat switched its tail.* **3.** to connect or disconnect by means of a switch. *Please switch on the lights.*

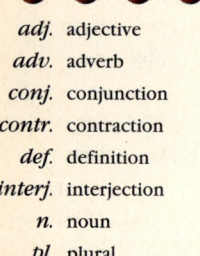

Taft, William Howard /taft/ 1857–1930, twenty-seventh president of the United States (1909–1913), chief justice of the U.S. Supreme Court (1921–1930).

tal ler /tôl′ ər/ *adj.* of more than average height; not short or low.

tan gle /tan′ gəl/ *v.* **tan gled, tan gling.** to twist together in a confused way. —*n.* a twisted, confused mass.

tapped /tapt/ *v.* past form of *tap*, to hit lightly. *He tapped the lid.*

taught /tôt/ *v.* past tense and past participle of **teach.** *I taught my cousin how to play volleyball.* See **teach.**

teach /tēch/ *v.* **taught, teach ing.** to help a person to learn; show how.

ter ri ble /ter′ ə bəl/ *adj.* **1.** causing fear or terror; awful. *The volcano erupted with a terrible roar.* **2.** very bad. *We had terrible weather on our vacation.*

tent /tent/ *n.* a cover that protects from weather. It is made of cloth and can be moved.

test /test/ *n.* **1.** a set of problems or tasks; examination. *We will have a spelling test on Friday.* **2.** a way to find out the nature or quality of something. —*v.* to give a test to or check. *The baker opened the oven and tested the bread.*

thank /thangk/ *v.* **1.** to say that one is grateful to. *I thanked the teacher for helping me.* **2.** to hold responsible; blame. *I have you to thank for getting us into this mess.*

Thanks giv ing /thangks giv′ ing/ *n.* **1.** a holiday in the U.S. observed on the fourth Thursday in November to celebrate the anniversary of the first Pilgrims' harvest feast that was held

 adj. adjective
 adv. adverb
conj. conjunction
contr. contraction
def. definition
interj. interjection
n. noun
pl. plural
prep. preposition
pron. pronoun
sing. singular
v. verb

in 1621. **2. thanksgiving.** an act of giving thanks.

that /t͟hat/ *adj.* **1.** used to indicate a person or thing being looked at or already mentioned. *That teacher is very popular.* **2.** used to indicate something more distant than or contrasted with another thing. —*pron. pl.* **those. 1.** the person or thing being looked at or already mentioned. **2.** something more distant than or contrasted with another thing. —*conj.* **1.** used to introduce a clause in a sentence. *I think that I will accept the job.* **2.** used to show reason or cause. *I'm sorry that you can't come to the party.* —*adv.* to that extent; so. *Was it really that cold yesterday?*

that'll /t͟hat′ əl/ *contr.* shortened form of "that will."

that's /t͟hats/ *contr.* shortened form of "that is." *That's my book.*

theft /theft/ *n.* the act of stealing. *The person who stole the car was arrested for theft.*

their /t͟hâr/ *adj.* of, belonging to, or having to do with them. *The neighbors and their friends played tennis all afternoon.*

there's /t͟hârz/ *contr.* shortened form of "there is." *There's some cheese in the refrigerator.*

they /t͟hā/ *pl. pron.* **1.** the persons or things being talked about. *The travelers were late because they missed the bus.* **2.** some people. *They say that cats have nine lives.*

they'd /t͟hād/ *contr.* **1.** shortened form of "they had." *They'd better leave now or they will be late for the show.* **2.** shortened form of "they would." *They'd be too polite to leave without saying good-bye.*

they'll /t͟hāl/ *contr.* **1.** shortened form of "they will." **2.** shortened form of "they shall."

they're /t͟hâr/ *contr.* shortened form of "they are." *They're not coming today.*

thing /thing/ *n.* **1.** whatever is spoken of, thought of, or done. *That was an unkind thing to say.* **2.** something that can be touched, seen, heard, smelled, or tasted but is not a human being. **3. things.** the general state of affairs. *How are things at school?*

third /thûrd/ *adj.* and *n.* next after the second. —*n.* one of three equal parts; 1/3.

thread /thred/ *n.* **1.** a very thin cord that is used in sewing and in weaving cloth. **2.** anything that is thin and long like a thread. *Threads of paint dripped from the brush.* **3.** the main idea or thought that connects the parts of a story or speech. **4.** a curved ridge that twists around a screw or nut. —*v.* **1.** to pass a thread through. **2.** to put on a thread; string. **3.** to make one's way through a narrow or obstructed place. *I threaded my way through the crowd.*

threw /thro͞o/ *v.* past tense of **throw.** *I threw back the ball.*

throat /thrōt/ *n.* **1.** the passage in the body between the mouth and the esophagus. **2.** the front of the neck. **3.** a narrow opening that is like the throat. *Hold the bottle by the throat and twist off the cap.*

throbbed /throbd/ *v.* past form of **throb,** to beat or pound heavily and fast. *My heart throbbed with excitement.*

through /thro͞o/ *prep.* **1.** from the beginning to the end of. **2.** in one side and out the other side of. **3.** in or to various places in. *We plan to travel through England.* —*adv.* **1.** from one side or end to the other side or end. **2.** completely; totally. —*adj.* **1.** allowing passage from one place to another with no obstruction. **2.** having reached a point of completion; finished. *I was through with the task.*

thumb /thum/ *n.* **1.** the short, thick finger on the hand. **2.** the part of a glove or mitten that covers the thumb. —*v.* to turn and look through

/a/	at
/ā/	late
/â/	care
/ä/	father
/e/	set
/ē/	me
/i/	it
/ī/	kite
/o/	ox
/ō/	rose
/ô/	brought raw
/oi/	coin
/o͝o/	book
/o͞o/	too
/or/	form
/ou/	out
/u/	up
/yo͞o/	cube
/ûr/	turn germ learn firm work
/ə/	about chicken pencil cannon circus
/ch/	chair
/hw/	which
/ng/	ring
/sh/	shop
/th/	thin
/t͟h/	there
/zh/	treasure

pages quickly. *I thumbed through the book.*

thump /thump/ *n.* a dull, heavy sound. —*v.* **1.** to beat or hit so as to make a dull, heavy sound. **2.** to beat rapidly. **thump er,** —*n.*

Thurs day /thûrz′ dā, thûrz′ dē/ *n.* the fifth day of the week.

time /tīm/ *n.* **1.** the period during which all events, conditions, and actions happen or continue. **2.** an exact point in time. **3.** a portion of time in history. —*v.* **timed, tim ing. 1.** to arrange or set according to time. **2.** to measure the time or rate of. *The coach timed the runners.*

to day /tə dā′/ *n.* the present day or time. —*adv.* **1.** on or during the present day. **2.** at the present time. *Today most people in this country light their houses with electricity.*

tomb /tōōm/ *n.* a grave or building in which a dead body is placed.

to mor row /tə mor′ ō/ *n.* **1.** the day after today. **2.** the future. —*adv.* on the day after today. *We are going on a trip tomorrow.*

tore /tor/ *v.* past tense of *tear,* to pull apart by force. *I tore my pants.*

touch down /tuch′ doun/ *n.* **1.** a score made in football by carrying the ball across the other team's goal line. **2.** the act or moment of landing an aircraft or spacecraft.

tow er /tou′ ər/ *n.* a tall, narrow building or structure. —*v.* to rise high up in the air. *The skyscraper towered above the city.*

toys /toiz/ *n.* things to play with.

trag e dy /traj′ i dē/ *n., pl.* **trag e dies. 1.** a serious story or play, usually with a sad ending. **2.** a sad or dreadful event; disaster. *The explosion in the coal mine was a great tragedy.*

trace /trās/ *n.* a small bit or sign left behind showing that something was there. *They found pieces of pottery and other traces of an old village when digging in the field.* —*v.* **traced, trac ing. 1.** to follow the trail, course, or path of. **2.** to copy by following lines seen through a piece of thin paper. **3.** to mark out. *I'll trace the outline in the sand.*

tramp /tramp/ *n.* **1.** a person who wanders from place to place and has no home or job. **2.** the sound of a heavy step. *We heard the tramp of the soldiers marching down the street.* —*v.* **1.** to walk or step heavily. *The elephant tramped noisily through the trees.* **2.** to travel on foot; walk or hike. *They spent the day tramping through the woods.*

trash /trash/ *n.* unwanted things that are to be thrown away.

trees /trēz/ *n.* the plural of *tree.* large plants with wooden trunks, branches, and leaves.

trick le /trik′ əl/ *v.* **trick led, trick ling.** to flow or fall drop by drop or in a thin stream. —*n.* a small flow or thin stream. *There was a trickle of milk down the side of the carton.*

trou ble /trub′ əl/ *n.* **1.** a difficult or dangerous situation. **2.** extra work or effort. **3.** a cause of difficulty. —*v.* **trou bled, trou bling. 1.** to disturb or make uncomfortable. **2.** to cause someone to make an extra effort. *May I please trouble you for a glass of water?*

true /trōō/ *adj.,* **tru er, tru est. 1.** agreeing with the facts; not false, wrong, or made up. **2.** faithful to someone or something; loyal. **3.** genuine; real. *The koala is not a true bear.*

Tues day /tōōz′ dē, tōōz′ dā, tyōōz′ dē, tyōōz′ dā/ *n.* the third day of the week.

tum ble /tum′ bəl/ *n.* a fall. —*v.* **tum bled, tum bling. 1.** to fall in a helpless or clumsy way. **2.** to roll or toss about. *We could hear the box tumbling around in the trunk.* **3.** to do somersaults, handsprings, or similar feats.

adj. adjective
adv. adverb
conj. conjunction
contr. contraction
def. definition
interj. interjection
n. noun
pl. plural
prep. preposition
pron. pronoun
sing. singular
v. verb

tune /tōōn, tyōōn/ *n.* **1.** a series of musical tones that form a pleasing, easily remembered unit; melody. **2.** a song. **3.** the right pitch or key. *The old piano was out of tune.*

tur ret /tûr′ it/ *n.* a small tower on a building. *Some castles have turrets at each corner.*

tur tle /tûr′ təl/ *n.* a reptile with a low, wide body covered by a hard shell.

twelve /twelv/ *n.* and *adj.* two more than ten; 12.

twitch /twich/ *v.* to move or pull with a sudden jerk or tug. *The rabbit's nose twitched.*

U

un bear a ble /un bâr′ ə bəl/ *adj.* not able to be tolerated or stood. *The icy water of the lake was unbearable.*

un cle /ung′ kəl/ *n.* **1.** the brother of one's father or mother. **2.** the husband of one's aunt.

un der ground /un′ dər ground′/ *adj.* being under the ground. *The mole dug an underground tunnel.*

un der stud y /un′ dər stud′ ē/ *n., pl.* **un der stud ies.** an actor who learns someone else's part in order to be a replacement. *The understudy got his big chance when the star became ill.*

un less /un les′/ *conj.* except on the condition that. *Unless you return these library books, you cannot borrow any more.*

un time ly /un tīm′ lē/ *adj.* **1.** happening too soon. **2.** happening at the wrong time. —*adv.* at a bad time or too soon.

ur ban /ûr′ bən/ *adj.* in, having to do with, or like a city or city life.

V

Val en tine's Day /val′ ən tīnz′ dā/ *n.* the day, February 14, named in honor of Saint Valentine, an early Christian saint. It is celebrated by the sending of valentines.

var i a tion /vâr′ ē ā′ shən/ *n.* **1.** change. *In the tropics, there is little variation in temperature between seasons.* **2.** a different form of something. *This story is a variation of one I heard before.*

ver y /ver′ ē/ *adv.* **1.** to a high degree; to a great extent. **2.** truly; absolutely; exactly. *That is the very best movie I have seen.* —*adj.* **1.** mere; by itself. *The very idea of getting up early makes me groan.* **2.** exact; precise.

Vet er ans Day /vet′ ər ənz dā/ *n.* a legal holiday honoring veterans who have fought for the United States, formerly called Armistice Day. It is celebrated on November 11.

voice /vois/ *n.* **1.** the sound that is produced through the mouth by speaking, singing, or shouting. **2.** the ability to produce sound through the mouth; speech. —*v.* **voiced, voic ing.** to express or utter.

vote /vōt/ *v.* **vot ed, vot ing.** to choose an idea, a plan, or a person for an office. *I will vote for Jenny to be the president of the club.*

W

was n't /wuz′ ənt, woz′ ənt/ *contr.* shortened form of "was not." *My friend wasn't home when I called.*

watch /woch/ *v.* **watched, watching. 1.** to look at a person or thing carefully. *If you watch the magician's tricks a few times, you may learn how they're done.* **2.** to wait and look in a careful, alert way. *The prisoner watched for a chance to escape.*

wear /wâr/ *v.* **wore, worn, wear ing. 1.** to carry or have on the body. **2.** to have or show. *He wore a big smile.* **3.** to damage or reduce by long use or exposure. *The ocean wore the rocks.* —*n.* **1.** the act of wearing or the state of being worn. **2.** clothing.

we'd /wēd/ *contr.* **1.** shortened form of "we had." **2.** shortened form of "we

/a/	at
/ā/	late
/â/	care
/ä/	father
/e/	set
/ē/	me
/i/	it
/ī/	kite
/o/	ox
/ō/	rose
/ô/	brought raw
/oi/	coin
/ōō/	book
/ōō/	too
/or/	form
/ou/	out
/u/	up
/yōō/	cube
/ûr/	turn germ learn firm work
/ə/	about chicken pencil cannon circus
/ch/	chair
/hw/	which
/ng/	ring
/sh/	shop
/th/	thin
/ṯh/	there
/zh/	treasure

Speller Dictionary 209

Wednesday/work

would." **3.** shortened form of "we should."

Wednes day /wenz′ dē, wenz′ dā/ *n.* the fourth day of the week.

week /wēk/ *n.* the seven days from Sunday through Saturday. There are 52 weeks in a year.

week ly /wēk′ lē/ *adj.* one time a week. *Every Saturday, we do our weekly shopping.* —*adv.* one time each week, every week. *Our Boy Scout troop meets weekly.*

we'll /wēl/ *contr.* **1.** shortened form of "we shall." **2.** shortened form of "we will."

were /wûr/ *v.* a form of the past tense of *be* that is used with *you, we, they,* or the plural form of a noun. *We were home all day.*

were n't /wûrnt, wûr′ ənt/ *contr.* shortened form of "were not."

what /hwut, hwot, wut, wot/ *pron.* **1.** used to ask questions about persons or things. *What is today's date?* **2.** the thing that. *They knew what I was talking about.* —*adj.* **1.** which one or ones. *What books are missing from the shelf?* **2.** any that; whatever. *Take what you need for the trip.* —*adv.* in which way; how much; how. *What does it matter?* —*interj.* used to show surprise, disbelief, anger, or other feeling.

what's /hwuts, hwots, wuts, wots/ *contr.* **1.** shortened form of "what is." **2.** shortened form of "what has."

where's /hwârz/ *contr.* shortened form of "where is." *Where's the book?*

which /hwich/ *pron.* **1.** what one or ones. *Which of the players did you think was best?* **2.** any one or ones that; whichever. *Choose which of the records you want to hear.* —*adj.* what one or ones. *Which skates are yours?*

who /hoō/ *pron.* **1.** what or which person or persons. *Who gave you that pen?* **2.** that. *The student who wrote that story did a good job.*

whole /hōl/ *adj.* having all its parts; entire; complete. —*n.* all the parts that make up a thing. *Two halves make a whole.*

wig gle /wig′ əl/ *v.* **wig gled, wig gling.** to move from side to side. *The little worms wiggle on the ground.*

wild /wīld/ *adj.* **1.** not controlled by people; living or growing naturally. **2.** not disciplined or orderly. *Those wild children often play rough games and hurt themselves.*

winced /winst/ *v.* past form of **wince,** to draw back slightly from something painful, dangerous, or unpleasant. *The child winced when the doctor gave the injection.*

wind mill /wind′ mil/ *n.* a machine that uses the power of the wind. *Windmills are used to pump water, grind grain, or generate electricity.*

win ter /win′ tər/ *n.* the season of the year between fall and spring. —*v.* to spend the winter. *My grandparents winter in Florida.*

wise /wīz/ *adj.,* **wis er, wis est.** having or showing good judgment or intelligence. *It is wise to stay away from fighting dogs.*

won't /wōnt/ *contr.* shortened form of "will not." *The painters won't be able to finish today.*

wood /wŏŏd/ *n.* **1.** the hard material that makes up the trunk and branches of a tree or bush. **2.** an area of trees growing naturally. —*adj.* made of or consisting of wood. *The furniture on our porch is wood.*

work /wûrk/ *n.* **1.** the use of a person's energy or ability to do something; effort. **2.** what a person does to earn money; a job or occupation. **3.** something to be done; task. *We finished our work early.* —*v.* **1.** to use

adj.	adjective
adv.	adverb
conj.	conjunction
contr.	contraction
def.	definition
interj.	interjection
n.	noun
pl.	plural
prep.	preposition
pron.	pronoun
sing.	singular
v.	verb

one's energy or ability in order to do or get something. **2.** to have a job. **3.** to operate. *Can you work the tape recorder?*

would /wo͝od/ *v.* **1.** used to express something that might have happened if something else had happened first. **2.** to express something that might happen later. **3.** to express a request. *Would you please help me?*

would n't /wo͝od′ ənt/ *contr.* shortened form of "would not." *I wouldn't do that if I were you.*

would' ve /wo͝od′ əv/ *contr.* shortened form of "would have."

wran gler /rang′ glər/ *n.* in the western United States, a person who herds or tends horses or other livestock; cowboy.

wrap /rap/ *v.* **wrapped. wrap ping.** **1.** to cover by putting something around. **2.** to fold or wind as a covering. *The nurse wrapped a blanket around the baby.* **3.** to clasp or fold. *The monkey wrapped its arms around the branch.*

wreck /rek/ *v.* to destroy or ruin. —*n.* **1.** the act of wrecking. **2.** what is left of something that has been ruined or damaged. *The room was a wreck.*

wren /ren/ *n.* a small songbird.

wring /ring/ *v.* **wrung, wring ing.** **1.** to squeeze or twist so that liquid is forced out. *You must wring the wet clothes.* **2.** to hold tightly and press or twist. *Some people in the dentist's office were wringing their hands nervously.*

wrin kle /ring′ kəl/ *n.* a small fold, ridge, or line in a smooth surface. —*v.* **wrin kled, wrin kling.** to make or have a fold, ridge, or line in a smooth surface. *Some people wrinkle their foreheads.*

wrist /rist/ *n.* the joint between the hand and the arm.

write /rīt/ *v.* **wrote, writ ten, writ ing.** **1.** to form letters, words, or symbols on paper or some other surface. **2.** to be the author of. *My aunt writes children's stories.* **3.** to send a letter.

writ ten /rit′ ən/ *v.* past participle of **write.** *Has your friend written you a letter yet?* See **write.**

wrong /rông/ *adj.* **1.** not correct or true. **2.** not moral or good; bad. **3.** not proper; not suitable. **4.** not working. *Something is wrong with my watch.* —*n.* something that is not moral or good. —*adv.* in a way that is not right; incorrectly. —*v.* to treat in an unjust or bad way. *The salesperson wronged us.*

wrote /rōt/ *v.* past tense of **write.** *We all wrote down what the teacher said.* See **write.**

Y

year /yir/ *n.* **1.** the time from January 1 to December 31. A year has 365 or 366 days. **2.** a word that tells how old a person or thing is. Each year is a period of any twelve months in a row. *Dee is ten years old.*

yes ter day /yes′ tər dē, yes′ tər dā/ *n.* the day before today. —*adv.* on the day before today. *I bought a book yesterday.*

you /yo͞o, yə/ *pron.* **1.** the person or persons that are spoken or written to. *We'll go with you to the concert.* **2.** a person; anyone. *You can vote at eighteen.*

you'd /yo͞od/ *contr.* **1.** shortened form of "you had." **2.** shortened form of "you would."

you'll /yo͞ol, yo͝ol/ *contr.* shortened form of "you will" or "you shall."

your /yo͝or, yor, yər/ *adj.* of or belonging to you. *Is this your coat?*

you're /yo͝or, yor, yər/ *contr.* shortened form of "you are." *You're almost as tall as I am.*

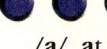

/a/	at
/ā/	late
/â/	care
/ä/	father
/e/	set
/ē/	me
/i/	it
/ī/	kite
/o/	ox
/ō/	rose
/ô/	brought raw
/oi/	coin
/o͝o/	book
/o͞o/	too
/or/	form
/ou/	out
/u/	up
/yo͞o/	cube
/ûr/	turn germ learn firm work
/ə/	about chicken pencil cannon circus
/ch/	chair
/hw/	which
/ng/	ring
/sh/	shop
/th/	thin
/t͟h/	there
/zh/	treasure

zipper/zodiac

Z

zip per /zip′ ər/ *n.* a fastener made up of two rows of teeth that fit into each other. Zippers are used on clothing, suitcases, and other articles.

zo di ac /zō′ dē ak/ *n.* an imaginary belt in the heavens. The sun, moon, and most of the planets seem to travel on paths through the zodiac during the year.

adj.	adjective
adv.	adverb
conj.	conjunction
contr.	contraction
def.	definition
interj.	interjection
n.	noun
pl.	plural
prep.	preposition
pron.	pronoun
sing.	singular
v.	verb

212 Speller Dictionary